MW00942482

Copyright 2011©Carey Rowland
-for pre-publication, 2011-2013, at:
www.careyrowland.com
-published book, 2014 by L. Carey Rowland

-cover by Terry Henry
-editorial advice with Katie Rowland
-printed by CreateSpace.com
ISBN: 1495330834
ISBN-13: 978-1495330834
Library of Congress LCCN: 2014902149

Prologue

Here we have an exploration of the year 1937; it was a perilous year, but not yet as explosive as the terrible forces of displacement and war that would soon overtake Europe and the whole world.

Through the eyes of a young American, Philip Morrow, we sojourn herein through an Old World that is slowly overheating with a new friction. Nazi militarism seethes clandestinely across the Rhine, cranking its vindictive *wehrmacht* machine, soon to sideswipe French bewilderment, and obliterate the peace and safety of the whole wide, unsuspecting world.

Through the slow smoke of that pivotal year 1937, we catch glimpses of a few scattered, disruptive sparks, soon to ignite a worldwide blaze. Kings and queens are startled, losing sight of their exalted positions in the ancient corridors of power.

A child emperor of China is made to perform by his Japanese puppetmasters.

In the middle of the world, Palestine begins its long, slow boil as restless Jewish immigrants from the north countries encounter resentful Arab natives.

Back at home, in the sleepy hometown of Philip's America, folks catch glimpses in the newspapers of the first glimmers of worldwide conflagration.

In London, Philip is doing business, representing an American tobacco company. He's a curious, ambitious young man who has forsaken the new world—his mercantile beginnings in a small mountain town, his university education—to embark on a roundabout odyssey in the Old World. The path Philip chooses, or that has chosen him, compels the young American along a trail of discovery. It becomes a sojourn in which he begins to understand how and why his father had a fateful appointment with eternity on a Belgian battleground in 1918.

In a Europe still weary from the last War, Philip gets his first real history lesson—not the kind of lesson you receive in school, but the kind you get when the torrents of history, and the current of love, get a hold of you.

1

Royals

Philip's cigarette burned a hole in the air. A thin plume of smoke danced up to the ceiling. Glass pendants on the chandelier above his typewriter accepted another ominous microdeposit of tarry film. After caressing the light fixture, his smoke wafted along the ceiling unseen; it ducked down at the wall to scuttle through an open window, then scurry on a breeze across Tottenham Court Road, from whence it could blow just about anywhere, maybe all the way around the world.

Philip was hurrying to finish a business report. As soon as the monthly was done, he would hit the street hoping to find a suitable place in the crowd to get a glimpse of the new King of England, whose crowning would be today.

For the love of a woman can change the course of the world. As Helen's face had launched a thousand Greek ships, so the affections of an American divorcée had turned the tide of royal authority from one brother to another. From one duke to another. Made ostensibly of sterner, though stammering, stuff than his older liege, Albert--soon to be called George VI--would, in only a few short hours ascend those few hallowed steps in Westminster to sit upon the throne of Edward, James, Henry and all those other regents who had ever commanded the armies or fleets of British empire.

The American, Philip Morrow, whose typewriter rang its final return as he completed his report, anticipated the mounting pageantry with distant, though wondrous, curiosity. He stood up, walked over to the open window, and surveyed the stream of English yoredom migrating south on Tottenham Court Road toward Trafalgar and beyond where the royal procession would pass in a few hours. His cigarette had died; he flipped its butt in the ever-present ashtray on the window sill.

The people of England were expectant, exultant. No mean Mr. Mustard here. No, they were ready to receive a new king, now that the whole affair of Edward's abdication had resolved itself into the ashtray of history. And all the more so, since the role of the regents was now largely ceremonial, having little effectual responsibility except to maintain that proverbial stiff upper lip with a vigilant eye upon the horizon where an eternal sun was perpetually setting, but never, of course, on the British Empire. God save the King, but it would be Mr. Baldwin, or Mr. Chamberlain, Mr. Churchill, or some such privileged commoner who would ultimately compel English hearts and guts to bear sacrificial defense of their storied shores.

Only a hundred and fifty-odd years ago, Philip's yankee forebears had fired the shot so-dubbed "shot heard 'round the world." Upstart revolutionists in that hotbed of rebellion, Massachusetts, had sparked a powder keg of free-thinking independence that had since set the whole of civilization ablaze with yearnings for liberty. But not here, no, not here in the realm, in the Albion of old. No, the very Magna Carta that had implanted, in former times, plucky zeal in the hearts of Englishmen--the very document--languished in a glass case at the British Library just a few miles from here. Who knew? These limeys were streaming like lemmings to a Dover cliff, like vassals to a gilt coronation, like white on rice. How many of them, this very hour, paraded right by the sacrosanct text unaware of the incendiary ideas embalmed within, in inky arcanity? How many?

Philip couldn't fathom these English; he had been here almost a year now, representing Brigham Tobacco Co., and slowly converting them from their stuffy old pipes to the new, improved method for smoke delivery, cigarettes. No, he couldn't figure these people out. The very people who had invented the industrial revolution now were so obstinate in their pipe-clinging. But Philip knew that in the midst of such tradition the wheels of progress would inevitably turn. Slowly would they turn, step by step, inch by inch. Not like in America where everything was push coming to shove. Clang, clang, clang went the trolley, down on the street; ding, ding, ding went the bell; beat, beat went the heart of an ancient nation yearning for prosperity and security.

Someone was knocking on Philip's door. He opened the door to see Nathan Wachov's laconic face. The tall friend, flipping a shilling coin, looked down at Philip and said, "If we can get a view at Trafalgar, it'll be because we either crawled under a thousand legs, or got to an upper story window. The King's subjects are packed solid like sardines from here to Parliament and beyond." Nathan was walking into the apartment as he spoke.

"It seems we've waited too long," observed Philip. "You'd think eight o'clock in the morning would be a good start on getting to a procession that's to pass some time this afternoon. You want some coffee?"

"I think not, old chap. We'd better get a move on. The faithful have been congregating since yesterday evening. I've already tried to negotiate my way onto Oxford Street, with no success; it may be a lost cause."

"So you think we can make a go of it?"

"Sure, why not? Nothing else to do today. Shops are closed, nobody doing business. You surely won't be servicing any accounts in this mob," Nathan speculated. "Grab your mac and let's see how far we can get."

Philip locked the door behind him as they started down the stairway toward the ground-floor entry. "Well, what'll it be then? The crawling approach, the sardine strategy, or the high road?"

"The submarine strategy, old chap." Nathan displayed a wide grin as he retrieved two metal tubes from his satchel.

"Periscopes?"

"Righto, spyglasses, actually. I bought 'em yesterday at Steward's, over on the Strand."

"Must have been a pretty penny, eh? They look like good ones."

"Quite dear, my friend, but how many kings do we crown in one lifetime?" They were stepping from the stoop now, entering the stream of slickered humanity that was moving, not quite quickly, in the exquisitely-fine morning mist.

"Well, this is the third in my lifetime," quipped Philip, raising his voice now to overcome the din of Tottenham Court Road's passing throng.

Nathan was surging into the crowded sidewalk, leading their way. He handed one of the spyglasses to Philip. "Edward doesn't count." He laughed out loud. "...no thanks to Mrs. Simpson. His was just a dress rehearsal for his brother's coronation. But King George VI is the real thing; I can feel it in my bones, as can, I surmise, these other thousands of British citizens."

Philip wanted to look through his sypglass, but found that to be a clumsy task while moving in the wake of Nathan's tall frame.

Half an hour and six blocks later, upon reaching Oxford Street, the duo was confronted with choc-a-block humanity straight ahead along Charing Cross, or the same madding crowd if they were to opt for a westward turn onto Oxford. They chose, with the obstinacy of youth, to plow straight ahead toward Trafalgar, even though the likelihood of thinner crowds was greater in choosing that route. It would be the path of more resistance. "I might have third-floor access at the Midland on Pall Mall," said Nathan.

Philip was vaguely aware, in his yankee pragmatistic funk, of the regally-directed energy that now flowed along Charing Cross. He could see, ahead and behind, a channel of motive hats—fedoras , bowlers moving, tweedy and herring-boned, felted, folded and tilted o'er English faces, high and low, noble and yeo, tethered with silkish neck-tied cravats upon legions of liegemen, and accompanying rose-cheeked ladies festooned with beads and laced bodices, covered in shiny mac wetness. All were flowing at street level in the London fog as one loyal realm, toward that coronary procession which would soon culminate like an Elgar promenade beneath their high holy spires of Westminster, and which would be validated in ancient, sacred words spoken o'er a stammering sovereign lord soon to be anointed during this very solemn hour, to receive the mantle of destiny that would-- little did they know at this gathering moment-- within just a few spare years, commission English RAF and compel British resolve to sacrificially prevail o'er the bellowing, belligerent Teutonic beast that only now began to breathe *wehrmacht* fire on the other side of the channel.

Nathan nudged Philip rightward when they arrived at Cranbourne Street. "I think we'll do more speedily along Haymarket. Let's go in that direction," he said. Trudging among the horde along Cranbourne and Coventry, they turned onto Haymarket, and the pair soon came upon the bowed windows of Fribourg & Treyer, a classic tobacconists' shop.

Philip grabbed Nathan's arm. "Let's stop here for a minute. I want to see their most recent blend." said Philip. Philip peered intently through the window at an array of snuff packages on display."Oh, what I would do to convince these old farts to accept cigarettes into their selections. I've made three visits in order to persuade them of the wisdom in adopting modern tobacco enjoyment, but so far to no avail."

"Young man," came a strained voice from behind.

Philip turned his head to see Nathan being addressed by a white-haired man leaning weightily against the rounded window storefront. The old fellow, quite dapper in a brown derby that shielded bright blue eyes over a pale, fleshy face, double-chinned over a red bow-tie, seemed nevertheless to be slowly collapsing beneath the burden of his own weight.

He clutched Nathan's arm. "Young man," he insisted, though weakly, "Would you be so kind..." He was faltering. His cataracted blue eyes closed slowly, then managed, laboriously, to open again. He looked up at Nathan's expectant face. "...currency stabilization...on the gold standard...perils...bloody monetary experiments...reverse...a calamity...Here, my boy, take this, please." The old man proffered a small notebook, which Nathan, puzzled, and attempting to support the fellow's faltering constitution, managed to accept with his left hand. Then the old fellow collapsed.

"Doctor! A doctor!" yelled Nathan, frantically. A thread of drool dripped from the old man's open mouth as Nathan struggled to lay his limp body down gently on the sidewalk. At the nearby corner on Haymarket, the lights changed, and traffic commenced.

Nathan and Philip, speechless, knelt beside the stricken man, whose portly, suited body now lay motionless on the sidewalk. His eyes stared blankly upward into the morning mist. A crowd of people stood and stared. Nathan began pressing at the man's chest in what appeared to be a vain attempt at stimulating heart operation. In a sort of desperate gesture, Nathan gently slapped the man's joweled face as if to provoke him to attention.

Then there was a parting in the crowd; a bobby was on the spot. "Stand aside, please," said the policeman, with accustomed authority. The two young men rose to their feet and backed off, allowing the bobby full access to this fallen gentleman's predicament. After conducting a few more ineffective chest compressions, the policeman gingerly turned up the old fellow's gold watch, which now lay inside his open coat on the ground, attached to the end of a gold chain that had strayed from the vest-pocket. Philip could see that the watch showed 9:33.

The officer looked up at Nathan. "Do you know this man?" he asked, while checking the pulse at his risk.

"No sir."

"What happened?"

"I was standing here by the window, looking in. I looked to my right. He was turning away, and slumping against the window. I took hold of him, trying to give him support. But I was in no position to bear his weight, so I let him down as gently as I could. He was, uh, blubbering, and that drool was beginning to come out of his mouth. I called for a doctor, and tried to, uh, somewhat, to stimulate his heart."

The bobby stood up. He looked directly into Nathan's eyes. He had a gentle, though official, demeanor. "Did he say anything?"

Nathan thought for a moment. "He did. He was going on about, uh, about the gold standard. . ." Nathan turned toward Philip. "Wasn't that it?" he asked.

"Yes, he said something about the gold standard, and monetary experiments," replied Philip, looking at the policeman.

The bobby looked down again at the body. He spoke slowly, "Do you remember. . .what his last word was?"

Nathan and Philip looked at each other. Nathan was pursing his lips, trying to think about what had just happened. He shrugged his shoulders. "It was all so sudden."

"Calamity," said Philip.

"Yes, that was it, calamity." Nathan affirmed, with relief, as if it were a matter of importance.

The bobby cast his analytical eyes around to the gathered crowd. "Does anyone here know this man?" he shouted.

The only response was the din of Haymarket's bustle as Londoners continued their pilgrimage in anticipation of coronation pageantry.

"Have any of you people ever seen this man before, or can tell me anything about him?"

Then came a reply. "Yes. I know him. He is a member of the Travelers Club. In fact, officer, I saw him there not a half-hour ago." The speaker was a thin gentleman, well-dressed in a blue, vested suit. His pale, gaunt face was thin, moustachioed, and spectacled.

"Step up, please, sir," the bobby commanded, gently, gesturing with his right hand for the informer's approach, as he retrieved, with his left, a notepad from his uniform pocket. Then, having another thought, the bobby looked upward and addressed the crowd. "You people would do well to move along now. Please make way for the medical team who will be here shortly."

Setting his cartridge pen to the notepad, he began to quiz the man in the blue suit. "Do you know his name, sir?"

"His name was Paul Wallris."

"How do you spell that surname?" inquired the officer, cocking his head slightly.

"Wallris. W, A, L, L, yes I think there are two L's, R, I, S."

"And you say you saw him at the Travelers Club just a while ago?"

"Yes, he was having breakfast there with some companions."

"I see." The policeman jotted for a moment, then looked up into the other man's eyes. "And what is your name, sir?"

"Greeneglass, Itmar Greeneglass."

Nathan and Philip were preparing to walk away. The officer, writing, glanced up at them. "I'll need you gentlemen to remain here for a while. Just stand aside there for a moment, please." The two younger men lit up cigarettes.

The officer directed his attention once again to the man in the blue suit. "Very well, then, Mr. Greeneglass, please describe Mr. Wallris' circumstance there at the Club this morning, if you can."

"I was not privy to their conversation, of course, as I was sitting nearby in a chair, taking tea and reading the *Times*. Mr. Wallris and the two other members were having breakfast together at a table by the window."

"Who were those other members?"

"I don't know, sir. Their faces are slightly familiar, as I believe they are both fairly new members, whereas I have been there myself for about ten years now. I do, however, know this about Paul Wallris. He was rather grief-stricken just now. His nephew was one of those seamen killed last week in the fire aboard the HMS Hunter, on non-intervention patrol off Gibraltar."

Philip took a long pull on his cigarette, a *Bullseye*, his best- selling brand. The smoke of it swirled upward into London mist, disappeared into the cloud, and wafted his thoughts far above and far away from the ancient gray city in which he now stood. Across an ocean, and across many miles of verdant, productive earth on both sides of that vast water, he had traveled, about ten months ago. Leaving the hardscrabble North Carolina hills and furrowed fields behind, he sought fortune and a better day, and maybe some adventure along the way. It was a reversal of the sojourn taken generations ago by his ancestors.

The old man's sudden demise reminded Philip of one dark day, back home in North Carolina, when his grandfather had died. Right in the middle of his burdens grampa had given up the ghost, in a half-plowed rocky field behind the business end of a crotchety mule, while breaking up red clay earth for the season's tobacco planting.

A foreboding pall crept across Philip's young consciousness--a kind of smoky wet blanket. Unanticipated, the mood now cast over his strappy vigor a condensing gravity. In the dampening London fog this portly gentleman had just been ferried to wherever it is that people go beyond the pale. Philip had, for whatever reason he did not know, just witnessed the passing.

It was a death. It arrested Philip's youthful attention more obtrusively than his grandfather's passing had done; and yet he didn't even know the man-- this old chap, Mr. Wallris, who now lay still and cold by the quaint, dusty window of a tobacco shop. The old fellow's collapse was noticed by a hundred curious eyes as strangers trundled by, but none of them commemorated it. No memorial for Mr. Wallris' passing, so far.

This stalking death could arrive at any moment, thought Philip, and yet it seemed that one would want to make some minimal arrangements for the dreaded appointment. Had the old fellow made an appointment? Had someone else made arrangements for his passage? Would a man meet God like a prospective client? More likely, the man was the prospect.

His grandfather—Bucky they had called him—had toiled many a growin' season between those spring plantings behind the mule and the 'baccer harvesting in the fall. Ah... the fall, the bright autumn. It seemed for a moment that Philip could almost smell the flue fires, curing and toasting golden leaves in their loggy barns, back on the other side of the Atlantic and the other side of childhood. But no, it was nearby aromatic Turkish, stoked in a gentleman's briar pipe, which now beckoned to Philip's olfactory.

Smoldering within his pipe dream was a pungent memory of grampa's ole back forty, and how their collective toil would later be soothed with the smoky warmth of family and hearth. That's how the laboring farm family laid to rest another damp autumn day of layin' baccer into the barn, after mama had at long last called them in for supper, reminding the young'uns to wipe their feet.

But death wouldn't be like that. Death wouldn't be like some impressionist painting softened with the dappling of romanticism.

No, death, he had just seen today, is a rude and cruel thing, an intruder. Death is an unholy fire, with unwelcome smoke to screen its noxious consequences. Its burning destructiveness was set quite apart from those gentle, flickering home fires of his memory. Death would be something like the bonfires which now blazed across the channel, far from England, beyond the Rhine and the black forest, in a Berlin stadium, where nazified extravaganzas now prepared to set ablaze national pyres of incendiary hate. The flames of those fires would ultimately cauterize Saxon conscience with a scarring beyond civilized sensibility in the smokestacks of Dachau.

But Philip didn't know that. Few people did, not even the soon-to-be-anointed King of England.

There's quite a lot that people do not know about what they do in this world. Why, Philip couldn't even fathom the lethal power of the thin cylinder between his two fingers.

But now the policeman was speaking to him.

2
Notes

The policeman asked Nathan if there was anything else he had noticed about the deceased.

"He handed this to me," said Nathan, "even as he was falling to the ground." It was a folded white paper, with this handwritten message largely scrawled in black ink:

Wallris--
John Bull's ransom will smoke out the black shirts tomorrow. If not, your bridge could burn.   *Chapman*

The bobby, raising his eyebrows, looked up at Nathan. "Mr., uh..., your name sir?"

"Nathan Wachov, of Islington."

"Mr. Wachov, did the gentleman, Mr. Wallris, did he display any signs of struggle?"

"He was struggling to stay on his feet, sir, but was incapable of it. He was losing strength rapidly when I went to his aid."

"Did his death appear to you to be, ah...natural?"

"He was gasping for air, and mucous was dripping from his mouth. I don't know; I've never had anyone die in my arms before now."

"Gasping?"

"Yes. Wouldn't you say that would be a natural response of anyone who is taking his last breaths?"

"Yes. Quite so." The policeman looked down at the body again. "I'll need to take this note, you know. Since this incident has resulted in a death, I'll need to retain any items that could be evidence."

"Evidence... of what? He gave it to me."

"While he may have handed it to you, that doesn't mean he gave it to you for keeping. This is routine procedure, I assure you, Mr. Wachov, in such a case as this."

"Certainly, do your duty, sir."

Two medics arrived with a gurney. Officer Morley began to facilitate their task of removing the body. "Stand aside, now," he commanded to the onlookers," raising his arms to shoo them away. "Move along now. We've a new king to crown today. Better get on with it."

Stepping aside, Philip looked quizzically at Nathan. He was curious about the note. "Black shirts?"

"Fascist renegades," replied Nathan, "Mosley's rabble upstarts." He spoke flatly, while gazing blankly at the body. The medics were preparing to carry the deceased man's rotund body away from the point of his last stand on this earth. Nathan began thinking out loud. "But who knows if contentious politics—the infamous black shirts group--has anything to do with this man's passing? That's doubtful. I mean, look at the old guy. Does he look like a man who would have anything to do with radical politics? He probably had a heart attack. My guess is that note is a random scrap of paper that he happened to have in his hand when the final moment came."

"He looks like a man," observed Philip, "who might be the object of some radical's discontent. He looks like, well, like a John Bull."

"Ha. You mean the blackshirts might have been out to get the old boy?" asked Nathan. A corner of his mouth turned up in a faintly incredulous grin. "He wasn't shot, or stabbed. He just. . . . died."

"A fat Tory," said Philip. "Look at him. He's not the sort of man who has ever stood, I daresay, for one moment, in an employment line."

"He hasn't missed any meals," agreed Nathan, looking up and around for the first time since they had suddenly encountered the unfortunate Mr.

Wallris. "I'm thinking, though, about that note: '...your bridge could burn,' it said."

For a perplexing moment, the loud murmur of the Haymarket crowd eclipsed their pensivity.

"His bridge to eternity," mused Philip.

Nathan's green Moravian eyes flashed with mild amusement. His wide mouth registered a thoughtful grin. "Perhaps he managed to cross that bridge before the burning. . ."

The man in the blue suit caught up with Nathan and Philip as they commenced their slow plodding through the crowd down Haymarket Street. Nathan felt a tug on his arm.

"You were the last person to talk to Paul?" the man blurted as Nathan stopped to turn around.

"If you can call it that," said Nathan, inspecting the speaker's face. It was a gaunt face, gray-bearded and etched with a testament of some affliction. A canopy of bushy eyebrows hung like a tallith over his expressive brown eyes. Nathan was standing still now, looking at this man in the blue suit, the man who had spoken to the policeman about Paul Wallris. Carefully, slowly, as if he were unsure of this circumstance's propriety, Nathan explained, "He said a few words. I didn't speak to him. I didn't know what to say." Nathan used a long pause to assess his questioner. "And then, well, you know..." Nathan started to turn away, as if to continue his walk, though he knew the man's persistent demeanor would prevent it.

"Sir, I need to talk to you. This was no insignificant man whose death you witnessed today," the man insisted.

Nathan reversed his direction again. "I knew this man for about one minute." He looked intently into those large brown eyes, eyes brimming with a need to know.

"What did he say to you?"

"I didn't hear it all. It was more like a mumble than...Who are you, anyway? Who gave you permission to ask so many questions?"

"I am Itmar Greeneglass, and Paul Wallris was a friend of mine."

"Well I am sorry for your loss, sir. But I must be on my way."

"What is so urgent that you cannot soothe an old man's curiosity about his deceased friend's passing?"

Nathan's decision to move forward was again arrested. "The crowning of an English king, sir."

"I see," said Itmar, "and is it you who are going to crown George the sixth?"

Nathan felt a sudden inexplicably defiant levity. He looked over at Philip's rather dumbfounded countenance, and registered an odd mirth, as one corner of his mouth turned up in a smirk. "I do bite my thumb at thee sir," said Nathan. He gestured with an upraised thumb, but he didn't bite it, and turned again as if to attempt another departure.

Philip was plumbing the depths of his understanding for some accounting of his friend's prickly reticence to accommodate the stranger's entreaty.

"He gave you something, didn't he?" Itmar was undeterred.

"That's none of your business, sir," was Nathan's awkwardly resolute response. There was a mild quiver in his voice. "Who are you anyway? Who appointed you the inspector on this case?"

Philip heard in Nathan's voice a subtle modulation toward cooperation; it seemed that Nathan was posing an authentic question to which he really wanted an answer.

"I told you, Nathan, Paul was a friend of mine."

Nathan looked long and hard at Itmar Greeneglass. Their eyes were locked together for a few seconds, until Nathan blinked.

"I need to talk to you, Nathan. Please come up to my office for a few minutes; it is just down the street here. Would you like some tea? Or something stronger if you prefer."

"How did you know my name?"

"You spoke it to officer Morley when he asked you the same questions that I've been asking."

Philip interjected. "I think we should do this, Nathan. Men don't just die on the street every day, you know. There may be something going on here that needs. . . a follow up, or something."

"I realize that, Philip. That's what concerns me. I wasn't expecting an inquisition, after I've already had one from the officer." He looked intently at the stranger again. "So if this deceased fellow was a friend of yours, how have you...how long have you known him?"

"I've known Paul for a year or so, met him in the Travelers Club. Recently, though, he has helped me greatly, or I should say, he has helped some friends of mine greatly. He was a very generous man." Itmar offered a hesitant smile.

"How so?"

The stranger lowered his voice a bit. "It is a matter of some confidence. These are precarious times, you know. My office is just up the street, where we can speak with some privacy."

Nathan was thinking. "Come on, Nathan," urged Philip. " I could use a cup of tea." He pulled out a cigarette. The dull roar of a thousand footsteps and voices became for a few seconds a surreptitious covering for the stranger's next statement.

In yet a lower voice, the intruder drew his face closer to Nathan's and spoke quietly, yet deliberately. "Mr. Wallris had furnished two ships from his fleet for refugees to escape from Guernica, and from Spain, to France."

That got Nathan's attention. His eyes widened. Surprised, he looked askance at his friend. "How about one of those cigarettes, Philip?"

"Better yet." Itmar looked at Philip and gently put his hand on Philip's sleeve. Then his eyes riveted back to Nathan's. "I've got a Cuban cigar with your name on it." He thumped Nathan lightly on the lapel.

"With my name on it," repeated Nathan, skeptically.

"So to speak." Itmar offered the little grin again, and shrugged. "Come on, Nathan. Three minutes, and you're in my office where we can talk." He slid past the tall man as if to lead the way.

"I don't know you from Adam," protested Nathan, with what seemed to Philip a touch of humor. "How do I know you're not one of them?"

Itmar wheeled around. "One of who?"

"I don't know, ah...one of the blackshirts."

The stranger, speaking low again, asked, "Mr. Wallris said something about the blackshirts, did he?"

"Not exactly," quipped Philip.

There was the silence of street noise again as Itmar considered his words. Then he said, "Maybe you don't know me from Adam, my friend." He stuck his face at Nathan's again. "You've heard of Moses, *n'est ce pas*? He was my great uncle."

Nathan laughed, and began walking in the direction Itmar was suggesting, down Haymarket Street toward Pall Mall. Despite the drizzly weather, a festive atmosphere inhabited the crowds of people who moved steadily as one mass of humanity, on both sides of the street, in the street, and just about everywhere you could see. The British people were gathering expectantly to crown their new sovereign. After a few minutes, the newfound man in the blue suit diverted Nathan and Philip to a clothing shop with its name, *Greeneglass*, painted in green and gold script letters on the display window. Itmar pulled out his keys, opened the door, and the three men entered a small, well-appointed store that smelled of fabric and dye. The sudden quiet as Itmar closed the door behind them was startling.

Although the shop seemed small to Philip, his survey of it presented a richly impressive inventory of goods, mostly women's blouses and dresses, in a variety of rich, though sedated, colors--lace here, wool there, a plaid or two, cream and burgundy, forest green, a burnt orange hat tilted upon a mannequin with a string of pearls beneath,. a compact men's selection over on one wall, colorful children's on the other. A folded ivory card with sizably printed script rested on a glass case; it read: *We assure you the best fit in London. Our alterations are guaranteed to please.* But Itmar wasted no time in conducting them to the back, through a draped doorway where they ascended a creaky stairway to an upstairs apartment. "My wife has our grandchildren out on Trafalgar to catch a glimpse of the royal procession," explained Itmar.

"We don't want to deter you from joining them," said Nathan.

"No worry, my friend. I'll be joining them at the appropriate time. We have some arrangements with friends who have a third-story view of the square. I can assure you there is nothing more important for me right now than to hear from you, if you willing to tell it to me, what my friend Paul said before he passed...Cigar?" He offered the hand-wrapped smoke which he had just retrieved from a humidor.

"Don't mind if I do," said Nathan, accepting.

The spritely gentleman offered a cigar to Philip. "And your name, sir?"

"Philip Morrow, thank you."

"Pleased to meet you, Philip...Itmar Greeneglass. May I ask, what brings this American to London?"

"I represent Brigham Tobacco Company."

"I see. I hope this Cuban wrap is to your liking."

"Surely it is. You were saying earlier, sir, that Mr. Wallris had provided some boats for evacuees from Spain."

"That's right, Philip. You understand," said Itmar, getting right to the point, "...don't you, that Franco's rebels in Spain would be powerless without the Italian and German support."

"I've gathered that from reading the papers. It seems that all of Europe is getting involved in this Spanish bloodletting."

Itmar was boiling some water for tea. The two visitors had followed him into the kitchen. "Please sit down, gentleman." He issued them to chairs at a quaint wooden table appointed with a ceramic vase of fresh peonies. "There's much more to that war than meets the eye. The rebels don't have an air force to speak of. The bombing of Guernica two weeks ago was carried out almost entirely by the German *luftwaffe*, and it was inhuman what they did there."

"I have read that almost the entire town was destroyed." said Nathan.

"It's true. Five thousand people, or more, were massacred under the German bombs. Very few survived, but those who did fled to Bermeo on the coast, about twenty miles away, which is one location where Paul Wallris' two ships stopped to retrieve refugees, eluding the blockade, of course. Most of the refugees who've been able to get out, though, came through Bilbao."

"Mr. Wallris owned two of those boats?" asked Philip.

"His company did. He himself had given the order for their use in this rescue operation. So you see, we do not know how his death will affect the availability of those two ships. And I daresay we need every available vessel to get those people out before the damned Germans get back to their wicked destruction."

"Who is 'we'?" Nathan posed the question.

"We who support the legitimate government of Spain—the very government that is now standing solely against this rising tide of German and Italian militarism." He was pouring hot water into their teacups.

"Communists?" asked Nathan.

Mr. Greeneglass laughed. He set the kettle back on the stove, turned around and faced his visitors again. "Do I look like a Communist?" he asked, shrugging.

"No," replied Nathan. "Obviously, you're not a Communist, nor a Spaniard, because it is not likely that a Jewish tailor fitting clothes in the heart of London would be either of those. So, whom do you represent?"

"I represent anybody who is willing to stand against Hitler and Mussolini, and their beastly stormtroopers who are trying to take over Spain, and probably all of Europe. It is bad enough we've got two dictators on the Continent without them setting up a third one. Furthermore, I have documentation, gentlemen, that my people—the Jewish people who are unfortunate enough to be citizens under the Third Reich--are being systematically arrested in large numbers, deprived of their property, forced to relocate into appalling places, and even, in some cases, murdered by Hitler's SS."

Nathan's spoon clattered noisily against the saucer as he had dropped it after stirring in sugar and milk. "Sorry," he said.

Mr. Greeneglass continued. "So, no, my friends, I am not a Communist, and I do not represent or support them. There are a few of their stripe who are part of the coalition that supports the Spanish government against those bloody Fascist insurgents. Most of the Spanish who are trying to retain their government of the center are just hard-working folk who do not want to be ruled by a dictator or a corrupt king. And they need help from outside if they're going to protect themselves and their government from being taken over by the beasts." He set a few scones out on a dish for them, a mere formality with the cigars already being fired up. It was something his wife had taught him to do. "Furthermore, the urgency of this situation is why I was so insistent that you accompany me here. If you have any information about Paul's last communications, I need to know what they were, if you are willing to help us overcome the effects of his untimely death. I gather from observing your talk to the policeman that there was a note. Can you tell me what was in it?"

"The officer had to take the note," Nathan obliged. "He said it was legal procedure in this circumstance that the police should retain it, as evidence, or some such. However, I can tell you that it was brief; it was addressed simply to 'Wallris', and it said that the black shirts would be smoked out...what was it, Philip?"

"The note said," offered Philip, that 'John Bull's ransom would smoke out the black shirts...ah...tomorrow.' ...and 'If not, your bridge would burn.'"

" 'If not,'" Nathan corrected, " 'your bridge—meaning presumably Wallris' bridge—could burn.' It said the bridge *could* burn. And it was signed, 'Chapman.' Do you know who Chapman is?"

"I do not," said Itmar, his brow wrinkling.

Their puzzlement over the Chapman signature lapsed into a lazily long silence, as cigar smoke curled upward. Itmar was not smoking, though his guests were 'raptly appreciating their Cuban rarities. The two young men found themselves punctuating this morning in unexpected smoky meditation over the deathly appointment. Finding themselves, after a blur of sidewalk events, at a toasty kitchen table, they began to ponder the significance of it all. The pumping empire heart of the old city swirled roundabout them outside; it teemed with mounting anticipation for the sacred coronation. There was today, in all England, a rare, sovereign presence that seemed to inhabit every lad and maid, every lord and lady of their ancient kingdom; it hung upon the London mist in glistening magnificence, even unto this very room, and proclaimed with silent certainty that all would be well in the realm of George VI.

The telephone jangled. Itmar answered it. "Hello...Yes, love...I am still at home...Soon, dearest. I'll explain later. I may bring some guests."

Far beyond the coronary flow of Coventry, Piccadilly, Haymarket and Westminster, long distant from Albion shores, westward across the thousand miles of Atlantic expanse, past a few hundred miles of North American coastal plain and piedmont, nestled between greening Appalachian ridges, a low fire was licking through two acres of bottom land. Smoke of a different weedy aroma crackled quietly upward into brisk Blue Ridge mountain dawn. Philip's brother Robert was burning fields, preparing their ground for this year's tobacco crop.

3

Plants

Only a few ridges and valleys from Robert Morrow's controlled burn, in the sleepy North Carolina town of Trail, Heidelberg presses cranked out the weekly edition of the *Trail Ledger*. Pete the pressman inspected the first impressions as his whirlygig printing machine turned pages out with rapid mechanical efficiency. On page 6 was a photograph of the soon-to-be-coronated king of England with his queen and two princesses, a lovely family. The half-tone looked good; there was no story here about King George, just a picture with caption, an item of some passing interest for provincial American curiosities. The page was properly registered and the type was sharp. Having surveyed his work, Pete the pressman approved it, and cranked the press speed up to make its run. With familiar relaxation that accompanied the soon completion of his early morning's work, he began to comprehend the informational content of his May 12 newspaper product.

One item of interest was, he noticed, in the Agricultural News column. It was a notification to farmers about documenting tobacco acreage, with information about participation in the new federal conservation and allotment program. Upon obtaining some paper forms from the local

Agricultural Extension office, the article said, the farmer could . . ."fill out a worksheet, and find out just what he needs to do to get the most out of the program. Then if it suits him to do whatever he must do to earn his payments he can do it and get paid for doing it."

"Hmmm," thought the pressman, "I'll have to remember to do that." As he was planning to set out an acre of his own on the old home place to generate some extra cash, come fall.

In the next room, Henry the typesetter was hurriedly composing, from the leaden trays of his typographic and photogravure armature, an ad for this edition's last page soon to be printed. The large display ad read:

Mr. Kool will broadcast the Kentucky Derby Day, May 21.
Accompanying the message was a background photo of a racehorse and jockey poised for their speedy start.

Being almost done with his work for this edition, Henry's mind began to wander, having been prompted, even by the lead-gray cast image not-yet committed-to-paper, by the galloping prospect of Derby day on a warm spring breeze, Henry could almost taste the mint juleps that would be imbibed by attendees in celebration of that annual contest, only a few weeks from now in a bluegrass eden far away, but not *very* far away, only a couple of hundred miles or so. Such was the power of a well-composed advert upon a man's imagination, furtively competitive imagination, which could be readily ignited by the suggested equestrian scenario.

Of course there was, in the black/white iconoture, no *Kool* cigarette dangling from the jockey's mouth, as he was, no doubt, pretty intent on what he was about to do—spur his prancing mount onward through Kentucky wind, dirt, cinders, and the other steeds' pistonating arses, past thousands of screaming spectators, toward that gloriously-fleured necklace of victory— certainly that bouquet of triumph—rather than, rather than the agony of defeat that would inflict tragic dismay upon a host of his wagering fans. If the jockey were to partake of a *Kool*, surely it would be after the occasion of jubilation, during some moment of reflective celebration after that ground- thundering event had rendered the powerful steed and his cool jockey champions.

But the *Kools* were surely being enfumed by so many excitable horse- watchers in the grandstand, most likely the coiffed and costumed women, whose appreciation for newfangled flavored filtered cigarettes far surpassed that of their men, whose smoking preference generally wafted toward the Lucky Strike, the Chesterfield, or the manly Bullseye.

It was damn-sure a lucky thing, anyway, for the nation and for, indeed, the whole eastern half of Kentucky that they even a had a Kentucky derby anymore, after what had happened just a few miles from that derby track not even thirty years ago. The renegadin' night riders had near'bout destroyed that middle third of the bourbon state with their fiery protestations and midnight raids burning barns and tobacco warehouses, casting forth terror and soiled britches as they rode nocturnally incognito, in rebellious upstart Ku Kluxy hurly-burly to compel Mr. Duke and his Trust to turn loose the tobacco market like it used to be before their monopolizin' capitalist asses had rumped the prices down to 3-2-even 1! cents a pound on the hogshead. The whole string of incendiary events had pret' near ripped the great state of Kentucky into shreds, like the 'baccer leaves that were even now being packed into godforsaken Bonsack machines driving Buck Duke's factories and escalating fortunes, even though the big magnate man himself had passed on to that great golden leaf patch in the sky about ten year ago. The old bull would have bucked all the leaf farmers across southern 'baccer belts into scurrilous servitude, given half a chance, if the Lord hadn't taken him on home into Methodist gloryland.

Henry's daddy had told him about it, the Kentucky Black Patch tobacco war, on account of Uncle Ralph had told them about it, seein' as how he had unfortunately unawares moved right into the middle of the so-called Black Patch region of Kentucky, just before all that goings-on had gone down. Why if it hadn't been for Teddy Roosevelt and the Supreme Court in 1911 the farmers today might be a-payin' the Tobacco Trust to take the blasted leaf off their hands just to get shed of it!

But all daydreamin' about horses and smokin' women and Uncle Ralph's misadventures aside, Henry and Pete and a few other dutiful newspaper personnel managed to crank their weekly *Trail Ledger* out and get it loaded onto the backs of trucks to carry it to every nook and holler of Wechola county. So about nine o'clock in the morning of this fine May the twelfth day in the year of our Lord nineteen hundred and thirty-seven, the two good ole boys stepped out onto King Street with a hankerin' for a cup of coffee and some biscuits and gravy from Joe's drugstore diner only a minute-walk away.

"I'm gonna stop in here a minute, if'n you don't care, to pick up some smokes, and I need some .22 shells for the crows." said Henry, in post-

Elizabethan English, though not the Kings' version. Entering Morrow's Store, the two men greeted a well-fed woman behind the counter. "Good morning, Sylvie."

"What makes you think it's so good, Henry?" replied the portly lady, her cheeks rosy with some indeterminable emotion. Sylvie's expression was deadpan serious, as if she were truly posing the question, not just making small-talk.

"Well sweetie," replied Henry. "All of Wataboudit county gets to read another excellent edition of the *TrailLedger*, for one thing. "What's got you looking so worried?"

"Somehow, I just never thought I'd see the day. . ." she said.

"The day that what?" asked Henry.

"The old man didn't wake up this morning."

"Mr. Morrow? He didn't wake up this morning?"

"Nope."

"You mean he died, Sylvie?"

"That's. . .that's what I'm sayin'. He died." Her eyes were tearing.

"Last night? in his sleep?. . ." Henry reached slowly across the counter, put his hand gently on Sylvie's shoulder. "Oh honey, I'm so sorry. . ." Sylvie began to weep.

"My gran'ma always said we'd all wake up dead one morning," said Pete.

Henry cast a wary look sideways at Pete, and furrowed his brow. He moved around the cash register to the end of the counter. Sylvie instinctively moved in the same direction to meet him there, and Henry administered what they call at church a holy hug. "Oh hon', it happens to all of us, some time or other. We've all got our appointed time to go be with the Lord." Henry spoke with reassurance, in an appropriately mournful tone. He rocked the grieving woman gently side to side with the holy hug. "Ole Roby was a great man; he lived such a life here! A lot of people gonna miss him. How old was your grandfather, Sylvie?" He stepped back and looked upon her with compassion.

"He would have been eighty-four today," Sylvie sad, composing herself. Just a hint of recovery smile crossed her countenance.

"Today? Roby died on his birthday?"

"That's right." Now she produced an actual smile, and wiped tears away.

"How did you hear about it?" asked Pete.

"Robert called on the telephone about an hour ago. He had just come in from burning off their field, and grampa hadn't got out of bed yet. Robert went in and found him, said he looked as peaceful as he could be."

"When it's my time to go, that's the way I want it to be," offered Pete.

"Yes, yes," agreed Henry, "and I've heard it said among the wise that the best a fella can hope for is to die in his sleep."

"And to know where he's a-goin' when he wakes up on the other side," added Pete.

"Why, sure." Henry put his arm on Pete's shoulder. "He's gone to be with the Lord now, Sylvie. You can rest assured of that. What about, uh, what about the family, all the young'uns, and the grandchildren?"

"Justine has called everyone on the telephone, except maybe Philip. He's all the way over in London, England now. She said she was going to send him a telegram." Sylvie retrieved a hankie from her blouse pocket, wiped the tears away. She shook her head as if to wipe away the emotional distraction. Customers were walking in the door. Recovering, she looked up and managed a smile. "Well, that's neither here nor there, Henry. People die every day, and we've got a store to run here, thanks to grampa. . . I mean, thanks to the hard work that he put into this place, and it wouldn't even be here if he hadn't worked and sweated all those years after papa, I mean. . .his own son, never came back from Flanders field. . ."

"He and Emma sure did do right by all you youn'uns, didn't he, Sylvie? He was a fine man. I think God broke the mold after he created your grandfather," Henry said softly. His effort to comfort her had met with success.

"Thank you. But what'd you come in here for, Henry? What can I get for you?"

"Are you sure you're alright, Sylvie?"

"I'm okay. I appreciate your encouragement, and we really do have a business to run here. Its what he would want done. . .its what he did every day of his life—get up do what needs to be done."

"In that case, you can get me a pack of Camels, and I'm going over here to get me some .22 shells to keep the crows off my seed corn."

Other customers stepped up to the counter. Sylvie checked them out with a courteous greeting and restored sense of duty. Henry ambled over to the shelf he was looking for, picked up his box of bullets, and returned to the cash register, paid for the purchase. "You'uns will call me if we can help, won't you?"

"We will, Henry. Thank you so much, you too, Pete."

"We'll see you at the funeral home, then, Sylvie, if not before. Don't hesitate to call if you need to," Henry assured her. Then he and Pete were out the door and back on Main Street. "That'll be one helluva big funeral," said Henry to his friend. They crossed the street, entered Joe's drug store and went back to the diner area. Henry took a seat on his usual stool at the corner of the counter. An old fella was sitting on the stool at the other side of the corner. "How you doin', George?"

The man nodded minimally at Henry and Pete. He slurped coffee. "Can't complain, nobody listen," said George, curtly.

"You're right about that, George. There's no point in complaining about anything. We oughta just thank the good Lord we're here for another sunrise."

A matronly waitress reached around the napkin holder and condiments, placed two coffees on the shiny formica. "The usual for you boys?" she asked.

"Your hair looks lovely this morning, Maybelle."

"Why thank you, Pete."

"I'll have waffles," returned Pete.

"No biscuits and gravy for you this morning?" said the red-haired woman of dignified maturity.

"No, ma'am. I've got a hankerin' for the waffles this morning, and some blueberries." He smiled.

"I'll have the biscuits and gravy," said Henry.

"Comin' right up." With no wasted effort, Maybelle whisked to the other end of the counter to refresh coffee cups for here charges there.

"Yeah, George, we're lucky to be alive today, don't ya know," said Henry belatedly.

"I guess you heard about Roby," said George.

"Yessir. We were just in the store and Sylvie told us he died in his sleep."

"He was a fine man. I'd like to have a dollar for every time he extended credit for folks around here."

"I hear ya, George. I wish we had more like him." lamented Henry.

"Roby was a generous man. He just about kept this whole town going, six year ago when burley prices went down to nine cents," said George.

"Tell me about it. I think he spent that whole year selling our papers and never took a dime for it. We were cutting in pretty close back then," Henry agreed.

"That was when Roby gave a peppermint stick to every kid that walked in the door after Thanksgiving, clear on past Christmas," Pete recalled.

George chuckled. "Yeah boys, I remember that. I had to stop my grandkids from going in there so much, so's they wouldn't abuse the privilege."

"He was generous to a fault. I don't know how he ever managed to prosper so well," wondered Pete.

"Make no mistake about it, Pete. Roby was as shrewd as they come. He was merciful on the small change stuff, but he knew how to keep his accounts. I mean. . .you see that place across the street. That kind of enterprise don't just happen without some mighty skillful wheelin' and dealin," George said.

"What year was it he started the store?" asked Henry.

"1893."

". . .when I was ten years old," mused Henry.

"Yep. I was 22, and I think Roby was about ten years ahead of me. Boys, I'll tell ya, it was a hard day for him when he got the word about Clint."

"You're talking about Sylvie's daddy. He never came back from the war."

"That's right. Clint died on Flanders field, in Belgium. Our boys, under General Pershing, drove the Germans back to the Hindenberg Line—and that was the beginning of the end for them."

"The beginning of the end for the Germans?" asked Pete.

"Yeah, but it was the end of the line for young Clint Morrow, God bless 'im."

"Yeah, that's a damn tragedy," Henry lamented.

George continued his tale of World War woe. "But really, the damnedest part of all was that Sylvie and Philip were just little ones when their daddy joined the army." George turned a little wistful, looked deeply into his half-full coffee cup. "Boys, I tell ya, it ain't right that a young man like that should have gone off to a goddam terrible war like that was over there, and then never make it back here to raise them young'uns. Its tragic, and him with a beautiful wife."

Maybelle eased the breakfasts onto the counter for Henry and Pete. Silently, she filled their coffee cups. The terrible cost of armistice was heavy upon that corner of her gleaming short-order domain this Wednesday morning of the year of our Lord 1937. You could have cut George's sudden solemnity with a dinner knife, but she didn't. Lifting her coffee urn, she retreated to other duties.

"Yeah, it's a damn shame," George continued. "And now that little Hitler fella is stirrin' up the German hornets' nest again. You've heard about the bombs they're dropping in Spain?"

"Up in the Basque, up in the mountains, you mean?" asked Pete.

"Yeah, that big bombing a couple weeks ago, the village—what was it?"

"Guernica."

"Yeah, that place—those were not Spanish bombs coming out of the sky. It was Nazi bombers doing Franco's dirty work."

"Isn't General Franco trying to run the communists out of the Spanish government?" asked Pete.

"Hmmph," George let out a big incredulous grunt. "Who cares about the wimpin' communists when you've got the Germans disregarding all the treaties that our boys died for—the peace that Clint Morrow died in Flanders field for." George stuck his finger up in the air, pointing eastward. "I tell you boys, this ain't good—what's happening over there between that little German mustache and his bald dago sidekick. They're trying to set up another dictator just like them in Spain, so they can take over the whole continent of Europe, maybe the whole world."

Another diner walked to the counter, set a wet raincoat aside, and occupied the stool to George's left. His raincoat was dripping, and it was obvious to all that rain was falling outside.

"Well all I can say, George, is I hope you're wrong. I hope Hitler and Mussolini and Franco don't take over the world. "Where did you hear that about those bombs being from Germany?" asked Henry.

George let out a big sigh, a tension-breaker. He took a gulp of coffee. "Hell, I don't remember. I heard it on the radio, and I think I read it in the Charlotte paper a couple days ago. Some congressman, I think, or one of them fellas in Washington was saying that it was the German air force."

"The Luftwaffe," added Pete.

"Right. That's what they call it. For all we know it's the Baron von Richthofen ghosts come back to haunt the French and the Brits.

Heavy silence fell upon the three men as they listened to the newcomer at the counter order ham and eggs.

"Maybelle?" called Henry.

"What, hon?" The dignified waitress stepped sideways in their direction.

"Do you think Baron von Richthofen could come back to haunt the world?" asked Henry, raising his eyebrows.

"Oh, God, no.' She flashed a slight smile, did an about face and returned to her life's mission. "God forbid," she called, turning her head back slightly as she walked away.

"Well, George, that was a great sacrifice that the Morrows made, sending their young Clint over there."

"Yes, it was. And then, in spite of his terrible loss, Roby took Clint's widow on, and them two kids, and raised 'em up. And he had a heart of gold, even though he knew full well how to make a dime or two. He knew how to walk that fine line between mercy and judgment."

"Like God," Pete spoke. "Behold the mercy and the severity of the Lord."

"Yeah, Pete, a little like God. It's a damn good thing there's little bit of God's work spread around in this world; otherwise the place would be all shot to hell," George opined. "And Roby was a true saint, in spite of what he had to go through. He could have turned real bitter. But he didn't. Instead of turning bitter, he got better."

"Right, George, a good man he was. And he did carry a lot of folks in these parts, back in '31 when the burley went down to nine cents, and the cabbage wasn't too plentiful either that year,"

A mischievous smile crept across George's face. "Ah, boys, but we don't need to worry about such things as that any more."

"What do you mean?"

"Mr. Roosevelt and his gang of New Dealers got it all figured out. They're gonna take care of the farmers now."

"They will, George," chimed in Pete. "I saw that this morning as I was printing our paper. The County Agent is going to have paper forms for all the leaf producers to fill out, so they can get paid a decent amount for their crop no matter what happens in the weather and the fall market."

"Really, now. Who says they got money enough to insure everybody's tobacco crop?" asked George.

"That fella in Raleigh—I think his name is Cobb, Billy Cobb or something like that—he says the AAA is getting set up to protect all the farmers against hazards, and guarantee them cash at the end of the season—"

"Yeah, buddy, what do they have to do get that guv'ment deal, huh?"

"Well, I think they have to cut back a little on their crop, plant a little bit less, so there's not too much 'baccer being traded come November. That way the price will be decent, and the Agriculture administration won't really have to pay out that much, because the price will stay high."

"Hmmph," George grunted. I think you're dreaming if you think that's gonna work the way it s'posed to. How much 'baccer will you be plantin' this month anyway?

"Just about a half-acre," answered Pete. "I don't do near what dad used to do, what with my job at the Ledger and all."

George laughed out loud. His earlier sombriety had definitely swung around now to something lighter. "Why, you're just a fly on the wall, boy, to those fellas in Raleigh, and in Washington. You think all that crop-bustin' shenanigans is gonna do anything for the little guy like you? No. It's the warehousemen, and the big growers down east, 'round Greenville, Wilson and those parts. They're the ones gonna rake in on that deal."

"And the tobacco companies," Henry tossed in.

George laughed again. "Yeah, buddy. They've got it figured out."

Maybelle was just now setting a plate of ham and eggs on the counter for the gentleman in the seat to George's left. "Can I get you anything else with that, sir?" she asked.

"No, thank you," said he. But before he got into the food, he turned toward the other three diners and said, "The Supreme Court ruled in January that the Agricultural Adjustment Administration is unconstitutional. So how are they going to run such a program if the highest court in the land has ruled against their power to do so?"

George was laughing again.

"Oh, they'll figure out a way to do it," said Henry. I think the state Ag agents and the Farm Bureau are going to come up with something that will work along those lines."

"That Cobb fella is a director of the AAA, as the Charlotte paper reported yesterday, and talked like they were just going right ahead with the plan. Do you know how they're going to do that?" asked Pete.

"I do not," said the man, with a wry smile. He sliced a piece of ham, lifted it to his mouth on the fork, and consumed it.

Henry pulled out his new pack of Camels, opened the cellophane, put the cigarette in his mouth and lit it.

4

Dreams

A hundred miles from where Henry unwrapped his pack of Camels and lit up to partake of its smoky pleasure, the manufacturer in Winston-Salem was busily churning out thousands more of those same packets. A piedmont gal named Glenda Brown was inspecting the little finished boxes that had been made attractive to the eye with camels and pyramids printed on their fronts; she operated a machine that collected the units into cartons of ten packs each. From that eastern US location the Camel cartons would be shipped all over the world.

A shipment of dreams they were—millions of little white cylinders to enflame smoky flights of fancy and nicotinal moments of repose from here to Shanghai and Shangri-la and everywhere in between. What had been in ages past magical pipe dreams were now being conjured *en masse* from the little white cylinders.

The most potent cloud of smoky profitability in the history of the world was wafting market-to-market, continent-to-continent, clueless of the surgeon general's report that would be issued decades later. Such are the historic enterprises of ***homo sapiens:*** They go and go, they run and run in frenzied productivity until their business plans are exposed one day to be a mere wisp of metastasizing smoke that contributes to   dark clouds of gathering futility.

All is vanity, saith the Teacher.

An imaginative marketer in the employ of the tobacco company had, at some point in the product's development, figured out that tobacco ruminations could be kindled even at the points of sale, before a purchase was made by any eager smoker. Why, just the sight of those strange humpy-backed mammals on the package was sufficient to vastly initiate wild imaginations among the legions of smokers. *Give me some Turkish tobacco* said the smoker to his wallet, upon seeing the camel and his mysterious background pyramid.

This little scenario had worked quite well for the Winston-Salem company. Although the rich heritage and reputation of Turkish tobaccos was actually found many hundreds of miles from Egyptian pyramids, the scene depicted on the packet's cover had accomplished exactly what it was intended to do—inspire the sales of millions of cigarettes.

What an odd-looking creature was the camel to the American eye, quite exotic.

It might be just such a golden-hued camel as that one on the cigarette packet. Probably just such a camel was, at this moment, tromping through real, Egyptian sands. It might be transporting a young officer-in-training, a young Egyptian of humble origin whose saber-sharp mind would one day embark upon a great destiny—a *coup d'etat* to depose, fifteen years from now, the very king of Egypt. That military trainee, Anwar el-Sadat, would ultimately preside over the Arab independence that would extricate itself from John Bull's colonializing exploitation, although the Brits would call it civilizing.

It might have been just such a sauntering camel that transported the dutiful cadet, almost in the shadow of the great pyramid, from his barracks to a class in military discipline that was a part of his training with the honorable Egyptian army. The camel's rhythmic pace may have pumped young Anwar's active mind into a forceful understanding of the task that was, even now, being passed to him across the muezzined Arabian world. The legacy of Kemal Ataturk was mobilizing in his direction. Magnifying its urgency was his childhood remembrance of the ballad of Zahran. Perhaps even now, at this early phase of his life, the ambitious officer-to-be was pondering plans for Arab unity that would someday solidify Mohammedan unity between Turkey, Egypt, and all points between and beyond.

Alas, in the distance, northward from ancient Egyptian pyramids, across the waters of Suez and the Sinai sands, there labored a young American-born Jewish woman whose cigarette-fueled life mission was parallel, though at-odds with, Sadat's. Golda worked tirelessly toward actualizing the dreams of her displaced people—dreams of an Israeli socialist state that would someday somehow exist, miracle of miracles, on that same narrow *eretz Israel* which was now unfortunately connecting Turkey and Syria to Egypt.

A square peg in a round dreidel was this long-hoped-for eretz Israel, saddled inconveniently between a fading Turkish star and the Camel on the Nile.

He the plus, she the minus—together they would spark brightly between a charged volatility of rival Abrahamic elements. Even now, their reactivity began to bubble up in intense heat of middle-easterly human strife.

In the Germanic fatherland of the next continent over, a contentious little Austrian usurper with a stunted moustache was wildly maneuvering to become, among other things, catalyst in the incendiary reaction between impetuous Arab and wandering Jew. In recruiting the grand Amin el-Husayni of Jerusalem, der fuehrer would entertain no tolerance for Jewish dreams of statehood, and no sympathy for wailings at the Wall.

Their strangely swastikified collusion was soon to be direly opposed by sacrificial Allied effort. Between a resolute British bulldog, an intrepid Russian taskmaster, and a consummate yankee politician with a cigarette-holder jutting from his jaw, the unholy duo would be snuffed out on the ashtray of historical disgrace. But that was still a long way off.

Back in the wilderness, in the midst of pyramidic antiquity, a camel's plodding pace was about to kick up a triple-stranded fuse to ignite all hell breaking loose:

-Ataturk, Abdullah, mufti al-Husayni, Hitler

- Herzl, Weizmann, Rothschild. Ben-Gurion

- Balfour, Lloyd George, Allenby, Churchill

The resultant smoke plumes would darken skies for many years to come, but not yet. It was still only 1937, and a king was being crowned in England, probably at this very moment.

His loyal administrators were striving to walk a global line somewhere between the constructs of civilization and the perquisites of exploitation. On this day, a merely mortal man sat expectantly upon an 870-year-old chair in Westminster Abbey in London. He sought the relative immortality of that functional anointment into which he had been born. But more importantly, he sought the endorsement of his enduring government, the fealty of his people, and the very unction of God.

For, as the *Times* would reflect a week later, there resided in the anointing of the British sovereign an "obstinate unanimity beyond the power of republican rationalism to touch." And while the principle of kingship seemed to some an "outworn superstition," and to others in the wide world a perpetual enabling of classic injustice, it nevertheless persisted among the resolute Britons as a "permanent instinct in human nature itself."

And so a stammering prince was awaiting, this afternoon, an endowed authority that would draw its strength from "powers outside human life." The *Times* of London could still opine, with resolute naïveté in the year of our Lord 1937, this conviction. The King would accept those powers not for himself, but for the life of his tribe. And yet, along with the timeless noble aspirations of his monarchy and its trained empire, all the base and selfish manipulations of humankind would surely accompany the king's subjects wherever they would set foot to represent their collective interests.

This was the perpetual problem that confronted his highness' loyal subjects in all the dominions of his vast empire--this the confounding yoke that vexed men and women throughout the wide world who found themselves beneath the "civilizing" thumb of John Bull's heavy, though benevolent, hand. It was the same oppressive power-gathering hegemony that had provoked us Americans to reject, one hundred and sixty-one years prior, the authority of George's namesake. It was the same meddlesome administrative tinkering that now irked Muslims and Jews in the holy eretz land of Palestine. It was the empire-wielding, irksome administrative intrusions that so frustrated the king's hapless subjects in every duchy, province and state from Hong Kong to Bombay to Bethlehem, and even unto Birmingham and Belfast.

Such feckless authority, though quite calculated and systematic, was nevertheless all too arbitrary and oppressive in its effects upon colonialized populations. In spite of all efforts, whether well-intended or ill, from the

King's dutiful minions, the consequences of their empire-building generally proved just about as predictable as rising smoke.

Back in London, continents away from the labored shuffle of camels' feet through Judean sands, far from the breezy flap of elephants' ears in distant Asian dominions, and landward from the decks and draughts of all His Majesty's ships at sea, here, here in the very heart of the empire, the American Philip Morrow stood at a window, watching crowds go by. The cigar that Mr. Greeneglass had provided for him emitted a pungent aroma trail, curling upward and seeming to disappear into the thick, indeterminable haze of striving civilization that enveloped the city. An incoming tide of expectant Brits, one floor below them on Haymarket Street, sent up low rumbles of pedestrian noise, mutedly audible through the window glass. Hundreds of hats, slickery macs and dripping umbrellas passed beneath the dry warmth from which he surveyed their bottlenecking passage. Most were headed from his right to left, north to south, in a slow stream toward Trafalgar Square, as if there were still enough room in that cobbled expanse to accommodate them all.

Itmar Greeneglass had guided their conversation to an explanation of the deceased man's maritime assets, especially two freighter ships, and his use of them to transport food to the refugees from civil war in Spain.

"The Government's non-intervention policy is, whether our comfortable MPs will admit it or not, working against the good people of Spain, and most assuredly working against their progress toward democracy," said Itmar. "Mr Wallris' bold willingness to support the Basques, in spite of the blockade, will strengthen their fight against Franco's Fascist insurgents."

Nathan said, "I've always thought that those cranky Basques in the north fancied themselves independent from the government in Madrid. Are you sure they are acting in the wider interests of Spain? They could be fence-sitting up in the Pyrenees, just waiting for this thing to blow over."

"While that is true, Nathan, the Basques are starting to feel the heat of Franco's push in a big way. The bombing of Guernica two weeks ago clarified the issue for them. And since that time—and especially since Franco's assault on Madrid was repelled, General Mola has unleashed a fierce attack, but the Basques have, so far, managed to drive them out. Now Mola is besieging Bilbao and trying to starve the people into submission. Hell, there are 400,000 people driven into Bilbao; more than half of them are women and children. This is precisely where Paul Wallris' two ships, the *Brickburn* and the *Olavian*, made such a big difference. His crews were able to, almost at a moment's notice, get those two carriers into the Bilboa river loaded with food and supplies—and who knows, maybe a gun or two down in the hold—and then after unloading them, pulling two full loads of refugees back out, and over to France at St. Jean de Luz."

"And the British government is working against this effort?" asked Philip.

"They've been debating in the House of Commons, but the Guernica destruction has made the truth painfully obvious what is really going on in Spain. The people of Britain should have no interests in abetting Franco in any way, whether by non-intervention or otherwise, especially when it becomes clearer every day that the insurgents are getting heavy military support from Mussolini and Hitler."

"And you think the Basques are siding with the government in Madrid?" Nathan queried again.

"The autonomous government of the Basque country is being represented in London by the Spanish ambassador," insisted Itmar.

A moment of silence crept in; they could hear the low rumble of the people in the street. An ambulance passed by with its whooping Doppler horn crescendo and then waning as the vehicle managed to crawl through the street.

"You know," said Nathan softly, "the Basques helped us greatly in the War. They are a brave, hearty, God-fearing race of fisherman and peasants. They got food and raw materials through to us in their own ships when our danger was very real, so I've been told. And they lost thirty ships in doing it."

"Exactly so, Mr. Wachov, and this is how we, a generation later, express our gratitude? By standing aside and allowing the Luftwaffe to bomb hell out of them? By pretending that Mussolini's goons aren't being sent in there to install another fascist *coup d'etat* on the Continent?"

Philip, standing at the window, noticed that two men who had been let out from the rear doors of the ambulance were now standing at the curb in front of the Greeneglass shop, and looking upward in his direction. It seemed as if in a dream, but suddenly he could see, without explanation, one of the two men was pointing at him, directly up at him—Philip Morrow, and trying to get his attention.

Philip blurted out loud, "Me?" He pointed to himself, and he spoke again to the window, "You wanna talk to me?"

The man, dressed sharply in brown suit and bowler hat, pointed upward at him again, and then back at himself, and was mouthing a silent, though quite understandable message. He wanted t o talk to Philip. Philip reached for the window lock, carefully removing a blue glass star of David artpiece that hung on a string, as he did so. With a somewhat clumsy motion, he opened the window sash. "Mr. Greeneglass, I hope you don't mind me opening your window, but there's a man out there who...uh..."

Then Itmar and Nathan were beside him at the window. The three of them looked down at the unexpected sight of this man in brown, with an unopened umbrella in his raised hand, pointing toward the shop door and obviously communicating a request to be admitted therein.

Philip, not an audacious sort in this nation of unfamiliar proprieties, was clueless. Itmar put his head out the window and yelled, "Certainly, sir. We'll be right down."

Without closing the window, Itmar turned on a heel, proceeded toward the door and the stairway. "I can tell by his suit, he's a policeman, probably a detective. Come along now." Philip and Nathan followed, back through the door of the flat, down the creaky stair, and through the clothing shop to the front door. Itmar opened it with a broad gesture. He stood aside as the two men entered, their clothes sparkling with London fog. "Good afternoon, gentlemen. Welcome to the Greeneglass shop," said he.

"Good morning," said the man in the light brown suit. He took his hat off. "I am Inspector Neville Crossbough, of Scotland Yard. This is my assistant, Dr. Harold Pepper."

"Do come in, gentlemen," said Itmar, and shut the door behind them.

"Thank you," the tall man obliged, stepping in, with Dr. Pepper following.

The inspector was a wiry man of about 60 years. He was wearing a starched white shirt, and necktie of deep scarlet background with small, leonine emblems of gold patterned on it. The khaki brown of his suit seemed to meld seamlessly with a ruddy complexion. Beneath untrimmed, arched brows that were darker than his sandy hair, the inspector's penetrating eyes assessed the young men skillfully. He spoke first to Nathan. "You, sir, are, I take it, mister. . . ah, Mr. Wachov?" He glanced at an open notebook in his hand, then back up, planting his eyes firmly on Nathan's.

"Yes, sir."

"So you are the man in whose arms Paul Wallris expired just two hours ago?"

"That's correct."

"I know you have given an account of that incident to Officer Morley. I am the detective whose task it is to correctly document his untimely death. Would you mind describing for me what happened back there in front of the tobacconist's shop?"

"Not at all, sir. He had gotten our attention with what seemed to be an incoherent statement about monetary policies, or some such. I could not really understand what he was trying to say. He did mention the gold standard." Nathan looked at Philip and continued. "But before he got too far into it, the next thing I know he's collapsing. He would have hit the sidewalk quite heavily if I hadn't grabbed him. Then I. . .well, I eased him down slowly. It seemed like the best thing to do. When he was down on the sidewalk, he opened his hand and the note fell out. He was. . .uh. . . gasping, and drooling. And then the life just passed out of him."

"I see." The inspector was silent for a moment. He looked at Dr. Pepper, then back at Nathan. "How old are you, Mr. Wachov?"

"Twenty-eight, sir."

"Have you ever seen a person die before today?"

"No, sir."

"Was it what you expected?"

Nathan wanted, for some strange reason, to laugh a bit, but stifled the impulse. "Well, no, I, uh, I didn't expect to have a man dying in my arms today. I mean, I never. . . no, it wasn't what I expected. Death is not a welcome event. It was quite disturbing, actually."

"Did his death strike you as . . . natural? Was it, do you think, a natural death?"

"I really have no idea. I mean, the way he was gasping was quite alarming, bordering on something like, like some internal violence. But then, like I said, I don't have anything to compare it too. Isn't death, by definition, a kind of. . . a kind of tearing away, a wrenching away?"

Inspector Crossbough was gazing intently at him. After an uncomfortable pause, he responded slowly, "Yes, yes I suppose it is." Then he shifted his gaze to Philip. "What about you, Mr. Morrow? Is that the way you saw it?"

"Pretty much, sir. Yes, and like Nathan, I was on unfamiliar ground with this. I don't think I've ever even seen a dead person, unless they were in a casket."

"How old are you?"

"The same. Twenty-eight."

"How long have you been in England?"

"About ten months, sir. I arrived on the White Star line last July."

"Is there anything more you can tell me about this man's demise, then?"

The two young men, looking at each other, shook their heads. Nathan said, "That's about the whole of it sir."

"I may, of course, have more questions for you at some other time, you understand?"

"Certainly, sir," Philip responded readily, as Nathan agreed with a nod.

The inspector looked at Itmar. "I do have a few questions for you, Mr. Greeneglass, but I prefer to ask them in private."

"Surely," agreed Itmar.

"Then, with your permission, I will dismiss these gentlemen from your shop, and we'll get on with it." Turning again to the younger men, he offered a formal smile, though it seemed quite benevolent.

Though he was a little surprised with the brevity of the Inspector's enquiry of them, Philip addressed Itmar. "Well, we know where you are, Mr. Greeneglass. I will certainly visit your shop again some time."

"As will I," added Nathan. "Thank you for your hospitality."

"You are both most welcome any time. In fact, I will likely be calling you on the telephone soon. You may need my services some time. Certainly, Philip, you will need a tailor's speciality at some point, as I know you are a salesman." He smiled broadly, and shook their hands.

Inspector Crossbough and Mr. Pepper stepped aside. The two younger men departed. Itmar Greeneglass closed his shop door gently behind them. Philip, turning left, southward, toward Trafalgar, entered the pedestrian stream behind Nathan and they were once again engaged in that same slow, crowd-encumbered walk, and in the same direction, that they had been doing before all this unexpected deathly occurrence had been thrust upon them. It seemed like a bad dream as Philip's feet, or the flow of humanity and hats and faces surrounding them, swept him along, almost involuntarily. Maybe death itself, he thought, is something like this—just drifting suddenly, without sufficient explanation or forewarning, into some kind of moving confluence.

With an unfamiliar perplexity, he looked back at the Greeneglass shop, and almost wondered if the whole string of events had really happened. Looking back, he noticed they were late, and a final image of the shop door with its green and gold letters gilded itself upon his memory. Even as every step took Philip further away, his gaze lingered upon the shop where he had found his way upstairs and had a smoke. Then somebody spoke and he went into a dream.

A dream shared by an entire nation, yea, an entire empire, a broken empire, a faltering realm, a fractured commonwealth of stumbling dominions. It was a dream of peace, almost seen. Yet the British people would be slowly discovering, beneath the luster of this giddy coronation euphoria, an unwelcome truth that there would be no peace in the continent of Europe. The 1918 Armistice dream was slowly being cast down, beneath a million uncaring feet, and trodden into the gutters of history.

It had been a dream of peace. Now it was being slowly ripped apart by two marauding beasts—two fiercely animalistic entities of communism and of fascism. While English bankers and politicians appeased a rising blitzkrieg of Hitlerian genocide, a red blaze of arbitrary Stalinist cruelty gathered unnoticed intensity to incite a tinder box of despairing European order. Spain would be the magnifying glass that now focused deadly rays of explosive power on their shrinking world. *I read the news today, oh boy, the English army had just won the war. A crowd of people turned away, but I just had to look, having read the book.*

"For in one hour such great wealth has been laid waste! And every shipmaster and every passenger and sailor, and as many as make their living by the sea, stood at a distance, and were crying out as they saw the smoke of her burning, saying, 'What city is like the great city?'"

Nathan, plodding along just in front of his friend Philip, looked down at his watch: 11:55 a.m. At this moment, only a mile or so from here, a vulnerable man of faltering speech—though he was a man of pre-ordained, ancient authority—was taking his seat at Westminster, and preparing to take a sacred oath. The appointed man was about to take upon himself the ceremonial masthead of a most seaworthy vessel—a warship that would turn back that tide of dreadful smoke, for a generation or two, or three.

5

Ghost

Oliver Cromwell found no eternal rest at Westminster Abbey. Soon after his burial there in 1658, the son of the king whose death warrant Cromwell had signed nine years earlier ordered Cromwell's body to be taken out of the sacred ground and publicly humiliated. Such heathen practices are nonetheless an undeniable part of Christendom's culpable history.

Oliver Cromwell's ghost wasn't an actual haunting spirit, of course, but rather the ever-present vulnerability of accumulated human power and wealth to be overthrown and redistributed by some upstart band of rebels. Since the royalist supporters of King Charles II of England had proclaimed Cromwell a regicide, or king-killer (along with the other 58 souls who had signed King Charles' death warrant in 1649), the presence of his contentious body, though dead, could not be tolerated in Westminster Abbey.

So Cromwell's body was not there beneath the pavestones of Westminster Abbey. Such was not the case for Charles Darwin, whose body was buried there at Westminster Abbey, along with a host of many other foundational persons whose life's works had formed the character of Britain's legacy to the wider world. Although the subsequent effects of Darwin's 19th-century biological research had done much to undermine orthodox church theology, his body nevertheless had been interred beneath those hallowed gravestones, along with so many other luminaries, notable persons, and kings and queens of England. Darwin's impact having been of a different quality than Cromwell's, his ghost exposed a different vulnerability to the institutions of human power and wealth.

Despite all that Cromwellian displacement of politics and all that Darwinian unearthing of sacred orthodoxy, the kings and queens of England were still, in this year of our Lord 1937, managing to reign over their people. So they were quite fortunate, yea, even abundantly blessed, when compared to, say, Alfonso of Spain, who had been deposed from his monarchy by a republican movement a scant six years ago. So today's overwhelmingly popular coronation in London was no small feat for a royal house.

The seven thousand or so people who had gathered at Westminster Abbey were entranced in the occasion's grandiose solemnity and magnificence. It is not likely that most of them entertained thoughts of the ghostly vestiges inhabiting this millennial edifice. On the other hand, it could be that many of them were aware of the lingering ethereal legacy of powerful personages from ages long ago. So many of the congregants at Westminster today had to sit for hours, perhaps contemplating the historical and ecclesiastical meaning of the cavernous hall, as they awaited the crowning of King George VI.

Langlis Afton, a very notable lady among the contemporary crop of British potentates, sat expectantly among those who had been invited to enter the cathedral. She listened carefully to the momentous passing of every sacred second during the ceremony. Attentive intuitions had attuned her to those ghosts of the former ages, though she was fully aware of the imminent gravitas of what was happening right here, right now, and quite thankful to be a part of it. Though she had been born a common American, Langlis' skillful conductions of intrigue among English societal and parliamentary potentates had propelled her far into the gilt halls of power. Her magnate husband, Sir Wilbur Afton, sat beside her. As an endowed aristocrat who had expanded his fortunes toward ever greater horizons, he was quite pleased with the proceedings. But Sir Wilbur had not yet heard that a partner in one of his companies had, only three hours ago, passed into eternity while babbling incoherence to a startled young stranger up on Haymarket.

Now began the coronation.

With all the King's promenade having entered from the west door and been ceremoniously positioned, a small, strong voice broke the Abbey's expectant stillness. The Archbishop proclaimed, "Sirs, I here present unto you King George, your undoubted King: Wherefore, all you who are come this day to do your homage and service, are you willing to do the same?"

"God save King George!" shouted those people present in the east parts of the building.

"God save King George!" affirmed those present in the south of the church, in response to the Archbishop's second call.

"God save King George!" pronounced the people in the west of the church, when the priest had sent forth his third call.

"God save King George!" spoke Sir Wilbur and Lady Langlis, along with all others in the north of the church.

Wouldn't Alfonso of Spain have welcomed such proclamations, had they been spoken over him by his own people in these turbulent times!

Wouldn't Pu Yi, the last emperor of China, have been comforted by such agreements if they had been likewise shouted by his own people in the midst of today's perpetual revolutions! But instead, his defunct Qing Manchurian rulership was being puppetized at this very moment by invading Japanese overlords.

This 20th century was no friend to monarchies, except the one in England.

Now the most solemn moment of the service was upon them. With the people having affirmed their allegiance to the King, it was time for, as the *Times* would later report, "the contractual to be lifted to the sacramental level." And so this prayerful song wafted through the air, "Let my prayer come up into Thy Presence as the incense; and let the lifting of my hands be as an evening sacrifice."

But listen! Listen to the small, strong voice, ascending as if smoke, with shouting affirmations and gentle melodies.

The Britons had been o'ertaken ages ago by a greater presence, an inhabiting spirit that manifested a longevity infinitely more pervasive than that of such mortals as these humans be. Occupied long ago, they were, with sprite more spunky than Darwin's or Cromwell's ghostly legacies, or even that of long-dead Archbishops of Canterbury. This holy strengthening ghost would be one whose Lordship, when entreated, can from time to time make straight the contorted sinews of human institutions.

This spirit's incisive tweaking had supplanted the genetic birthright of a distracted prince, displacing it with the resolute character now arising within his younger brother--an appointed brother, now to be an anointed brother, whose stuttering speech would by divine means ensure a most essential humility. And such humility would be sufficient, when supported with the liberty and good will of a resourceful people, to ultimately beat down a brutally destructive arrogance now rearing its beastly head on the continent. It would defeat, with blood, sweat and tears, the intrepid *wehrmacht* foolishness of a usurping so-called Aryan maniac whose militarizing horn was even now rising beyond yonder Channel in the lands of Anglo-Saxon origins. Such were the raging torrents of a flood that would soon engulf old Europe with modern warfare.

Sitting in Westminster Abbey, Langlis' Afton had, as yet, no understanding (though she thought she had) of the immensity of those historical forces. Those forces were presently mustering iniquity into a ghoulish pile somewhere beyond the cold currents that separated Dover from Dunkirk. She had been, like so many other Britons of her persuasion, looking quizzically at the newspaper mirage of an unannounced colonel from some Austrian abyss. It was naively hoped among her circle of influential friends that his vehement reassertion of German power would erect some kind of effective barrier against the Bolshevik menace to the east. Alas, one evil against another does not a defeated evil make, as the world would learn, the hard way, in years to come. But Langlis could not know that now.

"*Veni Creator Spiritus*," sang the choir.

"Come Holy Spirit" must be the prayer of a civilizing people. Surely it is the heart-cry of an ancient kingdom that seeks protection against that dreaded malady of old—barbarism. The people of the King, knowing that the reprobate dragon had long ago been slain, nevertheless understand that the beast periodically thrusts his ugly head from misty bogs of obscurity. It then threatens mankind with odious devourings. As superfluous as the ceremonial Holy Spirit entreaty may sound, it rises now as a primal response. Some suspect odor of lurksome carnage, having drifted across the Channel waters on fierce winds of anarchy, hath provoked it.

Now Westminster Abbey functions anew, as in ages past, as a great cultural nest from which the wild Anglo child, having crawled out from beneath a bloody Saxon rock, cries again for safe nurture.

Deliver us from evil had been the instructive prayer of their religion's founder, the saviour whose crucified body had been nailed upon a Roman cross nineteen centuries ago. A stylized likeness of that torturous cross was positioned high in their cavernous space of architectural grandeur. It hung, almost camouflaged, amidst the high pomp and ceremony, as symbol of some primeval yearning for deliverance from savagery. Ironic icon of death and hopeful resurrection, the damned thing had been erected by the church of England upon a stony Golgotha of every English heart—except, of course, those red-pumping cardiacs of the communists. And the atheists. They were on their own. And the Catholics. But never mind about that now.

Deliver us from barbarity. Give us, by God, a King! Now within this great cathedral of ascending visual splendor, beneath its converging spires of triumph over hell and death, a mere mortal man of unsure speech knelt before his priests and among his peers to accept the royal commission. It had been laid upon him long ago by his people and by his blood.

Another thing that had happened long ago was the reign of King George VI's great, great, great grandfather, George III, whose powdered-wig authority had been laid on the chopping block of history by a bunch of upstarts in America, one of whom—not this time a turbulent priest but rather a zealous colonial patriot, had said, "Give me liberty, or give me death!

Thus had the demise of the British empire begun, even as its great machinery of colonial development was gathering full steam a century and a half ago, on the unruly New World coast. Those infamous words from the mouth of one Patrick Henry had sounded forth beneath the reverberating rafters of a different kind of English church--a Virginia assemblage much humbler in structure, but a lot cockier and more impetuous—than its Westminsterian forebear. Mr. Henry and his compatriots were tindering within discontented colonial hearts a strange new fire, a blaze of republican revolution.

Nor would it be the last time in the next century or two that such a conflummucks would erupt. It was a new summoning spirit, a democratic *zeitgeist,* that had set the world aflame with yearning pangs for liberty. Although not the holy spirit for which good Anglicans prayed, there was something sacred about its demand for freedom among the opinions of mankind.

King George III had married a German princess, Charlotte, of Mecklenburg-Strelitz, in 1761. And so it happened that, during the next year, 1762, the young queen's name, Charlotte, was chosen in her honor as the name of a frontier town in the colony of North Carolina. Also in honor of the Queen's heritage, the name Mecklenburg had been selected for the county in which Charlotte town was located.

Alas, the Carolinians' obeisance toward King George III and his queen was short-lived. A mere fifteen years later, and they had been caught up with their American brethren in the hotspur spirit of the age. The Mecklenburgers' untethered frontier freedom generated America's first formal declaration of independence from Great Britain, May 20, 1775. General Cornwallis later referred to the place as a "hornet's nest of rebellion." Subsequent history revealed that Charlotte/ Mecklenburg would not be the only problem spot for King George III and his soldiers. A year later, and all thirteen colonies had agreed to a unified Declaration of Independence. When American sovereignty had been firmly established by defeat, in 1783, of the King's armies and his colonial intents, the citizens of that energetic North Carolina region hit the ground runnin'. They didn't miss a beat of that manifest destiny drum beginning to be heard between Atlantic and Pacific. Setting out on multiple paths of exploration, ground-breaking, crop-cultivating, animal-raisin' high-falootin' shenanigan-shootin' expansion like you never seen, why, 'afore anybody knew what was a-happening folks was well-established with farms and ranches out in the tamed parts of the wild land. Mercantiles and blacksmiths, cobblers and coopers, and all manner of enterprises on main street, prospered in one of the fastest expansions of human free market productivity in the history of the world.

By 'n by, after the Americans had confounded themselves into a civil war—even as their English progenitors had done three centuries before—after the rebs and the yanks had bled into their forefathers' verdant American dirt on account o' that contentious revolutionary zeal not dyin' down for such a long while, and after they had fought the damn thing out to its bitterest Antietam end and then buried their dead four score and seven or so years later, and after things had settled down a bit and folks was feeling a little bit normal again...one enterprisin' young fellow by name of Cornelius

Wolden saw some opportunities pertaining to money and wealth in the city of Charlotte.

Before the war fever had stricken the nation in 1860, a better kind of infection had earlier broken out—gold fever. The precious yellow metal was discovered in California in 1849, which led to the gold rush most folks know about, because everybody wants to be, you know, in California.

Not everybody, though. There had already been some serious, and productive, gold prospecting down in North Carolina, and it had been going on for nigh onto fifty years. That Mecklenburg hornets' nest of rebellion previously mentioned by General Cornwallis had of course wound down their rebellin' ways, and then also reined in their wild streak of civil war contentiousness, and had henceforth converted, by n' by, their feisty revolutionary zeal into evolutionizin' wealth acquisition. By late 19th-century, Charlotte had worked itself into a honey beehive of intense money-making buzz. They even established a US mint there to coin all the gold that was coming out of them Carolina hills.

So this Cornelius Wolden fellow set up shop right in the middle of Charlotte, selling clothes for every member of the family, from baby to granma, because keeping young'uns in threads was something that he and his wife Virginia knew something about, especially since their first four were girls. They didn't have a boy until the fifth child came along, and then another girl after that—six children altogether: Cornelia, Langlis, Emma, Roberta, Spencer, and Adele. The whole lot of them were excellent young folk, as children go, but daughter number two was an independent filly of what seemed to be a different breed.

Langlis Wolden, born in 1886, having eagerly availed herself of her parents' business acumen, caught an early whiff of what would later become suffragette liberality. In 1904, she attended the University of North Carolina in Chapel Hill. Having earned an English degree from that school in 1908, she returned to Charlotte and worked in Wolden's, her parents' thriving enterprise, which had now expanded to three stores. Unlike most of her southern sisters, still unmarried, Langlis departed for New York City in September 1910, ostensibly to hone her merchandising skills at a department store on 5th Avenue. By 1912, the fair auburn-haired beauty with flashing blue eyes had met, and captured the heart of, a dapper Englishman seven years her senior, Wilbur Afton, who happened to be an MP in the House of Lords.

Seated now beside her husband, Lord Afton, Langlis watched, silently with the seven thousand other invited guests, as the Archbishop of Canterbury placed a crown upon the head of King George VI. The bonds of English-American fealty, previously broken a hundred and sixty-two years ago by her ancestral Mecklenburg neighbors, were now in a state of repair.

Back in the USA, a hundred foothill miles from what had formerly been the Mecklenburg hornet's nest of anti-George III fever, Adele Higgins was training schoolchildren. Adele was the youngest of the Wolden brood. Born sixteen years after Langlis, she was a smart woman possessed of an exploratory nature. While her older sister had followed a path of worldly wealth, ultimately positioning herself among the movers of London society, Adele's diligent curiosity had found its focus in that sphere of influence *oh so much* safer and more predictable than business and politics—the universe of knowledge. She loved passing it on to others, especially children. Adele was hearing the call to the teaching profession.

Having worked busily in the Wolden stores through most of the '20s, Adele's growing passion for the advance of literacy got the best of her. In 1928, she headed up the mountain to Appalachian Teachers' College, in the town of Trail, to obtain the Grammar Grade Education degree and a state teaching certificate.

While the blooming schoolmarm was being prepared at College, an old childhood friend, Harry Higgins, had found himself inextricably drawn away from Charlotte's bustle, toward the nippy winds and wild mountain thyme life up at Globestone. But mainly it was the presence of one sweet Adele in that rarified Appalachian air that drew him up there. Trail, the town where Teachers' College was located, was only five miles up the road from Globestone. During childhood summers near the resort town, he and Adele, along with their respective families, had together cultivated a love affair with the crags and coves and sweetwater steams of the land of the sky. Harry had, by and by, uncovered a truth with reasonable certainty that his pining for life up on the mountain probably had as much to do with Adele's placement there as with any other magical aspect of that elevated place.

Harry was a well-heeled Charlotte business prodigy whose family had prospered in textiles since before the war. After honing a sharp eye for business opportunity under the tutelage of his hard-at-it father, the four-year stint at Harvard hadn't done him any harm either, in propelling him headlong into the 1920s wheelin'-dealin' world of money, fabrics, and properties. Not only that, but after the mudhole that he'd been dragged through in France , and the bloodbath he had managed to live through in Belgium, in order to defeat the Kaiser and his minions, this American life was high cotton, comparatively speaking.

But in the fall of '29, all that whoop-fiz high-stakes dealing changed big time, for some folks a lot more than others. Harry's family was one of the "others" that had managed, fortunately, to come out on the receiving end of whatever maelstrom of trouble it was that had stricken the world of stocks and bonds into hopeless disarray in 1929.

Consequently, when the dust and what was left of the Wall Street dollars had settled in 1930, and Harry's sharpened opportunity eye had seen a shining lining around a dark cloud that hung over a blue mountain a hundred miles from Charlotte, it turned out, lo and behold, that the silver-lining opportunity was a hotel up in Globestone. On October 29, 1930, one year after the Crash, and himself at the tender age of thirty-three, Harry Higgins bought the old Globestone Inn for a song and a prayer and a pile of cash that his dad had helped him get. He wrangled a deal with the heirs of Adolphus Stringman, who had been, back in the day, the legendary timber king of western North Carolina.

So from 1930 on, Harry was spending a lot of time in that resort town in which Adele had fertilized so many summer dreams during his youth. Patching together his version of the hospitality business that had been established by the Stringmans, he found himself in need of a helpmate and a little tenderness.

In 1932 Adele obtained her degree and teaching certificate from Teachers' College. They had a big wedding at Myerson Park in Charlotte, went to England for a honeymoon and a visit with sister Langlis and her Lord husband. Harry and Adele returned to their aerie Globestone home, sharing not only a bed and a new household, but also the fulfillment of all those youthful longings that together they had felt during long walks in the peaks and meadows of the Blue Ridge.

It was there in that magical place that Adolphus Stringman had constructed his mountain gateway getaway in 1875. Now it was the sole proprietorship of Harry and Adele Higgins. Adolphus had called the place *Valhalla.* But Harry, with a more popularizing intent, had chosen to rename the place the Globestone Inn.

This morning, Adele asked her class of tenth-graders to write their names and today's date, May 12, 1937, at the top of their papers. She was instructing the students in the proper construction of a sentence in English.

She wrote a sentence on the blackboard. It was:

Come their time men is to the for country now good all the aid of to.

Adele's eyes displayed a subdued mirth as she observed the puzzlement in her charges' faces. After allowing the better part of a minute for the message's impact to register in their hairy heads, she posed a question:

"Who can tell me what the subject of this sentence is?"

Jane in the first row raised her hand.

"Go ahead, Jane," said the teacher.

"It doesn't have a subject," spoke the pig-tailed girl, with self-assurance.

"Oh, no?" queried Adele, raising her eyebrows. "How do you know that?"

"Because it doesn't make sense. A sentence has to make sense."

"Is that so?" replied the teacher. "Well, why not? Why doesn't it make sense?"

Johnny, in the third row, raised his hand.

"Go ahead."

"Because it doesn't have a subject.' A few in the class chuckled; Johnny was pleased with himself.

The teacher also laughed. "Okay, then. If I told you that this collection of words *is* a sentence, and that it *does* have a subject, what would be your guess as to which word is the subject? You don't need to raise your hand; just speak, and have respect for your classmates."

"Men"

"Time"

After a moment, Adele said, "Those are good answers. Tom, why do think that 'men' is the subject of this sentence?

"It's a noun," said Tom.

"Very good," Adele responded. She wrote on the blackboard: *The subject of a sentence is most likely a noun.*

Jane asked, "Why do you write 'most likely'? Isn't the subject always going be a noun?"

"Good question, Jane. We'll talk about that in a later lesson, when we learn about gerunds. But let's just say for now, that 'men' and 'time' are both good possibilities for being a subject because they are nouns. What about 'country'? It's a noun. Could it be the subject?

"It's too far back in the sentence to be the subject,' Roby opined.

"Hmmm..." The teacher folded her arms, furrowed her brow, and displayed a melodramatic scowl. "Who says that relative position in the sentence has anything to do with whether a noun can be the subject, or not the subject?"

"I do," responded Roby. "Plus—it's got a preposition it front of it. It must be the object of a preposition."

"That's good," said Adele. "I like that."

"Now!" blurted Elizabeth, excitedly. "'Now' is the subject!"

"Oh, yes? How do you know that?" Adele challenged, turning on her heel to respond to the student.

"Because I rearranged the words to make sense. It is a coded message. It should read like this: Now is the time for all good men to come to the aid of their country."

Adele was laughing. "How do you know that?"

"I saw it on a poster, pinned to the wall at my granmpa's house. There was a picture of the Uncle Sam fella, and underneath him on the poster was that sentence."

Adele was still laughing. "Very good, Elizabeth Morrow. Your are correct. 'Now' is the subject of the sentence. And our lesson today is, sometimes you have to put your thinking caps on and figure things out. And even if you don't know what is correct, it is always good to try something out—something that you think will work. In this case, Elizabeth was able to combine her prior knowledge of a patriotic phrase with her understanding of the meanings of English words, and come up with something that makes sense."

"But you taught us, Mrs. Higgins, that the subject of a sentence would always be a noun. Is 'now' a noun?" asked Tom.

"That's a good question, Tom. The word 'now' is a kind of noun, in this case. . . although most of the time it is not. Most of the time it is an adverb. . .er. . .well, never mind. This English language we speak is quite precise enough, most of the time, to communicate our meaning, but not always. Our language is, you see, a hotch-potch of several languages—German, Latin, French. It all goes back to 1066—well, even before that—when William of Normandy conquered England. But . . .you'll learn that in history class. Your homework for tomorrow is to diagram this sentence that we just talked about."

A gentle knock was heard, Turning to the classroom door, Adele saw through its glass portal the face of the school Principal, The students were busily writing the formerly-scrambled sentence in their notebooks. Teacher walked to the door, saw that Miss Prutin wore an uncommonly somber expression. Adele stepped into the hall and closed the door behind her.

Miss Prutin whispered, "I've received a telephone call from Hattie Morrow. Elizabeth's great grandfather, Roby Morrow, has passed away this morning. Her father will be here to fetch her home within a half-hour."

"Oh! That's Roby. I'm sorry to hear of it. He—he operated the store in Trail."

"Yes, he founded that store, over fifty years ago."

"Roby was. . .the great grandfather?"

"He was the grandfather of Elizabeth's father, Robert Morrow. Roby raised Robert , and his sister and brother, after their father had been killed in the war, in Belgium."

"Have they made arrangements yet?"

"No. This came to light just a few hours ago. Roby had been living with Robert at their old home place when Robert found him this morning. He must have died in his sleep."

"I'll send Elizabeth out. Should I announce this to the class?"

"Please wait until we have gotten back to my office. I will tell Elizabeth when we get to my office."

Adele hesitated, then spoke a thought that was crossing her mind. "So her father never returned from the war. He gave, to his country, his *last full measure of devotion.* We were just analyzing a sentence about good men who come to the aid of their country. Elizabeth's father must have been. . . one of those good men."

"He was." Miss Prutin offered a gentle smile, and placed her hand on Adele's. "And his father, Roby, who passed this morning, was surely a good man too. He had come to the aid of his country—actually, his county, by operating that store for all those years, before his granddaughter took it over. That Morrow store made Trail the town that it is today."

"What was the son's name?"

"Clint. Most folks called him Shooter, growing up. Then he was gone, and never returned until they brought him home in a box. He would have been—

or he was—Elizabeth's grandfather. It seems strange to think of a young man like that, who never made it home alive, as a grandpa. But he was, though he never knew about it."

"I suppose there is a lot that goes on in this world , a lot that we never know about, after we ourselves pass on," mused Adele, introspectively.

"Now you sound like a teacher of English literature," Miss Prutin remarked. Again, the gentle smile.

Adele sighed. "Better get back to it. Maybe I'll have them write a little poem about what it means to "come to the aid of " one's country."

"Maybe you will."

With that, Adele slipped quietly back into the classroom, just in time to redirect that ancient entropy which possesses young fourteen-year-olds when left for too long to their own devices.

6
Civilizations

"Civilizations are founded upon such men as Paul Wallris," said Inspector Crossbough to Dr. Pepper. "And now they've up and killed him." The dapper detective raised his eyebrows.

"What makes you think that?" queried the assistant.

"Oh, well, the great deeds—and what I mean by that is, the *necessary* deeds, be they small or great, that must be done so that properly civilized life can endure the slings and arrows of misfortune—*those* deeds. They are initiated and carried out by bold men, men who are willing to buck the tide of their own era's habitual mindset, and undertake new ventures of great import."

Dr. Pepper inspected his friend's face with an amused skepticism. "I was meaning to ask, sir, what makes you think that someone has 'up and killed' Mr. Wallris?"

"Ah. . .forgive my aside; the writer of this note that was recovered from the deceased man's hand contains the sentence: **If not, your bridge could burn.**"

"And?. . ."

"Mr. Wallris did not have a bridge, The writer of this note—this 'Chapman'—may have been referring to the deceased man's life itself, metaphorically. This was, perhaps, a veiled threat, or, more precisely, a coded threat."

"Seems a bit of a stretch, Inspector. How do you know that Mr. Wallris did not a have bridge?"

"His home was at Montpelier Square, #49. There is no bridge at Montpelier."

"Had he, perhaps, another property in the country, with a bridge?"

"I think not, my friend, although we will be expecting the fuller report , listing his properties, from our people upstairs. "

"I hardly think our records personnel are working today. More likely, they are out there on the street, waiting with these other thousands of English souls for the King's procession to pass by."

"Well, *we* are working, aren't we? And what about those thousands of bobbies keeping peace out there today! Some dedicated policemen have got to ensure the safety and security of this delicate realm while the royals rearrange their roles.'

"Certainly, Inspector, but the men and women of the records department have, I believe, for the most part, taken the day off, although many have undoubtedly re-donned the uniform to beef up the security details."

"What time, by the way, are we expecting the Coronation procession to pass by here?"

"That could happen in less than a half-hour sir. The time now is 2:40. The King and Queen were expected to be leaving the Abbey at about 2:30."

Inspector Neville Crossbough walked over to the window. He peered out through the gray afternoon mist, looking first across the Thames, then to his right at the peopled expanse of the Westminster Bridge, with the clock side of Big Ben barely viewable from his third-story window. The Embankment street below was completely lined on both its side, as far as could be seen in both directions. Down and to his left, he could see what appeared as a strangely bare sidewalk, in front of the Scotland Yard main entrance. Its small but passable area having been maintained as pedestrian-free, the sidewalk there was in fact the only pavement he could see, apart from the street itself, where the royal procession would soon pass.

"I'm wondering, Dr. Pepper, if Mr. Wallris was, perhaps, building a bridge before he died—a 'bridge', as it were, to Spain, whereby those Spanish citizens who are defending their government from Franco's rebels can be supplied with food and essentials."

Dr. Pepper drew on his pipe. "Yes, I suppose that would be a 'bridge' of sorts. Mr. Greeneglass said that two of Wallris' vessels—that is to say, two of the previously idled *Thames-World* freighters—had been loaded with relief supplies and sent to Bilbao. And you are suggesting that some devious person, or persons, may have wanted to put a stop to Mr. Wallris' supportive activities, by killing him?"

"Just thinking out loud, old chap, and considering the note's mention of the blackshirts, and so forth, it all seems a bit sinister."

"Indeed, and with the 'John Bull's ransom'. That word, ransom, is the very definition of trouble. What do you make of it?"

"Haven't a clue yet. This is tomorrow's enquiry, when some normalcy returning to London will enable a more informed pursuit of the facts. But. . . I wonder, is John Bull the ransomed one, or the one providing a ransom, or some extortionist demanding a ransom?" The inspector furrowed his expressive brows and looked again at the street below. "Ah, here we go. Here comes King George now."

Dr. Pepper joined Inspector Crossbough at the window. They watched quietly for a few moments, from the privileged third-floor perspective of Scotland Yard, as the King's Coronation procession passed on Embankment street below them.

Preceding the King and Queen were multiple horsemen, with exquisitely measured gaits: Headed by the Colonial Contingent, with Burmese regiments at the fore, followed by Rhodesians in their inclimate shorts, then the South Africans, New Zealanders, the Australian contingent, the Canadian Mounties with added splendor of their crimson tunics, and rifles at the ready. The Royal Air Force marched in a disciplined display of ceremonial drill, followed by colorfully exotic sentries of India, wearing pugarees and tunics of gold, white, blue and crimson. Then came small detachments from the Chaplains, the Nursing Service, Territorial Army in new uniforms of dark blue. Naval and Marine detachments proceeded dutifully in anticipation of the royal arrival. Most regally impressive in their high, prancing gait were the 'K' Battery of the Royal Horse Artillery. Interspersed among the military units were visiting dignitaries, Prime Ministers, Sultans, and Emirs.

Then came the State Coach with crowned King George VI, and Queen Mary, newly-enthroned within. Their equipage was drawn by eight magnificently reined Windsor greys, driven by four postilions in short red jackets and jockey caps. Beside and behind the slow carriage were numerous attendants, upwards of a dozen groomsman, footman, Life Guards.

Red, gold, red, gold, red, gold, white. Their uniforms shone with brilliant gold and crimson through the dreary London not-quite-foggy atmosphere. The State Coach itself rolled in as an absolute visual symphony of shining gold ensconcement, opulently ornate and lavishly overstated in its 18th-century baroqueness, with large rear spoked wheels, bearing an elongated carriage mythically propelled by muscular Poseidon-spawned tritons. The gargoylish god-figures, displaying facial expressions of obsequious dumbness, held golden tridents in ceremonially upraised chivalry. Sculpted golden royal palms adorned the four corners of the royal box in which the King and Queen could be dimly seen, as, at last, they paraded past their ogling citizenry with a pompously joyful solemnity. George III had spared no expense in 1761 with the commissioning of this elaborate, royal conveyor. The carriage embodied a gilt Bourbonic excess of some former age.

The man and woman within, however, were of nobler intent than their pomp and circumstance might indicate.

"I think the 'John Bull's' ransom' in the note must be some sort of encoded threat to the continuity of our British empire," mused Inspector Neville Crossbough.

"What makes you think that?" asked Dr. Pepper.

"I don't know; it's just a feelin' in me bones."

Dr. Pepper considered this for a moment. "Methinks you discern correctly. . .John Bull's ransom. . .if not a threat to the empire, a threat, in some way, to our English way of life."

"Ah!" exclaimed the Inspector, with exasperated emphasis. "We're making too much of this. Tomorrow is another day. The King will be safely installed at Buckingham Palace, and life will go on. Let's go home to the missus; I'm ready to call it a day." The clock on the wall read 2:55.

But on the other side of the world, everything was quite different.

Here's a young man who would have been emperor of China, if the smoky purgatory of revolution had not removed it from him when he was only two years old. That was twenty-six years ago, in 1911.

Tonight, in this waning last hour of what had been a fretful day, Puyi Aisin-Gioro could not get to sleep. He lay in bed wondering what his next move should be to preserve the last ounce of his royal family's Qing dynasty dignity. But his plight was not going well. What Puyi did not yet understand was the worldwide death shroud now being lowered upon ancient royal dynasties by twentieth-century militarism and politics. And while his own family's legacy of Manchurian Chinese leadership was collapsing into the dust-heap of historical irrelevance, across the sea in Japan the death-throes of empire were convulsing differently. The climax and collapse of Japanese Hiro-worship would inflict a much more explosive destruction of Asian culture—a much more profuse shedding of Oriental blood. Its nightmarish offal was as yet still covered in gauzy future obscurity. But of course Puyi could not know that now. He had been a pampered royal child, fed, even after his deposition, with a silver spoon and a carefully controlled stir-fry of zombifying courtly artifice.

In recent years, the militarizing Japanese had invaded northeast China, and they were setting up a government to serve the many requirements of their widening Hirohito empire. Naming their new mainland state Manchukuo, the fierce Japanese overlords sought to make exploitive use of what was left of Manchu royal authority. And pretty much what was left of it was just this one person—this one frail, confused 28-year-old Qing would-have-been-emperor—who possessed very little political clout and no formidable followers, except for a diminishing household of inbred, eunuchian devotees whose days of delusive self-importance were numbered. And so Puyi's withering Qing dynasty authority was being manipulated by the pushy Japanese taskmasters. They were jerking him and what was left of his emperor identity around, like a puppet on silken strings.

Even as Hitler's Germany was striving, in the other world hemisphere to bring Europe under its demoniac control, so was Hirohito's Japan imposing similar military-industrial bondages upon the eastern half of the world. Only a few years ago, *Der fuhrer* had absconded the German Hohenzollern mantle of authority; now he was coveting an association with the imperial sword that had long held sway in the land of the rising sun, the land in which great reverence was shown for the ancient *manji*, or swastika, which his thulish Nazi ruffians had lately inverted and misappropriated as a symbol for their ghoulish campaign to extinguish European Judeo-Christian civilization.

Five months had passed since Hitler had tightened his constrictive designs on the wide world by forging a treaty with Japan. The agreement expanded a trans-world military axis by uniting European Nazi and fascist power with the house of Hirohito in the form of an anti-communist pact.

Japan's Foreign Minister Mushokoji and the Nazis' Ribbentrop had signed the Anti-Comintern pact in Berlin in Novermber of 1936. Their peace-shattering axis of evil intent, being global in scope, had covered a lot of political and geographical territory. One part of it was on the Chinese mainland; Germany recognized what was left of the Qing Manchu legacy as the puppet state Manchukuo, with Puyi Aisin-Gioro, the last Chinese emperor, as ceremonial regent, and Japan as its protector.

It was this young Puyi who now lay captively sleepless in a bed in the provincial capital, Changchun. He was trying to figure a way to outsmart Yasunori, the Japanese lieutenant-general who had been assigned as the erstwhile emperor's handler. So far, though, the impotent ruler's strategies to outwit his controller had met no success. Puyi's dynastic downfall had retained very little of the trappings of royal power. His Chinese countrymen—both the Chiang Kai-shek Nationalists and the Mao Communists—had seen to that.

There was, for instance, no golden coach into which he would be ushered and then transported to points of great ceremonial and political import. His condition as a twentieth-century potentate had been immensely diminished compared to that of, say, George VI of Great Britain, whose coronation was being celebrated by millions today on the other side of the world. How and why such a vast difference of respectful legitimacy should exist between the two great monarchies is a mystery. But the smoky underpinnings of royal authority were not really what worried Puyi so much. His troubles were much more practical, more immediate, than that, like wondering what food would the Japanese lords of war provide for his household's meals tomorrow.

Puyi's golden-spoon childhood had not permitted him to readily realize a certain hard truth—people can lie while smiling. This was an odious attribute of human behaviour generally more evident to most common folk; now its shadowy malignity was proving more irksome to him with every turn of events. His sleep was disturbed by a recurring dream; it had crept into his fretful slumber several years ago.

Kemsoko, head of the State Council of Manchukuo, was sitting next to him in the dream. Kemsoko was smiling. Across from them, in a very proper Qing chair, was Lord Lyton, whose delegation of European inquisitors had been sent by the League of Nations to straighten out an untidy locomotive incident at nearby Mukden, having to do with crooked rails and a derailed train. This inexplicable sabotage had resulted in the death to some of Hirohito's enforcers of rising-sun power—that is to say, Japanese soldiers.

But Puyi had been warned by a few of his Manchu military compatriots. He discerned that what the Commissioners were really looking for was a way to maintain, even enlarge, the open door to China that the Brits and those other meddlesome devils from the west had so bullishly held ajar for lo these many years.

Lord Lyton was smiling, as Puyi was explaining: the ancient legitimacy of His Emperorship had been lovingly acknowledged by the Manchurian masses. Thus had their "nation's" independence and heritage been preserved. All of this had been accomplished with the very generous and persuasive help of their Japanese friends. A few renegade Manchurians sabotaging a train track didn't amount to a mound of old *kaoliang* under a dragon's nose; it was a mere puff of impotent smoke beneath the ominous plumes of international statecraft.

Puyi's nightmarish misery wafted from his intense desire to be saying, *instead*, to Lord Lyton: *Get me the hell out of here; take me back to London with you because these Japanese are driving me crazy with their savagery.* But the very delicate last emperor of China could say no such a thing, because Kemsoko, a dutiful protector of the Japanese-Manchukoan symbiosis, was sitting right next to them, smiling. Puyi understood intuitively what diplomacy and kingly propriety was requiring of him; he was, after all the very titular expression of Qing regality.

In the great billowing scheme of things, this torturous constriction of Manchu sovereignty was not a random thing, but a calculated advance in a grand design of Axis acquisition., The cunning vehemence with which it navigated across the sea of Japan would soon prove eerily coincidental to events of fierceful stealth half a world away.

In Tyrol valleys the phantom was even now slouching through Austrian countryside, with an envious eye on Viennese grandeur. Across border districts bound in divided loyalties, the reichish fiend would soon be detected, stalking for morsels of Sudetan germanity. And yet it would be permitted to pass, by Munich trickery, unobstructed. The thing possessed an undisclosed appetite for slurping Bohemian rhapsodies, and a voracious compulsion to pilfer agrarian spoils from the storehouses of Moravia. The yawning Polish plain would, by 1939, present an open stage for the beast to blitz its swaggering entrance onto our world stage. A woeful devolution into the darkest abyss of human cruelty would its predatory sorties ultimately be.

With unbridled ferocity the thing crept o'er a war-weary world, under cover of billowing diplomatic smoke, having no conscience, no decency, no good, no God.

7

Vessels

The People of China, manifesting their discontent through warlord leaders, had destabled the Palace of Established Happiness in Peking in 1924. That building and the many other arcane structures of The Forbidden City were no longer verboten to regular people. But even before that, since 1911, the ever-shifting warlord manipulations of the people were, with unprecedented disregard for ceremony or tradition, dismembering ancient Confucian order everywhere in China. Confusion was the new order of the day. Now severed from its Qing head, the dynastic dragon's train of ancient power and wealth was being unceremoniously sliced into little military pieces. Forceful new revolutionary strongmen flung the remnants of power among their adjutants like entrails from a slaughtered beast tossed to dogs.

An enterprising sage, Yu Lo, had shrewdly managed to acquire a store of Qing and Ming artifacts; the booty was distributed through smokily undocumented channels, from the no-longer-Forbidden City storehouses of Qing wealth. In November of 1936, Yu had made a lucrative deal with the English businessman, Paul Wallris, to ship a selection of the precious items to London. By February, 1937, when the Chinese were celebrating Year of the Tiger, Yu had assembled a small collection of four representative pieces. His assistant had carefully packaged them and shipped the crate from Tientsin, on the *Thames-World* freighter *Oriental*.

At the St. Katharine docks in London, a crew of *Thames-World* stevedores set the crate aside, as had been requested by the owners. After the Coronation holiday on Wednesday, this Thursday morning was a little slow getting started, especially since the news had gotten around that Paul Wallris, one of the two owners, had died the day before. But by mid-afternoon the *Oriental* had been unloaded. A slatted parcel, looking uncharacteristically handmade with red Chinese script on white wood, sat in a corner of the dock warehouse. Large black English letters, FRAGILE, were stamped on all sides.

In late afternoon, James Jarrow, driver for the Wallris household, arrived to retrieve the Chinese package, for which Mr. Wallris himself had made special transport arrangements shortly before his untimely demise. A crewman that James knew helped him hoist the crate onto the Wallris' lorry; then the dutiful driver set out to deliver it to the Wallris home on Montpelier Square, as he had been previously directed.

At about dusk, James was waiting for traffic to clear so he could turn left onto Cable Street. He was considering a detour to his home in Shoreditch to have supper with his family before completing the errand. The original instructions, as given by Mr. Wallris himself before his passing, now seemed malleable, as James thought the actual delivery could possibly be delayed until tomorrow, considering the lateness of the hour.

Presently, James was aware that the vehicle to his rear was flashing bright lights on and off. Glancing in the side mirror of the Daimler, he could see that Jack Scrimby, foreman of the dock crew, had emerged from the car behind him, and was walking to the driver window to have a word with him. James rolled the window down.

Jack had a tense kind of smile on his face. "Hey mate, you need to do a turnabout and bring this back to the shop. Mr. Afton has just called on the telly, and he said this crate is to be delivered to another destination tomorrow."

This was a little confusing. With a little hesitation, James replied, "'Scuse me, Jack, but Mr. Wallris had told me himself he wanted this taken to his home at Montpelier."

"I understand, James, but since Mr. Wallris has passed away, Mr. Afton's order is that this is to be handled differently now."

"Ah, don't forget, Scrimby, I work for Wallris—not for you, and not for Mr. Afton."

Jack was a little taken aback at the response. "Look 'ere mate. People are waiting to drive by here. You should pull to the side and we'll talk about this...decide exactly what's to be done."

"I already know what's to be done. I'm taking this crate to Mr. Wallris' residence at Montpelier; that 's what he had told me to do with it."

"He's dead now. Lord Afton is in full charge of the shipments."

"No, Jack. Afton's got the run of the company now, I s'pose. But this here box is personal; it's going to Madame Wallris, as his widow. She'll make the decision what's to be done wi' it.

"Get out'a the lorry now, James," Jack demanded, vehemently. "I'll take it from here."

"No! You blitherin' idiot!" With that resolute objection, James stomped the gas pedal, leaving Jack Scrimby stranded in the street. Under James' sudden acceleration, the Daimler careened onto Cable Street, making a right turn instead of the left that he had intended. Instantly he was speeding down Cable Street in the wrong direction. A sudden alarm feeling was intensified in his mind as James recognized his location. It was the block where, last fall, the fascist blackshirts had had a showdown with the locals during their parade.

But the street's features were flying by in a blur now; pummeling along too fast, he couldn't think of what to do, except to keep moving until Scrimby and his car would be out of sight. In the rearview, James could see that, sure enough, the stubborn foreman was in pursuit.

A nervous mile or so later, James managed to scoot under a traffic light whilst Jack Scrimby was stranded at it. After a while, he turned left onto Christian Street, somewhere in Shadwell, and headed northward; he would somehow get to Montpelier Square in Knightsbridge and deliver his precious cargo before Thursday was spent.

An hour later, James had managed to navigate his way through London streets to his late employer's home in Knightsbidge, despite the hollow fear that hung in the back of his mind from Jack Scrimby's strangely obstinate objection. *And in the middle of a public street!*

Relieved to have completed his transport duty, James eased the Daimler into its garage in the alley; for a moment, he savored the quiet there, at the end of an unexpectedly frantic mission. He ascended the back step and entered the house at the anteroom to the kitchen.

犰日开起，麻煨降临

This is what Julia Wallris saw, scrawled on the note she found inside a Chinese urn that she unpacked from the crate that James had brought in the night before.

"Is that Chinese?" asked Tabitha, her sister.

"I haven't a clue," replied Julia. "Maybe it's Japanese."

"...wonder what it means," mused Tabitha, cocking her lovely head to one side with puzzlement. "But surely it is Chinese, since this box just arrived from China."

"Yes. I suppose."

Julia set the note aside. The two young women redirected their inspection to the vessel from which the note had fallen when Julia upended it. It was a shiny white vase with a blue dragon painted in fine dark lines. The creature seemed to be writhing, as most dragons are known to have done through antiquity, especially the Chinese ones. He had a scraggly sort of beard, and large, bulbous eyes, two tentacles from the side of its long face, and of course all of those scales covering the body from head to tail, if one can call it a tail, for it seemed the entire dragon, except for the head, was one long tail. Oh, but here's a big claw with five sharp fangs.

The urn was shaped somewhat like an upside-down pear, but with a flared base wide enough so that it could stand upright. At the top was a small round opening with a lipped rim. It stood about twenty inches high, with the widest part of its pear-shape being about ten inches, three-quarters of the way up from the bottom.

The note, written delicately on old yellowed parchment dropped out of the rim when Julia had carefully upended the vase.

"What did father have in mind when he purchased this?" Julia asked.

"I don't know. That was months ago, when he was doing business in China. . . February, I think it was." In all of her twenty-three years as Paul's daughter, Tabitha and her older sister had seen many exotic items floated in from the four corners of the British mercantile world. Their father had acquired them, for one serendipitous reason or another, and had them sent back to London on one of his ships. Mother's joyous appreciation of free-standing classic art works must have been the primary determinant in his selections. Their home was exquisitely decorated with such pieces, a collection that had grown steadily during the girls' childhood, even until now, two days after father's passing. Now it seemed the enlargement of it would be at an end, but for this last crate with the red Chinese script on its crated exterior. It seemed to have arrived out of nowhere with neither rhyme nor reason, and certainly no solace. The scaly creature now panting at the young ladies from its glazed pottery lair brought no comfort.

This cobalt dragon was a rude intrusion just now. Daddy was dead. The Oriental pottery piece came as an unwelcomed surprise, a sad disturbance under these present funereal circumstances. It had seemed to Julia and Tabitha, and to their mother Claire, that father's interest had of late centered quite intensely on Spain, even to the point of eclipsing his persistent fascination with more universal acquisitions.

To have been up with the sun on this Friday morning, and unpacking a crate from China the delivery of which had been arranged by their deceased father three months ago—was incongruent with their o'ershrouding grief. Tabitha had wanted to tear into the box when she saw James bring it in last night, as if the thing might bring forth some significant remnant of her father's activity in this life. But the sisters' exploration of this untimely parcel was only a weird diversion, to fixate their attention on anything besides the grievous situation at hand. Pondering the alien reptilian figure, Tabitha found it bizarre, as if the beast were now burrowing some dark monster lair in the midst of what had formerly been their contentment. Surely he was mocking their loss, and growling at their grief. *Daddy is gone, and I now I show up in your house*, it roared in silent porcelain growls; *I am all that's left*. The dragon was surely taunting them; you could see it in his fierce blue-lined scowl. No substitute for a loving daddy.

Death was scowling at the Wallris girls this morning; yet the terrible task of laying their father in the ground was still ahead of them.

"What are these other items?" Julia wondered aloud. She began pawing the shredded paper padding away from another object, exposing a smallish wooden box with intricately carved red scrollwork all over it.

"A jewelry box," Tabitha guessed.

"Here. This front comes off," said Julia. "It's a removable panel."

The door of the anteroom opened, and Sue, the maid, walked in. "'S'cuse me, ladies. Your mother has a visitor in the parlor, and she would like for you to come, please."

So the sisters suspended their examination of the newfound jewelry box and joined their mother in the front room. Rising from the sofa to meet them were two well-dressed older men.

"Thank you for responding so promptly," said mother to her girls as they approached. "These gentlemen are from Scotland Yard, and they have a few questions for us." Julia could hear in her mother's quavering voice an appreciation for her daughters' presence.

Tabitha felt distracted, noticing an Oriental vase of blue and white, on the marble-top end table next to the sofa from which the men had just unseated themselves. It was strikingly similar in color to the piece they had just unpacked, though much smaller; but there was no dragon on it, rather, some sylvan scene that oddly resembled their present meeting except the people were robed, and Chinese-looking. But now the deer-eyed gentleman in a brown suit was touching her hand. He bowed his head slightly; he was not smiling.

"Good morning, Miss. I am Inspector Neville Crossbough. My condolences for you and your family."

"Thank you," replied Tabitha, tinnily. She could feel herself not smiling. She didn't know what to do or say; this had never happened before. The inspector released her hand and stepped aside to greet Julia. Then another fellow was suddenly holding her hand and looking into her eyes.

"So sorry, Miss Wallris. I am Dr. Harold Pepper, from Scotland Yard." Unlike his companion, the good doctor had a vaguely kinder disposition, with a gradual smile, as if to say *don't worry; things can get better in spite of all this,* although his attire was appropriately black.

"Please be seated, gentlemen," she heard her sister say. Mother was still sitting in her chair looking dazed. Julia would be in charge of this, whatever it was to be. And so they all sat down. Tabitha still felt that this whole episode was a bad dream.

The Inspector spoke. "We do have a few questions, ladies, about your father's passing two days ago, if you don't mind."

"Certainly," Julia accommodated.

"Quite routine," added Dr. Pepper.

"Yes, of course," said Julia. "Thank you for following up."

Dr. Pepper continued. "Was all well, do you think, with your father's business affairs, going into this. . .ah, this ordeal?" He was sensitive to their situation. The Inspector seemed to be, for the moment, looking beyond the ladies to a far wall.

"As far as we knew, yes," answered Julia.

"Was he in, ah, good spirits, on Wednesday morning when he left the house?" continued Dr. Pepper.

"My father left very early on Wednesday," said Julia. "He always did, actually. I'm sure he left before any of us were stirring."

"So that was his habit?"

"Generally, yes, although, that being Coronation Day, I've no idea what his intentions might have been. I'm sure it was not, on that day, to go immediately to his business at the St. Katharine docks. Father and Mr. Afton had called a holiday for all their men."

"He went to the club," mother volunteered, shakily.

"That would be the Travelers Club, Mrs. Wallris?" inquired Inspector Crossbough.

"Yes. On Wednesdays he usually started his day there before going to the office. Wednesdays and Fridays at 8:00, most weeks."

"You recall, then, that on that morning he left the house in time to get to the Travelers Club at eight o'clock, say, 7:30 or so?"

"He left much earlier on Coronation Day. It might have been as early as 6:30. I was slumbering. You may find more precise information from James, our driver, although he is on an errand just now." said mother.

"Very well, then," concluded Crossbough. "He had breakfast there?"

"Yes, Inspector, he did. We had agreed, on Tuesday night, he would meet us at 11 o'clock at Trafalgar, after breakfast."

"At Trafalgar? Where?"

"On the top floor of the Museum. Lord Afton, Paul's business partner, had arranged for a room there for us, and a few others, to view the procession."

"Did your plans include meeting Lord Afton there?"

"No, sir." Lord Afton and his wife were invited to Westminster."

"Yes, of course," said the Inspector, as he seemed to recede into some thought or other.

"Do you know, Mrs. Wallris, with whom your husband had breakfast on that morning?" asked Dr. Pepper, politely.

"Well, I'm sure it was Harry Bosworth and David Blum. They are old friends of his."

The Doctor wrote their names in his black leathered notebook. "So it was, ah, the three of them having breakfast as usual, then?"

A disturbance was forming itself in Tabitha's mind. At last, the annoyance found expression. "Excuse me, Dr. Pepper. Why all these *questions*? There has been a. . .a death here."

Hearing the irritation in her voice, Inspector Crossbaugh turned his attention upon the younger daughter with a quick turn of his head. "Quite so, Miss Wallris. I am sorry to intrude upon your grief in this difficult time, but we have an unusual item here that may require some further investigation."

"Investigation?" Julia blurted, with some alarm.

"What is it?" asked Tabitha, her voice-pitch rising.

Inspector Crossbough produced, from his vest pocket, a small paper. He stood, handed it to Mrs. Wallris, then took his seat again. The two daughters rose and knelt at their mother's chair, seeking a suitable view of whatever it was. In that moment, Claire's aging face acquired a new wrinkle or two, looking as pallid as Stonehenge on a foul day. Julia's face was taut, but with a sort of ire behind her eyes; Tabitha, dumbfounded, dropped her lower lip with mute confusion.

The two detectives sat quietly on their assigned couch, a couple of meters away. They had waited for almost two days to observe whatever response this moment might reveal, and they knew what the note said:

Wallris--
John Bull's ransom will smoke out the black shirts tomorrow. If not, your bridge could burn.   Chapman

After a stunned silence of half a minute or so, Julia looked up, and directly at Inspector Crossbough. Her voice crackled, as a kind of eruption, "Who is Chapman?"

But neither detective answered. The older daughter had uncoiled the very question already hanging in their minds.

Mother dropped the white scrap on her lap. She began to speak, but the words were hard to come.

"Oh, mother, you. . ." Julia raised her hand and caressed her mother's cheek. It seemed that Claire might faint. Her head tilted back a bit, but it was more sleepless exhaustion that fainting. Then she was looking up at the ceiling, as if seeking angelic help. She looked as if she'd been run over by a train.

"There is a. . .a Mr. Chapman, at the *Thames-World*. He works in the office. I. . .I'm trying to recall his first name. It may be, ah, Mark, or Mike, or somesuch."

"Do you know, Mrs. Wallris, what his job is?" inquired the Doctor.

"He, ah, scheduling. I think he schedules the ships' deliveries, and tracks their itineraries. Paul had. . ." She began weeping. Julia was holding her hand, and again touched her cheek, then stroked her mother's forehead. Tabitha, kneeling, laid her head on Claire's lap. "It's all right, dear girls," her voice droned, now more with tedious grief than the earlier nervousness. Her countenance displayed a kind of deliverance, a recovery. She was a strong woman. She looked at Dr. Pepper. "Paul had mentioned Chapman several times in these last two months or so. It's Mark—Mark Chapman, he had been carrying a heavy work load, on the food deliveries to Spain."

"Ships delivering food to the port at Bilbao?" asked the Doctor.

"Yes, I think so," said Mrs. Wallris, now distracted again, remembering circumstances before all this confusion and death had laid its solemn weight upon them all. "The *Olavian*. . .it was taking supplies to the Spanish government through Bilbao. Paul had talked about Mark's difficulty in working all that out—"

Tabitha cut her mother off, clumsily, with a vehement exclamation. "Yes, and those damned blackshirts didn't like it one bit. They were crawling around all over East London, like roaches, making trouble for everybody. Damned fascists!"

"Shhsh! Tabitha. This is no time for your political opinions," Julia injected, raising her hand, like a bobby motioning for stop. A reproachful glance at her sister then swiveled back toward the detectives. "Inspector Crossbough, may I ask where this note came from?"

"Your father managed to hand it to a young man who happened to be there in front of the Fribourg shop, just before he collapsed."

"And did my father collapse to the ground?" Julia asked.

"Actually, Miss Wallris, he was caught. That same young man arrested his fall, and eased his, ah, his demise."

"You mean this man prevented my father from falling to the ground, just before my father—"

"That's right. The man was able to prevent your father from hitting the ground directly, and thereby afford your father some, ah, some comfort." said the Inspector.

"So father was in his arms?"

"Yes, ma'am."

"My father then died in this man's arms?" Julia's demeanor was taking on a sad grief, as if the event in question were a scene in a tragic play. "Who was he?"

"It doesn't matter now," replied Inspector, with inappropriate coldness.

"It most certainly *does* matter now," Tabitha erupted, with urgent ire.

The Inspector realized his insensitivity immediately, and sought to repair the offense, but by his own objective means. "Excuse me." He seemed to turn apologetic, but with a sort of awkwardness. "Who was that young man, Doctor Pepper?" he asked his colleague, without looking at him. The Inspector's gaze focused again on the wall behind the ladies.

"His name is Nathan Wachov." the Doctor supplied.

"And?" Tabitha queried, with a nervous edge in her voice.

"And?. . .Excuse me. . ." the Doctor hesitated.

"Who is he? Who is this person? Who was the last to touch and hold my father alive, and. . . and speak to him." Tabitha's grief was overpowering the earlier atmosphere of enquiry that the two detectives had earlier established.

"Mr. Wachov, a little older than you, a very pleasant fellow. He 's with a radio shop."

"And it was to him, Doctor, that my father handed this note?" Julia held the note in her hand, and nodded her hand down at it slightly as she spoke.

The Doctor elaborated, "Nathan Wachov, of Islingoton. He works at the RGD shop on Doughty Street. And yes, Miss Wallris, he was the last person to hold your father, and also, as far as we can surmise, the last to speak to your father."

The widow Wallris, with a weak voice, asked slowly, "What did my husband say to Mr. Wachov before he died?"

The Inspector responded, "According to the gentleman's statement, your husband expressed consternation about the monetary policies now being implemented by the government. He spoke of what he called the 'monetary experiments' that replaced our fiscal policies since we have forsaken the gold standard. He mentioned that phrase—the gold standard—specifically— Was it an issue that he often spoke about?"

"Oh yes," Julia said. "He had some very definite opinions about that, and being in the shipping business, he was quite knowledgable about the currency destabilization, and its very real effects on our trade."

"Yes, Miss Wallris," said Inspector, eyeing her keenly. "I believe he actually used that term. Is that correct, Dr. Pepper? Mr. Wachov's recall included that phrase—currency destabilization?"

"Yes, Inspector, and Nathan had a friend with him there, an American— Philip Morrow—who also your father's last words."

"We should invite them to the funeral," said Tabitha.

"Yes, dear, we shall invite Mr. Wachov and Mr. Morrow," said mother, with a first indication in her voice of any respite from their grief.

Inspector Crossbough resumed his enquiry. "There was another gentleman there who knew your father, although he says he was not present when your father passed. Rather, he gave us a statement shortly thereafter— a Mr. Greeneglass, Itmar Greeneglass. Do you know him?"

"I have heard Paul mention that name yes," Mrs. Wallris answered, as the girls shook their heads. "He is—well, I am in no position to say. . ."

The Inspector spoke carefully. "We did obtain a statement from Mr. Greeneglass; we know who he is, and we know of his association with your late husband."

"The tailor, he was Paul's tailor."

"Yes, just as he said. . . anything else that we should know?"

Mother was hesitant. "Well, gentlemen, if you have obtained a statement from Mr. Greeneglass, then you know. . ."

"Well, I'm afraid I can't—this is a matter of some sensitivity. . ."

"Mrs. Wallris, we must uncover any facts that are pertinent to your husband's passing."

Tabitha was roused. "Oh, this is about the blockade, isn't it?' Mr. Greeneglass was—ah. . ."

"My sister speaks without discretion, Inspector," Julia interrupted. She turned to her younger sister; her voice took on an authoritative tone. "Tabitha, we should discuss this in private, later." She turned to the two men. "Have you requested an autopsy, Doctor?"

"Yes, ma-am, we have." he replied.

Julia continued, effectively silencing her precocious sister, "All indications, Doctor, are that our father's passing was of natural causes. Is that correct?"

"As far as we can determine so far, yes," said Doctor Pepper.

"There is, however, the note, Miss Wallris. The one you hold in your hand. Its contents would indicate that there are some circumstances in your father's final days that require resolution, a resolution that can only come through the questions that we now are now asking."

"Questions about what my father's ships were up to—is that right, Inspector?" insisted Tabitha.

"Tabitha, I said—"

Inspector Crossbough raised his voice. "*Questions,* my dear ladies, about this note, and, at this point, nothing else. For instance, the bridge. Look at the note. Can you tell us what bridge may be referred to in Chapman's note?"

But opinionated young Tabitha still had some axe to grind, despite her sister's admonition. "The royal Navy interfering with British commerce—that's what this is about," her voice rising again.

"Please! Tabitha," her mother managed to exclaim. "We will discuss this later, as Julia has said. Do you understand me?"

"Yes, mum," Tabitha conceded. "But the Inspector asked about the bridge."

Mother's jaw dropped in astonishment. "What on earth are you talking about, girl?" We're speaking of a bridge, not a blockade."

"Precisely, mother. And Julia is right, as usual. We'll talk about it later."

The sudden silence was awkward.

The Inspector broke it, after a few seconds. "I understand your concerns, ladies. We all have our opinions about these present controversies. . ." He raised his eyebrows. ". . . these policies with. . . Spain, and so forth. You needn't go out on a limb over this. Dr. Pepper and I wish merely to inquire about the meaning of this. . .bridge. 'Your bridge could burn,' was the final element of Chapman's note. Sounds a bit, ah, foreboding to me, definitely indicative of a few questions. And the 'If not' subjunct that precedes it, quite a puzzling little message to be found in a dying man's hand, don't you think?"

Mother was weeping.

Inspector Crossbough stood up. "Such a lovely home, and this room. . .exquisite. Do you mind if I get a closer look?"

"Not at all, Inspector. Most of these decorative items, my father has acquired from distant places all around the world. They are a part of . . . his legacy."

"As are you," said Inspector, turning rather abruptly to face Julia.

"Pardon me?"

"As are you, a part of your father's legacy. If I had been he, I should have been quite proud of this family."

Dr. Pepper stood. "Ladies, we must be going, but we will return soon, as our investigation progresses."

Julia and Tabitha stood. "Thank you for your work, gentlemen. Should we discover any more about this, ah, bridge, we will inform you of it at your next enquiry."

Dr. Pepper smiled. He had noticed the Chinese pottery piece on the marble top next to him. "That vase, is, especially, I think, a lovely piece."

"Thank you, Dr. Pepper. Just this morning we received a companion to it, very similar, except instead of the placid scene, the new one has a dragon, in the cobalt blue on white."

"I see." Dr. Pepper smiled, and bowed slightly. "We have another appointment, Inspector," said he, glancing at his partner.

8

Signals

When Tabitha entered the RGD showroom on Doughty Street, Friday afternoon wafted unexpectedly into a slow foxtrot. Sweet Ambrose saxophones were drowning her heavy spirit in melody; a woman's voice was crooning *As Time Goes By*, and a tall blonde-haired fellow was gliding to greet her, with a gray suit, a blue tie and blue eyes that twinkled.

"Good afternoon. Can we sell you a radio today?" he said.

"I've never been in a radio store before," said Tabitha. She felt as if she were hearing herself speak through a gramophone.

He slipped into a smile as easy as a bigband clarinet line. "You've picked the right place to start out." Her stylish black outfit bespoke a somber dignity. "RGD is the Aristocrat of the radio world."

. . .*The fundamental things apply, as time goes by*. . . The tunes floated across her grief like a black swan on a still pond. *Is he*. . .?

"I'll bet you're looking for something that's compact—a table radio. Take a look at this 512 model; it's brand-new this year, with a tetrode valve in the output, for absolutely the best sound quality available in the world today."

His blue eyes pierced right into her darkened heart; a ray of mirth broke through. She found herself smiling. *How is this possible?*

He turned a switch and the machine came on, tuned to the same station as . . .*its still the same old story, a fight for love and glory. . . As Time goes by . . .*

"Yes. It sounds very nice. I'll take this one. But I'm on the bus. Can you deliver it?"

"Why, certainly," His surprise at the effortless sale was obvious. "If you . . . if you'll step back here to the register, we can make the arrangements."

She was waltzing along the carpeted aisle among the menagerie of gramophone horns and radio dials. A new tune began to play, a peppier selection this time. . . bouncing clarinet . . . zesty rhythm section, latin caliente, *oh yes, let them begin . . and we suddenly know what heaven we're in. . .when they begin. . .*

He walked behind a counter and opened a little sales booklet. "Now, to what address shall we deliver your new RGD radio?"

"Number 49, Montpelier Square."

"OK, very good, then. And the name?" and the blue eyes again.

"Tabitha." She smiled. "How much is the radio? I'll, I'll pay you now." She was retrieving a wallet from her handbag.

"Certainly, Tabitha, ah. . .Tabitha. . .and the last name?"

"Tabitha Wallris, 49 Montpelier."

Nathan lifted his eyes from the sales pad; he looked at her more carefully now. The world stopped turning; the moment had suddenly narrowed into a vortex of tragic discovery; It became just the two of them, standing in a radio store, she on the customer side of the counter, he on the other. Rhapsody in Blue swirled down upon them from somewhere, filling the airwaves with a torrent of tragic recognition, a speechless discovery of some terrible, unwelcomed truth. He saw a tear roll down the pink delicacy of her face; she was looking up at him with large brown eyes, but then he caught sight behind them, behind those shimmering doe-eyes, the struggling progeny of a dying man's last look upon this world, and Nathan thought she was almost like a baby at birth, trying to scream for the first time in history. Something, someone in the history of this world was trying to cry out.

"W-wallris?" he asked, in what must have been a scratchy gramophone voice.

She nodded, lifting the handkerchief to her face. There was a large stuffed chair nearby to her left; she turned, weeping, walked over to it and sat.

Nathan didn't know what to do. This had never happened before. His mind was wrung up in an indecisive warp, whether to persist in the lame act of writing a sales ticket, or to walk suavely around the counter to address, with comforting caress, the issue of this damsel in distress. He felt as if he knew her intimately, or knew of her grief more deeply than any man upon the face of the forlorn earth. But of course he had never seen her until a few minutes ago when the bell at the door signaled her entrance into the store and into his life.

Nathan chose the latter. He would be a man, not a salesclerk, in this moment of time. Approaching Tabitha slowly, he wanted to touch the delicate shapeliness of her knee, which had slipped outward from a black hemline as she sat down in the big brown velvet chair. But he touched her hand.

She recovered. "I know what you did," she said. "I came here to thank you for. . .for ushering my father into the next world."

He felt clumsy. "I'm sorry. . . I. . ." But now he wasn't thinking of Paul Wallris' collapse two days ago.

She was a lovely woman. Brown hair, brown eyes, rather plain in a way, but hiding behind those eyes he could see an uncommon spirit. She lowered the handkerchief to her lap with the other hand, the one he was not touching. Her nose was long and thin; he imagined her a sort of queen from ages long gone. The pink blush of her cheeks faded down to a pale swannish neck that carried a ruddishly vague hint of freckles, bedecked with a string of pearls that lay upon her scapula like a row of opalescent dewdrops. A delicate lace collar crowned the top of her black woolen dress, to suggest some forthcoming bright salvation atop her grievous predicament, like a silver lining atop the dark cloud. He sensed that her presently exposed vulnerability would cloak a more resolute substance.

"Where were you when. . .it happened?" a rather abrupt question, he thought, after speaking it.

Then her countenance stirred with restless movement. With a sort of flinging of the head, she looked out to the front of the store, and beyond it into the street. Carelessly withdrawing her hand from his, she was remembering; she was regretting. "We were to have met him at Trafalgar, at eleven. Father had left the house early, in his usual way, to meet his friends at the Club." Then she tossed the line of enquiry back at him. "What did he. . .what did he seem like, in those last. . .at the end.?"

The store manager passed by discreetly. Nathan, now on his knees with the young woman, glanced up at his boss, but said nothing. A silent understanding passed between them. An inexplicable smile crossed Nathan's lips, as he remembered Paul Wallris' last words. "He was communicating a message. He, ah, he wanted to tell me, or to tell someone, that is, I think he wanted to deliver a warning of some kind. . ."

"About our economic demise, the decline of the Empire, the lapsed gold standard, all that—"

"Yes, you know him better than I did, what he was. . .ah, going on about, calamity, he said. Then he handed me a note."

"We saw it. The Inspector showed us the note."

"We?"

"My sister, my mother and I—he showed us the note. What did he say about it?"

Nathan gave a gently perplexed shrug. "It wasn't—he just handed it to me and said to take it."

Lost in thought for a moment, she turned her head to the street again, as if expecting some signal from beyond the glass panes of the storefront.

"Why don't we, ah, go somewhere? I'll buy you a drink. You want to talk about this," he offered.

Her perfect teeth gently raked across the lower lip. "I suppose I'm expected to be home soon." The Scottish-looking arched eyebrows furrowed.

"You're a grown woman, Tabitha."

Quickly she turned her head toward him, gazing directly into his eyes. A long moment passed. He held her gaze like a precious jewel. *Who is this man that doth challenge the very gravity of our grief?* "Where shall we go then?" she slowly responded.

"To the *Nightingale*, the pub down the block here." He looked at his watch. "It's after four. Late enough to call it a day. We'll have dinner, if you like." He stood up.

"What about your work?"

"Mr. Martin will be fine. We'll be closing in less than two hours. He won't mind if I leave a bit early."

"Not at all," spoke Mr. Martin, overhearing, from the nearby sales counter. "I'll deliver this radio myself with a few hours, if you like." He was completing the sales ticket that his assistant had left by the register.

Tabitha stood and walked over to the sales counter. "Are you quite sure, Mr. Martin?"

"Oh yes, Miss Wallris. I'm happy to deliver it. As it happens, I have some other business to attend to, in Chelsea. There's no inconvenience. I am pleased to be of assistance. I read of your father's passing yesterday in *The Times.* Please accept my condolences for your loss."

Tabitha placed her payment in pound notes on the counter. "Thank you."

"As he was ringing up the sale, Mr. Martin commented, "I daresay, Miss Wallris, that some of our inventory here has arrived on your father's ships. He was a business man well-respected here in The City." He handed her a receipt. "Thank you for purchasing your RGD radio." Smiling, giving a slight bow, the shopowner excused himself and proceeded to the front where a prospective customer inspected a large floor-model.

"Oh, Mr. Martin," said Nathan, quickly, "I will take care of this delivery, if you don't mind. I'll see to it after the lady and I have refreshment at *The Nightingale.* I will drive her to her home and deliver the radio at that time."

"Very well, Nathan," said the shopowner. "As you like it. Do enjoy your evening together."

"Thank you, sir. We certainly will, insofar as that is possible under these grievous circumstances."

A few minutes later Nathan and Tabitha were walking down Doughty Street. Friday afternoon was busy with pedestrians and motorcars passing to and fro. In the midst of the busyness two young people traipsed slowly along the sidewalk, appearing to glance at the shops along the way, but in reality seeking some solace or reconciliation far beyond the noise and haste of London hubbub. "What was your father like, Miss Wallris?" Nathan asked.

She was pleased to hear the question, a very timely question for her at this moment. The hint of a smile crept across Tabitha's lips at the thought of what her fathers's life had been, a productive life from which, among his many accomplishments, his union with their mother had yielded herself and her sister.

"He was a wise businessman," she answered. "Always was a hard working man; he grew up in Camden, started working at the St. Katharine docks in 1900 as a porter. When the dockers went on strike in 1905, he skipped ranks, got out of the labor end of it." She looked at Nathan carefully. They were walking quite slowly amidst the throng.

"How did he accomplish that?"

"His parents, my grandparents, had a nest egg. It seems that my father must have been doing things rightly. He had leased a small steamer and began a transport across the Channel to the Continent. Of course all that was interrupted during the war. But he managed to survive the war, serving in the Navy. He had established some business contacts in France. By the mid-twenties, he was running three freighters. I suppose his labor background helped him greatly." She smiled, and looked up at him.

"How so?"

"My father knew how to talk to men who knew how to work. He had a way with them. He always cut them an appropriate piece of the pie, as it were, and they must have appreciated it, because together they made the enterprise work. Much of the tension among the stevedores, it was. . .well, my father's venture was, it seemed, somehow exempt from all that strife. I suppose he got on well with them, for he had started out as the workers did. By 1925, Lord Afton took notice of their productivity, made my father a business proposition, and so they formed a partnership."

The pair ended their stroll along Doughty when they reached the door of the *The Nightingale* pub. It was a stately wooden door, dark green with gilt carving, in the middle of which was the carved figure of a bird, presumably a nightingale. Nathan opened it for her, and they entered. The place was pleasantly dark, with gaslight ambiance. They took a seat at a table for two, by the window. Tabitha looked out upon the street from which they had just emerged. It was a marvel that she had walked three blocks with her new acquaintance, this tall unknown man who had been the last to speak to her father and touch his hand, and yet it seemed she had seen nor heard nothing of their passage along Doughty Street. Nothing had occupied her mind but the memory of her father's life, which this radio man had prompted with his question. Tabitha knew that soon relatives would be gathering at her home, and that Mother and Julia could probably use her help with preparations for the wake and so forth, but Sarah the maid was excellent, and quite capable, and had said she would enlist some extra help, and anyway what could be more important this, what she was doing right now? Explaining to the man who had shepherded Father's passage beyond the veiled Channel of whatever it was into which her father just entered—heaven, certainly, that her father had been ushered into, explaining to this man, this bridgetender the exquisite mercantile grace of her father's earthly endeavors. Yet so much more than the businessman Paul Wallris had been; he had been a loving father, though somewhat distant at times; he had been one who managed to tend, while not the details of her life, the very broad strokes of her canvas, her juvenile explorations with brush and palette, her schoolgirl days, her university studies. But now he was. . .gone.

"They must have been doing something right," observed Nathan. "It is no small feat to build a business such as that, and make it prosper steadily."

But now he was. . . away. She was displaced for a moment. A lady with a little cap was at their table.

Nathan was looking at Tabitha; he asked her something, and raised his blondish eyebrows slightly. Then waiting a moment, he looked up at the woman and .ordered a pint of Newcastle ale. "Would you care to have something to drink, Tabitha?" he asked again. "Or to eat?," at her hesitation.

Tabitha heard herself, as if inside a gramophone, asking for a glass of Bordeaux. "Yes. . . In fact," she resumed somewhat unsteadily, " the shipping grew, ah, exponentially. " *What an extraordinary man he had been.*

"Lord Afton's capital infusion was, it must have been, perfect timing." Nathan observed.

What had been the meager *Thames* steamship line became *Thames-World Shipping Company.* "In 1927, father and mother moved us from Camden to Knightsbridge, Montpelier Square. That was quite a change."

Out in the street, a woman in a blue and white gingham dress was carrying a child asleep. Tabitha saw the child yawn. *I was once like that, in my mother's arms.* A small blanket fell from her shoulder to the sidewalk. The baby's father retrieved it quickly, and draped the cloth gently across mother's shoulder, tucking it gently beneath the infant's head. The little one stuck his tongue out and continued sleeping.

"What on earth were you, Nathan. . .thinking when you had this encounter with my father? I can't imagine. . .did it make sense to you, what he was talking about?"

"Oh, it made perfect sense alright. There's a lot of that talk here in the City. Your father was not, by any means, alone with his opinions about the gold standard, and. .. all that paper money that passes for currency these days."

"But, I mean," she was looking at him quite curiously. "How did you. . .where did you. . .come from?"

"Well, I was with my friend, Philip. We had just come from his flat on Tottenham Court Road. We were taking a, I suppose, a little breather. It seemed to us to have taken over an hour to get from his place to where were, there on Haymarket, just in front of the tobacconist's shop. The crowds were so thick, you know, so slow, it being the morning of the coronation. We were standing at the window. Philip was looking inside at something. He's an American, represents an American tobacco company, actually. He was saying something about the pipe tobacco in the window. I was looking down the street, toward Trafalgar, which was the way we had been headed. Then I, well, I felt this weight. It was your father's grip on my shoulder." Nathan lifted his right arm, crossed it over to his left shoulder, to indicate where he had felt the sudden pull. The next thing I knew, there were your father's blue eyes right in front of me. They were. . ." Nathan wanted to be sensitive in his description.

"What? They were . . .what did you see in my father's eyes?"

"They were. . . exhaustion. He just looked so very, ah, tired."

"But it was more than that. It was much more than exhaustion, wasn't it,? that was pulling him down."

"Yes." Nathan answered concisely. He felt himself not wanting to wander into any further accounting of the scene without her requesting it. There was the hint of a tear again in her eye.

The lady in the cap brought her a glass of wine, half-full. Tabitha gazed out the window. The couple with the baby had moved on. Three uniformed soldiers passed by the window, and businessmen with their bowler hats and doublebreasted suits, smartly-dressed women coiffed with curls and stylish hats. The street was darkening, paces quickening, streetlights glowing. "But you, Nathan, where did *you* come from?"

"Well, Tabitha, I'm from right here, in Islington. This is where I grew up, but I was born in Czechoslovakia."

"Oh?" She turned from looking out the window, and peered straight into his eyes.

"Yes. My parents came here in 1914, just as the war was starting. They left from Prague, where they had been living for a few years. Before that, they had come from Movavia." He pulled his cigarettes out, offered her one. She accepted it, and he lit the tobacco sticks. He snapped the lighter shut. Deep within the young couple, alveoli cringed in anticipation of the tarrish gunk that was about to constrict their hidden world of pulmonary infilling and going forth.

Their smoke drifted up to the ceiling, mingling as it went, with likewise wafts of wayward gas, human hot air expulsions, shape-shifting extractions of the falsely rising expectations of mankind, but not nearly so noxious as the smoke soon to be curling through Dachau chimneys, nor as despicable as Hiro-inspired weaponic expeditions occupying Manchurian heartland, far, far away, on the other side of the wide world. And yet, there they were, cluelessly confident Nathan and grieving Tabitha, sitting in a cozy pub in the hubbub City of the civilized world, while all around their tiny island hell was busting at the seams, seething to ignite trouble in any possible nook and cranny, and dark cavity where it could be incendiated, most ubiquitously, even in *homo sapien* hearts and lungs and wherever flesh is heir to.

But they were not aware of all that. "You are from Prague, then?"

He laughed. "I'm an Englishman, grew up right here, on Judd Street. I was five when mum and dad left Prague."

"So you are, what, twenty-eight, then?"

"Yes. And you?"

"Twenty-three." She looked at him thoughtfully. "The way I see it, Mr. Wachov—"

"Please, call me Nathan."

She lifted her head slightly, displaying a proud chin. "The way I see it, Nathan, I must have been the progeny of my father's last blissful union with mother before he sailed off with His Majesty's navy, to go defeat the Kaiser's philistines."

Nathan felt his ears turning red. "I, ah. . .what a little blessing you must have been to them, Tabitha, in spite of the war. You were able to slip into this life before all the world blew up."

"Yes. A war baby, I was, a last-minute forethought. My mother says I am such an independent woman because those first four years were spent, for the most part, in father's absence. During the war my mother nursed me, an infant, and managed to hold Julia on a sort of tether; she was three when father had to leave." Tabitha took a puff on the cigarette, leaving a trace of red lipstick on the filtered end. Her eyes challenged him, but to what he did not yet know. The blackness of her attire beshadowed a kind of mystery; it veiled a low, well-tempered impudence that was somehow endearing to him. Yet the whiteness of her collared lace presented some inexplicable propriety, lending her demeanor a kind of balance, like a diplomat upon a mission, constantly making adjustments to optimize her position. Now hard, now soft. Or maybe the soft side was just his imagination, just his wishful imagination. She took a sip of the wine, and lifted her chin again in that proud sort of way. Odd, there was something odd in the way her thoughts must rotate inside her smart head, behind the brownness of those eyes, between locks of her waving hair, which had drooped in elegant disarray when she earlier removed her hat. He couldn't tell if her hair was naturally wavy or not, but it had a unique fixity framing her delicate face. *But what? again she speaks,* "And now, dear Nathan, the Teutonic beast that my father and his fellows took four years to subdue—the beast is stirring again in his lair."

This was a surprise to Nathan. He had walked into this pub thinking to console the grieving daughter with words of comfort, but she was full of something, and whatever it was, it was a little more volatile than mere grief, more potent than a predictable morosity. Her focus wandered, for the first time, away from his face; she turned her head left, and surveyed the low-lit denseness of the *Nightingale.* It seemed to be a test; she was stretching him in some way, dipping her toe in the frothy tide of her own political, or perhaps moral, sensibilities. She was casting some signal, already, of her turbid thought-life into the lamplight of a London evening, into the very inexpectant, unfathomed depth of his soul, or the world-soul. It was a moment that would somehow define their future together, if there was a future. He looked steadily at her, but her inspection of the dark pub was still rampant. A few seconds of silence passed in the still tension of the 1937 air.

His sights, now yearning for some exploration of her beyond mere countenance, had drifted downward, to the row of luminescent pearls hanging exquisitely upon her neck. As he was considering their perfect roundness, carefully, he spoke, "That's what Mr. Greeneglass said."

He too was casting about in the turbulent waters of that Channel.

He saw the pearls move, all of them shifting together to one side, as she turned her head, with new quickness, to inspect his face. His eyes ascended to hers again. He could see their surprise. *Touch'e.*

"Oh. You know Mr. Greeneglass?"

"I met him just a few minutes afterward."

"After...?"

"After your father's passing."

She was caught up in a thought, maybe a decision, of some sort. Nathan continued, "My friend, Philip, and I visited him at his flat on Haymarket just after the bobby dismissed us."

She looked at him curiously. "At his shop, his tailor shop. *n'est ce pas?*"

"That's right. We went through the shop to get up to his flat, a very well-appointed place I must say, small but quite tastefully done. He had one of our radios, a console. He said he had a family, a wife, and I think, two children. The place was definitely a home. And they had a menorah on the shelf, a Jewish home, you know. A family place."

"I've never been there. I mean, I've accompanied my father a couple of times when he was being fitted and whatnot. And he bought me an outfit one time, very elegant cream silk blouse, with maroon wool skirt and jacket."

"That's sounds nice; it must be quite fetching on you. I'd, ah, like to see it some time." He smiled, innocently.

"On me?"

Nathan chuckled. He felt very clumsy just now, as if he had talked himself into a corner. "Well, sure. That is, is there any other way to view someone's outfit? It must be. . .ah, worn, on the lady."

She smiled at him; sipped the wine, and looked out the window. It was dark now. *Mother is certainly wondering about me by now.* Then she turned her head slowly back to him and said, "Did Mr. Greeneglass tell you that my father had been doing some special work for him?"

"Yes, he did, Tabitha. We talked about it at considerable length, before the detectives showed up."

"Inspector Crossbough? and his associate, Doctor. . ."

"Doctor Pepper, yes. They had some questions for Mr. Greeneglass. They were following up, you know, on information that the constable had passed along. The constable had interviewed Itmar right at the, ah, the scene, back at the tobacco shop where it happened. He is also a member of the Travelers Club, as your father was. Itmar had seen your father earlier at the club."

"I wonder," she wrinkled her nose, "how it was that Mr. Greeneglass happened to be near the scene of, near the tobacconist's shop, when my father collapsed?"

"Now that, I do not know. I didn't think to ask him. But of course, his shop is on the same street, so it could have been a coincidence."

"Quite so." He could see in her expression that she was again caught up in thought.

"Itmar told us, Tabitha, about your father's two ships. . . sending supplies to the Spanish government."

"Oh, he did?"

"He did. He thought very highly of your father because of it. . . and probably for other reasons too. That is, I myself came away from there with quite a respect for your father, in spite of the dreadful circumstances. This sounds strange, I know; I knew him for only a minute or so. . . but, ah, Itmar, later when we talked in his flat, seemed to be genuinely grieved about your father's death. I got the impression that their collaboration was much more than just business." He could see her eyes moistening again. "Tabitha, did you know about those special excursions to the coast of Spain?"

"Yes. I had asked him to help Itmar's people in Spain." She paused for a long moment, gathering words with care. She was still looking out the window. "I had a friend, Aunika Bruchis, who had come to me with a need several months ago. It was about the time that Franco began his insurrection. Aunika made it known to me that there's a lot more going on than meets the eye there. The fascists are supplying Franco with guns, even tanks and planes. There are terrible things happening on the Continent now, Nathan."

"I understand completely, Tabitha. I have relatives in Prague who've been saying the same thing."

"Oh?" She looked into his eyes again. Now he saw more than grief behind the tears; he saw fear. "What have you heard?"

"This is not just about Mussolini and Franco. Hitler and his gang of thugs are stirring up a hornet's nest of trouble among the Germans in the Sudetenland. That place could blow at any time." Smoke was curling up from his cigarette, but it was about spent. He snuffed the thing out in the ashtray, and drained the last of his ale.

The lady with the cap and apron was at their table again. Nathan said, "I'll have another Newcastle, please, and, for the lady, a glass?" His raised eyebrows asked the question.

"Yes, I'll have a glass of your Chardonnay, please, and some fish and chips,"

"That's what I'll have too, I'm hungrier than I thought."

"I must call my mother," she said.

9

Fumes

What had begun, in the shadowed origins of human experience, as the gathering of food and warmth had evolved into something else in the modern way of doing things. By 1937, people and their institutions were all about the accumulation of monetized wealth and political power. In recent centuries, great numbers of humanity were progressing toward unprecedented middle-class levels of prosperity and security. And those who were not succeeding in the race were at least trying to. Lately, with the Depression and whatnot, there was, on the face of the civilized earth, maybe a little more trying than actual acquiring. But pooling resources was what it was all about in most corners of society. In America, the deal had been every man for himself, but that was changing, and now it was a new deal being wrought between the politicians and the deflated capitalists.

Modernity's debut on the world stage had concocted a multiplicity of ways for men to enrich themselves. The most recent thrust of unbridled wealth creation was the American way., which had sprung forth largely upon the vast potential of having an entire continent of undeveloped resources, newly discovered and ripe for the picking. Thus did the wondrous wealth-generating effects of yankee ingenuity become exponential in their impact, because the historical timing of our American experiment coordinated so advantageously with the dawn of the industrial age. The so-called industrial revolution was picking up steam at just the same time that the new democracy was toddling out of its nascent Enlightenment conception.

In the latter 19th-century, tycoons such as John D. Rockefeller and Andrew Carnegie had harnessed the sod-bustin', steel-drivin' inclinations of an energetic, adventurous, young nation. Together they shook the earth with resource-driven productivity from Boston to San Francisco, and in every holler and hamlet in between. Many a fortune was made in the wake of the rails and the cars and the stars and bars of the new frontiering capitalism.

For instance, a smarter-than-the-average-bear dirt farmer in North Carolina had initiated a worldwide tobacco empire that rode on the coattails of those rails. Mr. Duke had initiated his smokin'-joe enterprise on the back of a mule-drawn wagon, along the dusty highways and byways of mercantile America. His high-powered thrust of leafy capitalistic expansion outsmoked his competitors. It happened when he perfected, during the 1880s, the most profitable use of a brand-new machine for manufacturing cigarettes.

Philip Morrow, the young American now in search of English markets for tobacco profitability, was in the employ of that smoking behemoth company of the bustin'-out world. He was finding that the way business is done in the old world is not the same as how it's tendered back in the States.

The accumulation of wealth in merry ole England was proving to be a beast of a different color. A centuries-old social and economic order dulled the cutting edges of raw ingenuity and sales bravado with which young Philip and his countrymen were accustomed to hawking their wares.

In the old world, accumulations of wealth were much more closely related to wealth that already existed. They were not just pulling money out of the ground like back in the USA. This stodgy old money resided steadfastly within the protective structures of feudal and military institutions. Surrounding every pile of assets was a web of power—political and military density.

But all that had changed radically in 1917. Now the Capitalists and the Democracies of Europe were running scared.

When the Bolsheviks tore down the Russian Czar's gilt empire, they immediately began exporting their revolution to the world. That's the way Marx had conceived their grand plan, and so that's the way they intended to liberate the working world from the rapacity of capitalistic exploitation. They stubbornly undertook their worldwide project in spite of severe infighting and confused disorganization. So in spite of themselves, the Reds were able to intimidate their moneyed nemeses to the West. Fearfully anticipating an onslaught of Communism from the East, the European houses of wealth and power were scrambling for defenses.

Thus did they mistakenly identify, in the late 1930s, the German reich, newly constructed under Hitler's forcefully vicious methodology, as a wishful bastion of European order and capitalistic vigor. Weren't the Germans the proud forgers of finely-tuned industry and disciplined authority?

The leaders of the western world were slowly deluding themselves into a tragically misguided assessment of Hitler. Too many of them saw his rise as a potential defense of European order, and the wealth that sustained it.

This confrontation of semi-biblical proportions would hold as captive a newborn republic, Czechoslovakia, soon to be orphaned at the doorstep of Western naiveté.

In Petrograd, and Moscow, and out in the wide Siberian steppes, the intrepid Bolshevik leaders purged themselves of dissenters as they went. Apparently this was an unforeseen part of the newly forged Marxist internal machinery—blood and vengeance.

What the Marxists and the Bolsheviks despised in the gathering of personal wealth they made up for in the accumulation of power—raw, coerced, gulaged power.

The revolutionaries' starting premise had been the dissolution of the old order, which was, in Russia, the Czar. Then they intended to rebuild society from the peasantry up, through collective power, collective action and collective ownership of the means of production, The whole plan looked workable on paper—appropriating the means of production from the rich and distributing it to the people, the new so-called proletariat. But the working out of their plan was a different animal. As time passed, it could be seen in the heartless manipulations of the Soviets that power was gravitating toward one man, Josef Stalin. And he was no nice guy.

By the late 1930s, this was obvious to Adolf Hitler, because he was doing the same thing, drawing power to himself, although he was casting his net in the German way, which was of course superior, or so he thought, to every other damned nation in the world.

Hitler and Stalin were both, at the same time, eliminating from within their own ranks those who resisted them. And they both used the same methods—murder and fear. Stalin purged those whom he considered enemies of the state, and thereby cultivated rampant fear of insubordination within the ranks. Hitler also killed those who resisted him from within, but his violent strategy went one step further: he elevated, by deceit, his own vengeful struggle (*Mein Kampf*) to an unprecedented level of hyper-decadent Third Reich policy.

That one man could inflict such putridity upon the world was an offense of demonic proportions. Even Josef Stalin was fooled.

Most folks, including the leaders of the so-called civilized world, were clueless about what was going on behind the scenes in Germany and Russia. The bloody business was being conducted in secret places, under cover of darkness. But there was one group of people who detected early on, as they always have, what was happening to our world. Because they, before all others, would pay the dear price for such highly-organized slaughter.

They saw through the diplomatic smokescreen.

On Friday night, and the next day, a lot happened in the city of London, and in the world at large—far too much to give an account of now. In historical terms, Saturday was the mere blinking of an eye, a candle lit and then snuffed out.

Saturday night, Itmar Greeneglass had found Philip's flat, and was knocking on the door. Philip answered it. "Mr. Greeneglass! what a surprise. Please come in."

"Thank you." The tailor walked in. and stood a few feet from the door. His face presented an inexplicable solemnity.

Philip had the feeling this was not a social visit. "Please, sit down. What can I do for you?"

Itmar's eyes seem to be unsettled. "I apologize for the intrusion. I have a situation, I . . ." His voice trailed off.

"Would you like something to drink? I have some good wine here."

"That would be perfect. Thank you." Itmar relaxed somewhat, sitting back on the sofa. His eyes landed upon a framed picture, hanging on Philip's wall; it was a print of Andrew Wyeth's *Christina's World*. "That's an interesting picture, Philip," said the tailor.

"I thought so too." He handed his guest a glass of red wine.

Itmar's attention seemed to intensify as he gazed at it, as if his mind were seeking a retreat of some kind, an aside into some other world, a world of art, or wide open space, or wide sky, beyond the confines of the smoky city and the troubled continent. "What is she. . .doing? in the painting, why is she in that position, that—it seems, helpless, position, or maybe, not entirely helpless."

Philip looked up at the picture. The Wyeth painting depicted a woman in the midst of a vast meadow, or, probably, pasture, with a grey sky overhead at the top of the painting, extending the full width of the scene, and a nearly-level, slightly curved horizon, punctuated with a distant wooden farmhouse. A thin, young woman in the foreground was on her knees, but leaning to one side, as if somehow crawling with powerless legs toward the wooden house. She was pictured from the back, wearing a long, simple cotton dress, her brown hair tied simply in a ponytail at the back of her head. "Not entirely helpless," said Philip, as he turned to look at Itmar.

Itmar's gaze remained on the picture, as if he were searching in its field for words, perhaps words to explain his unexpected presence.

Philip broke the silence. "I received that as a gift from my company, when I left the States last year, to come to England. My boss, Mr. Duke, presented it to me after a farewell dinner. And he gave me this. Philip extended his arm to reveal a gold watch.

"Exquisite," said Itmar, as he inspected the piece. Philip had sat in the padded chair across from the couch. "Swiss."

"Thank you." He noticed that Itmar had very bushy eyebrows, for a man as young as he. "Mr. Duke knows my aspiration to become a collector of art. He gave me that because it represents the best of American work, although it is not, as you can see, a painting, but a print. Still, a very fine piece of work from our Mr. Wyeth. I am told that the girl, Christina, has polio." Philip sipped his wine. "I prefer to think that she is not entirely powerless in that circumstance." He looked up at the picture again.

"That she is, in fact, moving slowly, despite the handicap, toward her destination, the farmhouse," added Itmar, pointing up at the object of their interest. Then his eyes turned again onto his host. The visitor allowed a hesitant smile.

"Yes. That's it, moving slowly, despite the difficulty, with eyes on the horizon, as it were," said Philip.

The tailor relaxed his posture again, taking a sip of the wine.

"Have you had a busy day?" Philip asked, searching.

"No, actually, quite restful. Sabbath."

"Aah. . . right." Philip stood up. He walked to the window, felt a cool breeze flowing. Across the street on the sidewalk, in front of the small grocery, two men were having some disagreement. He pulled out a cigarette and lit it. Across the street, one of the two arguing men began to walk away, while the other began haranguing him with a raised voice. 'Two thousand pounds' Philip heard from the mouth of the second man. The first man, retreating, raised his hat briefly in a gesture of feigned farewell. 'This is not the last you'll see of me, Mr. Montague,' shouted the second man to the first.

Out of the blue, it seemed, Itmar said, "You know, Philip, I know about you Americans. I have friends in New York."

"Oh? What do you know about us?"

"You are defenders of the free world, a world that needs to remain free."

"Is that so? Who told you that?"

"Well . . . ah, George Washington, Abraham Lincoln." The tailor shrugged and offered a curious smile.

Philip appreciated, in the words of the Englishman, this association with such a legacy of liberty. But Philip was a businessman, always seeking a more relevant, a more productive, manifestation of the yankee exposition of freedom and its benefits. "Ha. What about Henry Ford?"

"What's he got to do with it? Never mind. I could tell you a few things about his political opinions. The point is, ah, Philip, the Brits are dropping the baton on this. They are cowering at the bully's taunts. The MPs will be debating this thing until they're blue in the face, until it becomes too late."

"Too late for what?"

"Too late to stop the Nazis, the Fascists."

"There's the treaty—"

"Doesn't mean a damned thing," Itmar proclaimed, raising his voice, not in ire, but in emphasis, as if some neutralizing verdict on the treaty had already been decided. "The Versailles arrangement is Hitler's main indictment to the German people that they got a raw deal after the war."

"They should have thought about that before they started the war."

"In a perfect world, Mr. Morrow, perhaps they would have."

After a few seconds of silent consideration, *point well-taken*, Philip said, "You are expecting, then, that Uncle Sam will take up 'the baton', as you call it, because John Bull has dropped it?"

"One can always hope, Philip. Every communication I'm getting from Berlin and Prague is that my people are up against the wall under the heavy hand of this so-called 'Third Reich.' Mark my words. Hitler's stormtroopers are up to no good. And it does not appear that the British are willing, or even able at this point, to do a damned thing about it. As I said before, it is up to the Americans to rise to their task as the defenders of the free world. And you, Philip, are an American, and, I daresay, a well-connected one at that."

Philip emitted a low chuckle. "Look around you, Mr. Greeneglass. Does this look like the abode of a well-connected yank?"

"You are a businessman, representing a company that is doing business," Itmar's voice rising, "all over the world! Think of it." The voice dropped low again, like the dynamics of a Haifetz violin solo. What Itmar said next was premeditated, the principal theme of his case as he had, a few minutes before, walked through Philip's door. "Go to the *Thames-World* office on Monday and establish some kind of account with them. Do business, whatever it is you do to sell cigarettes. See if you can find out what is going on there—who is making things happen, making decisions on the day-to-day level." Itmar stood up, walked over to Philip's other window, looked out at the street. "Mark Chapman, who wrote the note, is working there, and has been, for many years. He was, you see, in Paul Wallris' employment," He paused, but Philip had no reply. Itmar continued, "And I remind you that it was Chapman's handwritten note that Paul handed to your friend Nathan at just the moment of his death."

Philip felt a little stunned. *What? Chapman's note? What's that got to do with anything on my business plan?* Puzzled, the young yank protested, "That's not the way it works, Mr. Greeneglass. My business plan includes calling on wholesalers and retailers, not, uh, not shippers."

"Doesn't matter. Think something up. Take a load of your product and make arrangements for them to deliver it to somewhere in Spain—Barcelona, right in the heart of the matter. That could be a good beginning to establish a working relationship with Wallris' company."

Philip sighed, He ambled slowly back over to the wing chair and sat, took a drink from his wine glass. He looked at his visitor and spoke slowly, "Mr. Greeneglass, what do you know, already, about this—this company? Who is running the shipping operation from day to day? What is Chapman's role? What were they—Have you been there?"

Itmar returned to his chair. He looked Philip in the eye. Now, it seemed, he had the young man's attention. "I have not been in the company office. My communications about sending supplies to people in Spain, and making arrangements for some refugees to be boated to France—this was all between Paul and me. He handled it . He was helping us because, I believe he had personal convictions about the threat posed by Franco's assault on the government. I do know this. He had a partner, Lord Afton, , a very powerful man here in England, a member of the House of Lords. What is worrisome about Wilbur Afton is that, as has been reported in *The Times* and other sources, including my personal associations, he seems to have some fascist political leanings.

"Do you know this? Or are you just speculating about it. You can't believe everything you read in the papers."

"Paul himself had expressed alarm about his partner's associations. Afton and his wife—she's an American like you—are known to host, with regularity, gatherings of influential people who unabashedly support German rearmament."

"Why? I mean, what benefit could come to Britain from that?"

"All indications are that Hitler is a rabid anti-communist. And you know we have a few of those here. They're deathly scared that the Bolsheviks will be able to carry out their plans for world revolution. But there are more than a few of our British potentates here who regard the Third Reich as a stabilizing force in Eastern Europe—a dam, as it were, to arrest the tide of the communist rabble." Itmar paused. His eyes were intense with conviction.

"Go on," said Philip. "I have noticed this myself, in the papers."

"Geoffrey Dawson, the *Times* editor, is one of these people. He, and Garvin, at the *Observer*—they're lapping up this fascist whitewash like it was yesterday's news. That deal that Hoare made with Mussolini over Abyssinia was a complete collapse of decency. They've practically given the fascists in Italy license to run rough shod over northern Africa, the same as what they're doing in Spain, at Guernica—a bloodbath! All our English money is starting to move in the wrong direction here. Why, three years ago the Bank of England bailed out the Germans' debt. Montagu Norman is practically a dictator with the way he handles our currency. Runciman, Rothermere—there's a whole gang of them who are sucking this German soup, and Afton hobnobs with all of them. It has been reported. . ." Itmar lowered and slowed his voice now. "I have heard reliably that Ribbentrop himself has dined with the Aftons—yes, the traveling mouthpiece of Nazi smokescreen—he and his stooge on this side of the Channel, Oswald Mosely—what a gang of heathens! Thugs! How unfortunate for our dear friend, Paul Wallris, to have been locked into a partnership with Wilbur Afton. Paul was in over his head. I daresay they didn't like it one bit that he was bucking their tide on the other side of the Channel."

"It's a wonder he was able to muster any physical support for your people in Spain."

"That's true. I definitely think he was operating under Afton's radar. I know he was skirting around the royal navy itself to get those two boats in and out of Bilbao. It's a travesty that our government was obstructing these benevolent transports to the people of Spain. I really think this Cliffdon group were pushing their weight around among the MPs."

"What about Mr. Chapman? What do you know about him? Why would he have written such a note—about the blackshirts, and a bridge that might burn—to Mr. Wallris? And why would Wallris pass the note to Nathan as his last act?"

Itmar leaned back on the sofa, gulped down his wine. The tirade had exhausted him. "That, my friend, is what I am hoping you can help me discover."

The telephone rang; its jangly intrusion startled Philip, although he felt himself strangely relieved at the interruption. "Excuse me, Itmar." "Hello," he spoke into the phone.

"Mr. Philip Morrow?

"Yes."

"This is London Exchange. I have an overseas call for you from the United States. Please hold, and I will connect the line."

"Yes. Thank you."

After a few seconds of static and a few other bell and whistlish sounds, a weak voice came on, "Hello, Philip?"

"Yes. This is Philip. Hello."

"Philip, this is Sylvie. Can you hear me? This is Sylvie."

His sister's distant greeting was as a voice from another world. "Sylvie! Yes. This is great! I'm so glad to hear from you." But then, just as suddenly as his sister's voice had penetrated the Atlantic Ocean to remind Philip of his origins so far from European strife, the telephone went dead.

"Oh, pshaw!" said he, the displaced American, regrettably.

10

La Cabeza del Toro

Philip's grandfather, Roby Morrow, was dead, but there was nothing to be done about it. Three weeks on a transatlantic voyage and then mourning with the folks back home would belatedly accomplish little. And then there would be, after who-knows-how-long, the long trip back. *What would Roby himself do in this situation?* Not that he ever would be in this situation, across the damn Atlantic in a flat over Tottenham Court Road in Bloomsbury, London.

The old fellow had loved Philip well, had raised him, taught him, through many hours and many days at Morrow's Store, everything he learned about business, before Philip had high-tailed it down the mountain at the ripe age of eighteen, and landed his inquisitive self in Durham, not Durham North Yorkshire, but Durham North Carolina, where Mr. Duke's worldwide tobacco empire had drawn Philip into the smoky enticements of wealth and privilege, which gilded heirlooms had formerly been in the domains of the nobility, but now, because of American ingenuity and Capitalism's genius, were accessible to any young buck who was willing to work hard and leave his humble roots back in the red clay claptrap of Appalachia.

This Sunday morning, Philip stood on a windy dock, just off St. Katharine's Street, watching the Thames flow eastward toward its confluence with the English Channel, across which all the trouble in the known world seemed now to be brewing.

But apparently that hell's-kitchen of European bloodletting had been brewing for a long time, at least thirty years or more. Philip's father, Clint, had breathed his last of this world's smoky contagion on a battlefield somewhere in Belgium, a place called Flanders' Field, beyond the estuary of that cold Thames and across the choppy Channel. Philip's only memory of his father was hazy. He couldn't decided whether Clint's tall image in his mind was actual, with a flannel shirt on it, or fantastical, with its knight-like armored brilliance blinding out the cold hard truth, that noble countenance having been summoned up in his child's mind from, either true recollections, or from some long-lost need to fill in the patriarchal blanks that somehow had not been supplied by his old grandpa Roby.

He did, however, remember his father chopping wood, back at their home place near Trail, in the Blue Ridge. He thought of this as a boatload of coal was being negotiated into its destination at the dock. On the other side of the waterway, Philip saw a smaller boat, although it was quite a large vessel by his landlubbing standards. It was taking on both cargo and passengers. The name *Guenivere* was painted on the bow. It would most likely be transporting them to Calais, France. Ten months now in England, and he had not yet been over to France. Why not? Philip wanted to get on that boat. To hell with all this talk about Spain!. His father had died just beyond the French-Belgian border. He wanted to go there and see the place for himself. Philip wanted, suddenly and unexpectedly, to go to Flanders and leave some flowers at the place of his father's demise. What had that moment been like for his papa? On the battlefield, probably not anything like this passing just five days ago, when the old Paul Wallris had slipped into eternity from Nathan's grasp while they watched helplessly there in front of Fribourg and Treyer up on Haymarket. His father's death had surely been a violent one.

And yet the violence was ongoing.

A gentle tap on his shoulder, and Philip turned to see Itmar and another man standing beside him. The other would be Mark Chapman, as Itmar had arranged. Mark appeared to be a red-faced Irish, with bushy eyebrows and a grave demeanor. On his head was one of those tweedy flat caps like the Irish wear, with longish strawberry blonde hair beneath. He extended his hand and they shook, exchanged hellos. Then Mark spoke to Itmar, "We'll be going over here to Borkenau's diner for breakfast."

"That'll be fine," said Itmar. "Lead the way."

The place was a hole in the wall, but roomy enough to take on a bunch of hungry dockworkers. The three men took a table by the window, looking out at the dingy street on one side and into the belly of English maritime labor on the other. They were drinking coffee, eating biscuits and waiting for breakfast. The smell of eggs and sausages was a welcome aroma on this brisk spring morning.

The Irishman took his hat off and tucked it on the window sill behind a napkin dispenser. As he launched into a diatribe, it seemed to Philip that the large bald spot above his head curiously reinforced what would prove to be unadorned preference for candid truthtelling as opposed to diplomatic nuance.

Mark Chapman looked intensely at Itmar, shot a glance at Philip. Then he began speaking. "Your dead friend, my late boss, tried to step into the middle of a damned hornet's nest of feuding Spaniards. And that, my friend, is why he is no longer with us."

"Do you think his death was not a natural one, not a heart attack, or. . ."

"I cannot say, exactly, Mr. Greeneglass," said Chapman, turning his head, ". . .what might have brought the untimely death of Mr. Wallris. But I know beyond a shadow of a doubt that threats had been pressed upon him very shortly before—"

Itmar interrupted, "The blackshirts, mentioned in your note?"

Chapman raised his eyebrows quizzically. "Ah, the note, you know about my note."

"Philip saw it clearly, after Mr. Wallris handed it to his friend just before he passed out."

Chapman looked at Philip. "I understand you were there when he died."

"Yes, sir. I saw him fall on the ground—or he would have collapsed on the ground if my friend Nathan had not caught him."

"Well what d'ya think, boy? Was it a natural passin' under the veil, or was there, did you see, anything to indicate otherwise?"

"I couldn't say, sir. I've never seen a man die before."

"Oh, the hell with this 'sir' business. Call me Chip. That's what my friends do." He allowed a faint smile.

"Well, okay then, Chip. I haven't a clue. He was. . .uh, he was drooling, and his eyes turned up before they closed."

"So it is, the way of passin' from this world. 'Tis not a pretty thing, no matter what the circumstance." Mark Chapman looked out the window. Some thought was rolling around inside his head. He turned his face to Itmar and began speaking, at a slower delivery than before, "Mr. Wallris was in over his head. He was caught between a generous commitment that he had made to you, Mr. Greeneglass, and his conflicted association with his business partner, Wilbur Afton, *Sir* Wilbur, as we call him around the office." The ruddy man raised his eyebrows with incredulous skepticism. "But let me explain to you, gentleman, what was taking place here, at the ThamesWorld shipping company, where I have worked for twenty-four years, where I have come to have great respect for the deceased, and not as much respect for the other partner. As I said, Paul was up to his arse in these complicated Spanish disputations, and he was trying to do the right thing. But you can't do the right damn thing when both sides are wrong! A man cannot do the right thing when both sides are bloody murderers!"

The waitress brought their breakfast, sausages, baked tomatoes, eggs, setting the warm plates on the table. "Thank you, Miss. You are a princess, I do believe," said the expressive Irishman. After the distraction, his thought had shifted, but Mr. Chapman continued, "Well, here's an indicator of the way things are, and what got Wallris into this fatal mess, although it is a turn of events that just happened yesterday." He looked out the window again. A dark, Spanish-looking fellow was passing outside the window, with a very large, burdensome rucksack on his back. The burly man paused and watched as the man passed. "You see that fellow. He just got off the boat, I'll wager, from Spain. Looks to me like he's been to hell and back, and that pack on his back is what he managed to get out with before some CNT anarchists shot him down, in the streets of San Sebastian or somewhere, because he wanted to work his little patch o' God's green earth instead of joinin' up with the rabble-rousers who want to take everybody else's goods." A flash of recollection crossed his face. "Yesterday, my friends," He looked intensely at them both. "Yesterday, Largo Caballero's government collapsed, and what remains of Spanish government cowers in Valencia, on the Mediterranean coast, about to be routed off by General Franco to God-only-knows where— Morocco?" Chapman cut off the end of the sentence with a flourish of his hand, with pointed fork-in-hand emphasis.

Detecting no response yet from Itmar, nor Philip, Mark Chapman continued with his treatise on the Spanish situation. "This is not a good sign for the government, as if the bloody Spanish weren't divided enough between Franco's assault, and the anarchists who are trying to tear the whole nation apart with expropriation—stealing farms and industry from the landed classes. The revolutionary groups who are pretending to support the government are, truth be told, tearing the very government apart with their bloody factions. They're so busy killing one another, they cannot unite to sufficiently oppose Franco's Falangist army. The government of Spain, my friends, is a lost cause! It will never hold together. Or if it does—" He raised a single finger, the fork still protruding from a fleshy palm. "If it does, it will be because they have gotten enough weapons and disciplined support from the Russian communists. And you may ask why the Russians. I thought you'd never ask. Do you think these John Bull capitalists in London will ever support a communist government in Spain?" Chapman leaned back in his chair, with an attitude of rhetorical completion, and some exhaustion. Then he lit into his sausages.

While Mark was partaking voraciously of their meal, Itmar answered, "They are going to have to support the Spanish government. General Franco's rebels are being supplied with weapons, and with *wehrmacht* bombers manned by German pilots,"

"Is that such a bad idea?" asked Mark, after a bite. General Franco will be the enforcer who prevents Spain from falling prey to the Marxist delusion.

"And what delusion is that?" asked Itmar.

"The delusion that communist intelligentsia can expropriate lands and industrial plants from the rightful owners and assign them to be managed by incompetent revolutionaries and bureaucrats." Chapman stuck his fork, upside down, in the air toward Itmar, to emphasize his point. Then he took another bite of the sausage, which was fast disappearing from his plate.

A long silence ensued. Then Itmar spoke. "Do you suppose, then, that General Franco will rescue the Spanish people from being overtaken by the Bolshevik horde?"

Chapman smiled. "It's not that simple. I understand that, and it is pretty obvious that Hitler and Stalin are up to no good in backing the Nationalists. The little German colonel is a troublemaker, a treaty-breaker, and probably a damned lunatic. Nevertheless, Franco's Falangists, and the Carlists with them, are perhaps the lesser of two evils. I'm not so sure that our deceased, Mr. Wallris, understood that. In fact, though I had a lot of respect for him, I never understood why he was so ardent in his support of the government. He was risking—I daresay I can admit this in your hearing, and perhaps that of the young American here—serious consequences from the British government itself, for defying their gutless non-intervention blockade. And there were elements of our business community here who had detected what Paul was up to in supporting the Spanish government."

Itmar retorted, "I don't think Moseley's blackshirts represent any legitimate part of our City or its business. Most of the fascists out on our streets appear to be unemployed workers who have nothing better to do than make trouble for the rest of us."

"Those unemployed ruffians are, like it or not, a consequence of our capitalist way of doing things," said Chapman. "God knows I have little sympathy for them; they are a constant pain in the arse over in East London where our office is. They are arrogant and rude when they come looking for jobs, acting as if they're entitled to work just because of their British citizenship. But they are just pawns in the game, and there are rooks, and knights—one in particular I can think of—who manipulate their disruptions for their own purposes."

"And what purposes might those be?"

"To prevent the damned communists from taking over Spain, or any other country—Czechoslovakia—that's what."

Another long pause. Then Itmar asked, in a low voice, "What would you say, Mark, if I told you—and I know this may be hard to believe—if I told you that Hitler's Nazis, the ones sending military support to Franco, are systematically rounding up people I know in Germany, then commandeering their personal property and sending them, on trains, to camps out in the country to do slave labor for the Third Reich?"

Mark Chapman thought for a moment. He looked quizzically at Itmar, as if this man-to-man encounter between an Irishman and a Jew in a dockside diner were an event of some fateful consequence, yet hanging in the stars. Slowly, he said, "You mean the Jewish people, your people, are being arrested, as if for crimes they did not commit, and then convicted and sentenced without trial, to some sort of prison?"

"Yes, exactly."

"I have heard that," said Mark Chapman. "I heard it, in fact, from Paul Wallris, about three days before he died."

Southward from the London diner where Philip, Itmar and Mark spoke of Spanish surnames and shifting power reins, and windward beyond the turbulent Channel, a vast arc of airborne terror recently had begun. It rained *luftwaffe* pain over the Basque towns of Durango and Guernica, and would soon sling incendiary suffering throughout the whole damned entirety of Europe. With unprecedented force and demonic cruelty, ancient Iberian self-sufficiency had been cut asunder by dreadful Junkers and Heinkels like a hot saber through cow's butter, without mercy. The tinder peace of 20th-century blood-bought civilization would soon be incinerated afire like a bat out of thermite hell.

At this moment, as three English men puzzled out transplanted ideologies and shifting Spanish loyalties. . . at this moment, Viscayan ruins still smoldered from the bomb raid that screaming *wehrmacht* air-monsters had inflicted three weeks ago at Guernica. Even now, the unholy cloud was escalating to previously unknown heights of stratospheric iniquity, having been spewed from godless National Socialist bombers as they dumped metallic sacrilege upon the sacred Spanish earth and its people. Now the smoke spiraled high into Basque air; it drifted over the Pyrenees, defying all the better angels of modern man, and strewing blasphemous carnage beneath the warring winds of a fallen world.

But over In Paris, a surreal bull's head was emerging from blank canvas. The unbridled painter from Spanish Andalusia smote brushstrokes of black and white oils, revolutionary paint, mournful black and gauzy white they were—to declare a pleading indictment soon to be slapped upon the face of clueless Europe, unveiled at the unlikely *venue* of a fashionable World Exposition in the French capital.

For such a time as this—a time of braying beasts and of mothers' mournful wailing, a time of unprecedented, experimental airborne perdition. . . for such a time and place as this, while yet the tender adagios of Segovian *guitarras* could still be heard to resonate across Castilla La Mancha, now so lowly slow and then so passionately picado, between the melting mountains and the weeping plains of old Spain, for such a time and place as this, the world sighed its vain refrain of denial pain. Even now, apart from the destruction, the passions of ancient Andalusia were being slung out in creeping artish protestations.

But the men and women were few whose prescient palette could taste these bitter libations now being poured out upon the sands of Guernica; Paul Wallris, the working Englishman, had been one of them who had begun to navigate against the rising tide of iniquity. But now he was laid in a north London grave.

Life goes on; yet movement stirs like swelling spring within it. *La Passionaria* still proclaimed resistance in *las plazas*. Over the Pyrenees, beyond the broken walls of Roncevaux, and across the plain of France, in the city whose lights always were burning while a thousand artists were burning for expressive deliverance from the world's smoky confusion, the Pablo from Andalusia wielded his skillful brush, and the smeared world of underspoken artful resistance was forever moved. Even the very world itself was snorting with apprehension, like a spooked horse that neighs nervously and paws at the air; it senses danger in such unaccustomed barometric descent.

Alas, a gathering ransom maelstrom was whirling in this continental storm, soon to be sacrificed on Europa altars by, and for, *la cabeza del toro.* The dear price to be paid for such bullish blunders would prove more costly than *les citoyens* of this world are prepared to pay, and its yawning deficit would be covered in blood. But Oh! lamentable day. Who knew?

11

Los Perdederos

"I suppose when a man has something once, always something remains," the woman said. She was speaking of her husband, who now was confined to a prison in Barcelona. The "something" that remains of Geraldo Kopa could not be known, since neither his condition nor the accusation against him had yet been revealed by the PSUC, or *Partit Comunista*, which seemed now to be more and more in charge of the Spanish government.

Philip was listening intently to the imprisoned *Comandante*'s wife, Plia, whose seasoned voice now issued from between her dark lips like slow smoke from some craggy Pyrennic cave, and the smoke enveloped her words in clouds of cynical hindsight.

Whatever it is inside a man that compels him to lead ragged, ill-equipped militias onto the frosty plateaus of Aragon and require those soldiers to hold a front line against trained fascist battalions—whatever it is that sustains him through such war, and then strengthens his resolve to do what is right—even even after his anti-fascist comrades have unjustly thrown the brave *comandante* into a dark prison; "Always something remains," Plia was saying, as lamplight glowed on the taut skin of her high Castillian cheekbones, while the cigarette shrouded her obscure hope in pathos.

They were sitting in a café at Perpignan, on the far coast of France, not the Channel coast, nor on the western bay of Biscay, but on the

Mediterranean side, just north of the border from Spain. Mark Chapman, the Irish whom Philip had met at the London dockside only five days ago, was with them.

Plia was explaining that fierce, factional infighting of Spain's embattled Republican government had landed her dear Geraldo on the wrong side of a CNT insurrection that erupted at the *Telefonica* building in Barcelona about three weeks ago.

"My husband had brought his men back to Cataluña to rest, and to recover from two months of fighting, in the wintertime, at the Zaragoza front, along the Sierra de Alcubierre. These men should be getting medals for their service, not accusations of treason!"

"And they arrived at Barcelona just as the police raided the Telephone Exchange? Mark asked.

"So sad to say, *Si*. This was an unfortunate turn of events—I mean, the timing. I wish they had stayed at the front. Franco's army would have been a lesser curse upon Geraldo and his men than the false accusations against our *Partido Obrero* that have now come out of the *Partit Comunista*." The smooth skin on Plia's long face, browned with fifty-five years of Cataluna sunshine, folded tightly around her large brown eyes, which displayed a fire of ire for her noble husband's unjust treatment by the PSUC. "*Los Asaltos* raided the Telefonica on the third of May; that was a Monday. Geraldo's brigade had come in from Huesca on Sunday, just the day before!" Plia's indignation rose up as she straightened her body against the wooden chair-back. Her eyes opened widely with exclamatory emphasis.

She is so...Spanish., thought Philip.

Plia's tirade was not over. She lowered her head, and her voice again, taking a tone more grave. "This revolution has been commandeered by the *Partit Comunista*. Negrin and his donkeys, with their Russian advisors, have pulled the bloody ground from beneath our feet. They've left our workers and farmers in the dust and the mud, out in the trenches to be slaughtered by Franco's Moorish goons and the German airplanes, while they make plans in Barcelona, and in Valencia, to steal our forward progress and turn it back into fascist oppression! And they call us the fascists! They call us the Trotskyists, as if it were a crime to struggle for the people's true revolution. I'm beginning to wonder if they are not worse that General Franco. I'm beginning to wonder if maybe we should have joined the Carlists in Navarre, and fought with them to bring España back to the old days, the times of dignity, and of faith. Even faith in the Church is better than being accused of

Trotskyist insurrection." She turned her head to the left, and to the right, suddenly aware of her culpability in uttering such doubts during this time of treachery and shifting alliances.

But Plia was in France now; she could speak freely, or so it seemed, especially here in the Café Liberte, where the proprietor and the clientele displayed an identifiable favor for the expatriates of the Spanish *Partido Obrera de Marxista*, better known as the POUM.

"I like your cigarettes, by the way, Señor Morrow. *Gracias*," she said, raising her hands to light another. Philip handed the woman a new packet of Bullseyes.

"De nada, Señora," said Philip, smiling. That's what I'm here for. Wouldn't you like to take a truckload of them back to Barcelona with you? There could be some sizable profit for you and your family in that."

Plia threw her head back and laughed uproariously. "Ha! Just like an American, always out to make a buck." But she spoke with amusement, not judgment. Obviously her Marxist mind could still somehow entertain the prospect of some personal advantage in this situation.

Her amusement at his yankish opportunism was a welcome response, it seemed, for the young American salesman. Her mirth was contagious. Philip felt himself smiling broadly. "Is that so terrible?" he asked.

"Oh no, mi amigo; esta bien. Your cigarettes are in high demand in Barcelona, although the foreigners and the monarchists at the Hotel Continental usually manage to procure the lion's share of such luxuries." Her head made another quick survey of the place. "If I had a lorry full of your tobaccos, I would drive out to Huesca and give it all to the men of the *Obreros* brigade who hold the line against Franco's pigs there."

"You would really give it away?"

"It is all for the people of Spain, mi amigo—for her people who work hard every day to build her goods and to grow her crops in the hot sun, and then rest in the cool of her welcome nights. *Viva Espana!*"

"But Senora Kapo, won't you need some money for legal fees?

Incredulous, but still amused, she responded, "Legal fees? What are these legal fees of which you speak?"

"For your husband's defense in court. You must get a lawyer to convince the court that your husband has served Spain well, in terrible conditions of war at the front, and that he is a noble comandante, and he is surely no traitor to Spain and its people."

Now Plia was serious. "Oh no, Mr. Morrow, oh no, no, no. You do not understand. This is not your American courtroom. What I am telling you—" She raised her hand, one finger extended for emphasis, as if she herself were a counselor in a courtroom. "What I am telling you is that PSUC have no such ...sensibilities. They are people without conscience. I fear, from this time on, if these Comunistas are allowed to run Spain, they will in the end oppress our people just as severely as the Fascists. The way they are going, there will be no justice in Spain. Already!—well, see for yourself. My husband, Geraldo, who has served faithfully, as a sacrifice, even almost, as Christ himself—at this moment he does not know what charges are to be brought against him. His imprisonment is for no other reason that he is a comandate of the *Partido Obrero*, and our party now becomes, it is said in Barcelona, the scapegoat in the insurrection at the *Telefonica*, and we are to be blamed because the Anarchists were using the telephone exchange as a base for continuing to carry on the revolution while the PSUC wants only to prepare the way for Russian domination of our people."

In the silence of Plia's last emphatic cadence, Mark announced, "Well, then, I'm going to order another bottle of wine."

"Si, Señor, Gracias." the feisty Señora responded. "That is very gracious of you." Her relief at the opportunity to express herself, in the midst of unaccustomed French *liberte* and English candor, was obvious. "And some bread, please,"

"Yes, ma'am. Absolutely," said Mark. He turned to the *garcon*. "Please bring us a bottle of your good Languedoc, and a large baguette."

This would be a good time for a little stroll to get some fresh air, before the evening became too chilly. "I'll be back shortly," said Philip, as he rose from their table.

This talk of Russian intervention was a surprise to Philip, although he had certainly read about the possibility of such an encroachment in the British newspapers. In Philip's uninformed mind, the greater threat to Spain was to be encountered from the rebel side, and Franco's fascist insurgents. It had certainly seemed that way after his lengthy talks with Itmar. Actually, he and Mark were on a mission for Itmar; they had come to this Mediterranean port to meet, and hopefully transport to England, two German refugees who were relatives of Itmar. But that rendezvous would be tomorrow.

He wandered out from the café, crossed the street, and found himself standing on a boardwalk facing the Perpignan harbor. The chilly air laden with salt smell was stimulating his sense of adventure, the air. The water had a bit of chop in it. Along the edges was an ashy scum, with corks and whatnot, and a little clump of fishguts that he could smell, just below his perch.

The dull grey sky was darkening as evening fell. His thoughts went back to their arrival in France, less than a week ago. Mark had provided passage for him on the Olavian, a coaster vessel of Sir Wilbur's Thames-World line. After their departure from St. Katharine's Docks in London on that Sunday with Itmar waving farewell, their night crossing on the Channel, and then down to the Bay of Biscay, had been uneventful, the boat arrived at St. Jean de Luz on Monday night, May 17.

Before a Tuesday embarkation with cargoes for Bilboa, the Olavian had released a few deliveries for the French port, one of which was a shipment of Philip's Brigham tobacco products. Lord Afton's involvement in the Thames-World shipping company was now, with the demise of his partner Paul Wallris, being expanded somewhat beyond its previous, relatively passive, status. At Sir Wilbur's request, Mark Chapman had made arrangements for sale of a lorry-load of the Bullseye cigarettes, which was Philip's best-selling product and a brand popular just about anywhere in the world. The buyer was a Mexican businessman named Lothario, who would receive the shipment at the St. Jean de Luz dock with a lorry, to be driven through Hendaye and across the border, then delivered to one Truncoso, a representative of Franco's army, for distribution to the rebel troops, now occupying the Basque coastal towns of Irun and San Sebastian. Having spoken with Itmar and understanding the tailor's detestation for fascist associations, Philip felt a bit uncomfortable in business dealings from which Franco's army would receive any comfort whatsoever, tobacco-borne or otherwise.

But Sir Wilbur seemed to be in full charge of Thames-World now, with Mr. Wallris' wife and daughters having the minority share, and their activity in the company ostensibly taking a backbench role. The influential Lord Afton's preference for Franco's cause was well-known. His employee, Mark Chapman had opposite political inclinations, but was in no position to set any directions for the shipping company's business dealings. So Philip's sale to the mysterious Mr. Lothario was not a source of satisfaction for him, except that the usual profit would produce a welcome credit to his monthly report, as well as a considerable commission, and a feather in his cap among the back-slappin Brigham 'baccer boys back in North Carolina, since now it could be said that he had personally sold cigarettes in the Spanish market, though indirectly.

But the sketchy arrangement at St. Jean de Luz and Hendaye was not Philip's only order of business while in France. After a somewhat uncomfortable night in a lumpy French bed, he and Mark rented a truck and drove a few miles up the road to Bayonne, where they received another lorry-load of Brigham tobacco, this one having arrived directly from the U.S.

From Bayonne, they drove through the greening Aquitaine countryside,. Spring was in full glory. Philip, riding with the passenger window down, breathed deeply, drawing in the delicate scent of lilac blooms beginning to show purple amidst the new, yellow-green of the leafing season. Southward they traveled, through quaint St. Jean-pied-de-Port, and across the Nive River. Winding through Basque hills, the ascending road afforded them a picturesque view of the red tiled roofs on stark white houses in the sunshine. Upward toward Roncevaux Pass they went until they reached Spain. At the border, a guarded gate prevented further passage. But just inside the French side a white truck was parked, and appeared to be waiting for them. A short dark-haired man, dressed in tailored a blue suit, leaned against the truck; he was smoking a cigarette. He smiled broadly upon their arrival, and tossed the cigarette down.

After introducing himself in French, as Rolando, the young man shook hands in a gregarious manner with Philip and Mark. He promptly produced from inside his jacket pocket a princely sum—400 British pounds— deposited the cash in Philip's hands, not mentioning a receipt. Together, the three men loaded forty tobacco boxes into his truck. When the transaction was complete, the buyer climbed merrily into his driver seat, started the engine. The guard, dressed in olive uniform with a red cap, opened the border gate for him and saluted smartly. Rolando waved and sounded his horn, then drove back into Spain. A gust of wind blew across the Roncevaux Pass, stirring rye grass meadows in the breezy sunshine with waves of jade-like brilliance.

Philip and Mark climbed back into their rented truck, and commenced the long haul to the Mediterranean coast where there was more French and Spanish commerce to be had, and an appointment with destiny for Philip, arranged by Itmar Greeneglass.

But that was then, two days ago, and this was now, Friday evening, with ominous darkness descending on Perpignan's choppy harbor, and fish guts floating in the murky water below him. Philip turned his back on the

Mediterranean wind and strolled, hands in his pockets, toward the restaurant where he had left Mark Chapman and the Spanish lady, Plia, about a half-hour before. Shaking off the seaside chill, he savored warmth, stepping back into the cozy place with candles, white tablecloths, and people speaking in low tones. Mark and Plia Kapo, still seated at the table, were sharing their new bottle of wine; but now two young women were sitting with them.

As Philip quietly approached the table, he heard one of the women speaking, "I don't know if this was a miracle, or if it was just our family making precautionary measures, or a little of both. . ." The lovely fräulein punctuated her story with a questioning glance upward at Philip. Her large, brown eyes were pensive, brows furrowed with trouble, and he felt their inspection on him now as he stood opposite her, behind Mark at the table; she had taken Philip's seat. Glorious brown curls framed her beautiful face like a dream, a dream interrupted as she had ceased speaking.

"Excuse me," he said, "I didn't mean to interrupt." He stretched out his best, glass half-full American smile.

Mark glanced around at Philip, acknowledging his arrival with a wordless nod. "Hannah, this is my friend, Philip Morrow, whom Itmar had mentioned to you in his telegram." Philip nodded, and extended his hand, palm downward to signal that the ladies should please not rise on his account, as they seemed inclined to do. "Philip, this is Hannah Eschen, and her sister, Lili."

"Ah." He looked directly at the lighter, younger sister, Lili, then back to the serious Hannah. "You were saying that it was a miracle that you got here?"

Her furrowed brow relaxed, the eyes twinkling in candlelight, "Yes, well, perhaps . . ." A wry smile twitched across her thin lips as Hannah hesitated. Her eyes dropped down to Mark, inquiring tentatively of what confidences might be required in this situation, during these troublesome times—times of hasty displacements they were—and unscheduled embarkations. But then, she had only just met Mark as well, although Itmar had spoken of him, so she could find in his Irish eyes no security as yet, although she had known him now for a full twenty minutes longer than the American. Then Hannah remembered that her uncle Itmar had arranged this meeting from London, and she realized how far they had already managed to travel in recent days upon the improvised rails of his financial and credential arrangements, which were nothing short of miraculous in their thorough anticipation of all their obstacles along the way. And so Hannah found herself blurting, rather carelessly, "We only just left Munich about a week ago," neglecting purposefully to mention that she and her sister had no intention of ever going back to their Bavarian home again. "And, and. . .all of this has to be from outside Germany and that is our miracle—what saved us."

"Saved you?" inquired Philip, with wonder.

"I have," stumbling over the German accent, "I have, perhaps, overstated my case. My English is—"

"Excellent," Philip said. "Your English is excellent.

She smiled. "Thank you. What has. . .ah, transported us. My uncle has made our travel arrangements to transport. . ."

"To transport you to where?" Mark queried.

Now the younger sister had an opinion. "We do not know yet what is our destination." Lili's accent was thicker.

"We have transit visas as far as London. This, Itmar has arranged for us," said Hannah, confidently. Then she added, a little unsurely, "if they are accepted when we leave France, and when we arrive in London."

"That—my dear fräulein Hannah, is what your uncle Itmar has sent us here to arrange for you, and also. . ." He smiled. "to accompany you." Having spoken so, Mark stood up, pushed his chair gently toward the corner of the table to make room for Philip. Noticing again their seasoned companion from Spain, he apologized. "I'm sorry. I have neglected to—Señora Kapo, please meet Hannah and Lili Eschen, and," looking at the young women, "please meet Señora Plia Kapo."

The Spanish lady placed her older hand, reassuringly, on Hannah's "I too have a miracle, señorita—that I am here alive! I understand these things. But I am even now praying for a miracle! My husband, who has been fighting bravely to preserve our Republic of Spain, and leading other brave men into battle, is now thrown—it is a terrible mistake—into a prison in Barcelona."

Hannah raised her eyebrows. This talk of prison was no stranger to her German ears. It seemed that these last four years in Munich—ever since the Nazis had come in—had been a slope tipping treacherously downward, tumbling family members and friends into a nearby dark prison, newly-built out in the countryside, at first unspecified but what had lately acquired the name *Dachau*. "*Konzentrationslager*" she murmured.

The waiter had brought more glasses, and Mark was pouring red wine for all. Philip was retrieving a chair from another table. "I have a brother who was taken two weeks ago by the SA, and put in prison," Hannah whispered, her eyes watering, to Plia, as the older woman broke bread from a baguette and handed it to her.

116

"What is your brother's name?"

"Heinrich."

"And on what charge have they arrested him?" Plia's radar was keen. Many years of marriage to the *comandante*, and especially during this year with such extremities of unpredictable atrocity and injustice, had sharpened her awareness to the peculiar perils of 1937. And the nation of France—in which they now sat, having just met, tasting so freely and recklessly of some fragile *liberte Francaise*, imbibing the candid sparkle of their newfound Gaulic *fraternite* over Languedoc, speaking so freely yet mournfully between the frightened *fräulein* and the embattled *Señora*—this France, into the air of which their low-spoken complaints now trickled, bloodlike, toward a convergence of some bottled rage—this France itself was now fermenting, in many places from Toulouse to Paris to Lille, with an invasive spirit of fear. It boiled up from the hot cauldron of *Espana*, frothing over the Pyrenees in the south, even as it sloshed from Nordic fissures of aryan cruelty that spewed beyond the Alps.

"It is too crazy; the charge against my brother is not—there is no authentic German law to—he was arrested for kosher killing."

"Oh no! Your brother did not kill one of the policemen, surely not!"

"No, no. He was taken because they caught him killing a cow in the kosher way, which the Nazis have forbidden. My family is in the cattle business. They took away the knives that he and my father have always used for kosher slaughter and preparation, and then they took Heinrich in the night to Dachau and that was two weeks ago. We have not seen him since, and they have not charged him with anything. But the SA have issued yellow stars of David that we must sew onto our clothing. Oh! that King David were here now to deliver us from these philistines." Hannah was weeping. Mark and Philip didn't know what to say. Plia stroked her hair. Lili excused herself, walked outside. The sky had cleared. The red sun was pasted in the sky like a wafer.

A thin swath of southern sky, pewter-bright between heavy clouds and the soggy coast of France, was splayed across the horizon, like a patient etherized upon a table. Young refugee Lili thought of her forsaken home in Munich. Here she was, her gaze glancing along that horizon until it settled on the fiery orb at the western end of the panorama. She felt freshly plucked, as if from some fungal overgrowth of National Socialist parasitism. The noxious 'shroom had puffed up its whitish, larcenic lumps with Aryan arrogance, and was now devouring generations of Germany's Jewish cornucopiae, including her father's cattle business and their Munich home.

Just now, standing upon the brow of an estuary's point, Lili could not see, nor could she comprehend, the full significance of that horizon's imminent peril. From Perpignan to Dunkerque, the eastern borders of France were being unceremoniously rendered naked, laid out as sacrifice before some beastly onslaught of military butchery now in the making. Stealthily was that minotaur of militant German wrath arising, having been stirred from its cavish slumber, falsely induced in the vertigo of Versailles mirrors. Now Lili stood at the southern foot of France. Suddenly flung, she was, into a cauldron of international manipulations, here at the border of boiling Spain. From southerly *Cote d'azur* glow, now dulled by dusk and dank, the once-proud, republican profile of France had proclaimed itself, for centuries, northward and eastward, then back westward, in a jagged arc. At the Alsace extremity of her ancient claims stood the stately *Grand Dame* of Strasbourg, vulnerable in her pregnant eastern protrusions. Now fragile with wounded *liberte*, she found herself in bondage, having little resolve, and naked in the hot Thorish breath of *wehrmacht* bellows.

France had been so weary of the last war's extremities of blood and carnage. She had exacted futile reparations through the dire treaties, so desperate in their misdirected graspings at peace and security. Those vindictive pacts had lately been Saar-tossed, with unflinching hitlerian untruth, into the swiftly flowing currents of the Ruhr, soon to be deposited downstream, at the yawning mouth of rude Rhein retaliation and choppy North Sea humiliations.

Persons, so small, fled in the lengthening shadows of these giant events.

"Papa is in Strasbourg," Lily heard her sister say. Startled from her trepidation, she turned to see Hannah, standing on the platform below her, wearing an expression of dubious wonder. Next to her on the platform was the American, whose name Lili had forgotten to remember. "Philip says he will accompany us there," Hannah added.

"How do you know that father is in Strasbourg? And what about mother?"

"Mr. Chapman went to the telegraph office down the street. He received a telegram from Mr. Greeneglass, who communicated that mother's train trip from Munich to Stuttgart went according to plan, and that papa was able to get out of Munich Wednesday night. Then they were able to meet at Kehl, on the border. Last night, they traveled by auto into France."

"Who drove them?"

"That, I do not know—must be some person with whom Mr. Greeneglass had made arrangements," Hannah replied.

A white seagull lighted on the railing, a few feet from where Lili was standing. Amused with the distraction, she approached the bird slowly, hoping to touch it. As soon as she was in reaching distance, the creature flew flappily away, into the sunset. With that whimsical encounter, Lili turned on her heel, descended the metal stairway to the lower platform where Hannah and Philip were standing. Now she recalled, from their earlier introduction, his name. With a curious smile, she looked at the American and spoke, "Mr. Morrow, why are you so willing to accompany two German girls whom you have just met, to Strasbourg?"

Philip laughed with delight. "I. . .I have, for a long time wanted to go to Strasbourg, ever since I took classes in French, at university. One of the first conversations we studied was about traveling to Strasbourg, for. . .I think. . . for a ski trip." Seeming to think further into the matter, he continued, "More important, however, may be that I would like to go beyond Strasbourg, if that is possible, up to the north of France—actually it is Belgium—to see the battleground where my father died in the war."

Lili's slight smile evaporated. "Oh, I am sorry to hear that." Her brows wrinkled with sympathy. "Where is that?"

"Somewhere in Belgium, according to what my grandfather has told me."

"What battlefield?"

"It is a place called Flanders field."

"How old were you then, when your father was killed at Flanders?"

"I was eight when the memorial service was held." He looked at her thoughtfully.

"Do you remember that well?"

"I remember the flag, and the 21-gun salute."

"You did not see his face?"

"No. The service was a flag and an empty coffin. His body is still somewhere in Belgium, in the ground." Then there was silence for a little while, except for the lapping of waves against a concrete seawall below, and little whistling breeze.

Her attention drifted. Looking up at the sky, now almost black, Lili nodded her headed directionally. The night was turning clear, and cool. "There is the North Star," she said.

Philip looked up at the pinpoint of bright light. "So it is." He smiled at her.

With a mischievous grin, she looked at him. Slowly, she said, "Vous souhaitez vous rendre a Strasbourg pour skier?"

"Oui, mademoiselle." He had an unabashed American accent, and southern at that. A bit unsurely, he continued, "Mais. . .uh. . .le plus important, je voudrais parler a ton pere." His expression remained serious.

But her expression was more lighthearted. "A mon pere? Pourquois?" she asked, with quizzical smile.

"J'ai lu. . .Je. . . I have heard that the new government in Germany has turned quite repressive. I would welcome the opportunity to talk first-hand to a man who lives there and can tell me more about what is happening in the so-called Third Reich."

"Cruel," she said, adamantly.

"Pardon me?"

"The Third Reich is cruel," she repeated.

"They are thieves and murderers," Hannah interjected. "Why don't we go back in the restaurant and get something to eat? It's getting cold out here, and I'm hungry."

Philip agreed. "It is getting cold. That's a good idea." He turned slightly, extended his hand toward the restaurant where they been earlier. "Apres vous, mademoiselles."

As the threesome approached *Le Diner Special*, Hannah inquired, "Philip, what is your business?"

"I represent an American tobacco company, the Brigham company." He produced a packet of cigarettes from his jacket pocket, the same packet from which he had earlier retrieved a smoke. "These are my most popular brand, *Bullseye*. Would you like to try one?"

"I don't smoke, but I think maybe Lili does, although our father does not approve."

Lili chuckled. There are many things of which our papa does not approve. Nevertheless, Philip, I should like to try one of your famous American cigarettes, after dinner."

"That can be arranged . . .with your father's permission," Philip teased.

"Our papa is not here, and anyway, his permission is not required in this matter," was Lili's riposte.

"I would, however, like to talk to him about the developments in your country, if you are willing to let me accompany you to Alsace. And your brother—what is his name?"

"Heinrich."

"Is he not able to come with your parents into France?"

"He was arrested two weeks ago. We don't know where he is," replied Hannah, her voice returning to a serious tone."

"Is there something you can do—"

"We have done everything we could think of, Philip, to get to Heinrich, or even to find out where he is. He is not the only one in Munich whose whereabouts are not known," said Hannah. She looked at him rather fiercely.

"It is not that we are leaving him behind. The truth is, those SS men— they have suspended all the laws to suit their own— they would most likely have come for father, if we had not planned our exodus from Germany at just such a time as this. That is why we all—the four of us who are left—have decided to flee while we still can. There are others who have failed to heed the signs of this Nazi pogrom, and themselves disappeared."

"Is it because you are Jewish?" asked Philip.

"The simple answer is yes. There are some who say they are going after people who have good assets, prosperous shopkeepers." Now the three of them were standing outside the restaurant. Hannah was getting upset. "It may not be a good idea to speak of such things while we are in this restaurant."

"But you are not in Germany now."

"I do not know if that makes a difference or not, Philip. These fierce Germans have been caught pursuing French people too. Their cruelty knows no bounds, especially toward the French, who have always stood in the way of the German bullies. They may even have covert agents in this very place, as close to the Spanish border as it. Our friends in Munich have said that Hitler is sending airplanes to Spain to bomb the cities so that General Franco can establish fascism, like Mussolini has done in Italy."

"How could they know that?" Philip asked.

But before Hannah could answer, Lili grabbed her sister's arm. "Let's go in, Hannah. You were the one who spoke of being hungry. There is enough noise in this place. If we do not talk too loudly we can explain this whole cursed thing to Philip. Let us eat dinner."

And so they went in. The garcon seated them at the same table where they had been earlier. Mark and Plia were not there, although Philip thought he knew where they had gone.

"J'amerais avoir soupe a l'oignon," said Lili to the garcon.

12

Rift

It was as if a great chasm were cleaving the soul of civilized Europe—a great tectonic heaving of opposite human compulsions—visceral, metallic, physical power goose-stepping from the darksome German east, against enlightened ambivalence in the dusky French west. On one side, a million Nazi arms stiffened in heilish salute. Their starkly parallel thrusts mimicked, or mocked, ancient spears poised and battle-ready over castle parapets of the fortified past. The rumblings of this richtering rift even now were shaking to dust the very foundations of Europe's cultural edifices; soon Frankish ramparts would tumble into heaps of startled confusion and mounds of fearful rubble.

On the other side of the great ideological rift of 1937, the French were in disarray.

"Do you think the border officials in Strasbourg have been compelled into collaboration with the Nazis?" Lili asked her older sister. But Hannah just turned her eyes, melancholy, to the window. To Philip, their trepidation had become palpable; it hung like a storm cloud.

The locomotive beneath their feet was rumbling with a gentle, hypnotic rhythm. Across the aisle, a mother with babe asleep on her shoulder crooned lullaby in the little one's ear, *Frère Jacques, frère Jacques, dormez vous?* she sang softly, as mama rocked her child with loving tenderness. *How long has this been going on?*

Their train was now an hour out of Avignon, rolling in the gathering dusk, for an overnight passage to Strasbourg, where the escaping Eschen father and mother would, it was hoped, be soon reunited with the refugee daughters. There, in the border town of Strasbourg, the irregular heart of French resolve beat in fretful suspension. Now Lili and Hannah, with Philip alongside, were barreling toward the shadowy edge of that great border divide. It was an old national fault-line, cleft now between stone-faced phalanxes of the Third Reich, and the startled cadres of the French Third Republic.

"Our leaving Munich was a sudden decision, and we were in a hurry. We were not even able to see papa or say goodbye," Lili explained, for the third time, to Philip. "Surely papa has made it safely it to Strasbourg, as your friend Itmar has telegraphed." Lili's dark eyes wandered to the windowed sky. Preoccupied, she unthinkingly surveyed an orchard of silhouetted fig trees as they were passing silently in the stark contrasts of evening light. The Lyonnaise horizon was ablaze with streaks of golden brilliance beneath distant black cloud layers. A silver-orange ribbon, the River Rhone, glinted from the far side of the fields.

 France was divided. Germany was not.

The Third Republic of France was torn with factions, tattered as an old tri-color that had flapped o'er *le guerre* for too long. Her white, social-centrist soul trembled now in existential dread, while red cadres of the communist Left barricaded the corridors of wealth with enforced *egalite*. Out on the perimeters of French dignity, colonially flung far-afield, blue cotillions of the nationalist Right stood resolutely in defense of the *ancien regime*, whatever that had been or would someday somehow again become. *Vive la France!*

But on the other side of the Rhein, the German former-prisoner, having been tethered and bridled in subjection around the Continental townsquare of Entente Europe for the last eighteen years, was now rather suddenly, unexpectedly, sprung loose from his public humiliation that had been decreed and cartographed in, of all places, a French palace in 1919. The prisoner had snuck out of Allied economic interment under a camouflaged cover of premeditated deceptive diplomacy, lying, as it was, upon the exposed cartilage of ancient, noble European expectations, and the comatose corpus of *Lex Europicus*, even as Birnam Wood had, back in the mists of antiquity, moved against Dunsinane. Unbeknownst to the well-intentioned, well-appointed and duly elected diplomatic scions and ministerial sycophants of European civilization, the slithering passage from Versailles accountability had been accomplished in 1933 by a lawless law-wielding corporal whose capacity for vengeance was deeper than the abyss, and whose genius for stealthily-equipped rearming retaliation knew no bounds.

This was not supposed to happen, but *Les Francaise* did not know that. Neither did the British, although there was a bulldog or two who was sniffing about, soon to ascertain that there was something rotten in the rebuilt ruins of that Great War that had been fought to end all wars. But that Winstonian assessment was almost too late, almost too defenseless, after the little mustachioed corporal had crawled out from under an Austrian rock. And so the Brits and the French and everybody else were about to come up a pound late and a franc short, playing catch-up ball, which is a damned dangerous game before. But hey, who knew?

The young American, Philip Morrow, surveyed darkening Provence countryside from a French railcar as the sun set on everything that had previously existed, or that he had even thought existed. The lovely Eschen sisters, formerly of Munich, held each others' hands as their train approached Lyon. They were worried about mama and papa, and would be for a while yet. Philip, for his part, surely did not know, had certainly not anticipated when he had departed the dock in London town a few days ago, that he would be pummeling across France in the dark of night toward Lyon and Strasbourg and the Rheinland and Belgium, and Flanders Field where his father had been somewhere buried. He did not know. But then what is it, when we get right down to it, that we really know?

France was not the only nation splintered by governmental factions; there was another. It was a vast land, of the north, ruled by zealous, newborn soviets whose revolutionary contentions would soon be resolved by the heavy hand of fierce leader.

As the train pulled into Lyon, the conductor informed Hannah Eschen that their request for a sleeping berth could be accommodated, but alas, only for two. So Philip accompanied the sisters to the sleeper car, which happened to be, happily enough, the next behind the one in which the threesome had been seated. With the German girls comfortably situated and primed for a night's rest during their passage to Strasbourg, Philip returned to his seat.

The train chugged out of Lyon station. Philip positioned himself for a nocturnal ride through the darkened countryside of southeastern France. He intended to sharpen his very elementary French reading skills with a newspaper he had found. Soon after the train had achieved cruising speed, and the night turned sedate while city lights outside thinned to reveal a panorama of dark windows punctuated by a crescent moon, the rhythmic stillness of the steel wheels below settled into a slumbery monotony. Philip knew its steady progress would lull this express train for many hours. As his cognitive grasp of an article about Leon Blum's government started to drift into sleepy, yankee incomprehension, the quiet humdrum was broken when a man entered from the rear door. The sound was startling, as Philip's ears were suddenly filled with the clickety-clack of steel wheels. The sliding rear door opened and Philip noticed a flash of red scarf as it silently moved, beneath a black beret, along the aisle to the next open seat, which was three ahead of Philip's and on the opposite side. A dark-haired man, thin-necked. Nothing new here. Time for a little snooze while his life and the two lovely German girls resting dreamily nearby were transported further into the starlit nocturne of May 22, 1937.

A dream of his blonde French teacher, Mdme. Metz, back in North Carolina, was torn asunder when the clackety roar of train wheels filled Philip's ears again as the rear door opened. What time it was Philip did not know. Maybe an hour had passed, maybe a minute. A man was slowly walking between the seats, looking for something or someone, or just a seat. He was heavy-set, with an olive wool military jacket, but no insignia, and a peaked cap of the same color tilted upon a blonde head. The man stopped at the seat where the other fellow had previously seated, and plopped his heavy frame down in the adjoining seat. Philip could easily lapse back into restful bliss, but there was something curious about the way the seated man had looked up at the other who had joined him. The look was not welcoming; it seemed more an expression of surprised dismay, even fear. The big man who had just entered spoke in a low, deep voice. Philip faintly heard, though could not understood the man's thick French, which sounded like Russian.

"You think you can evade me so easily, mon ami? I have not come down here for no thing. We do have some settlement that yet needs to be achieved," said Ilya Ehrberg to his comrade. He raised his eyebrows, as if they could become a question mark to complete his inquisition.

Philip could see only the back of the big man's neck as he spoke, and a jowly jaw on the right side of his face. The thin man's nervous profile was stricken with dismay. Philip watched the thin, close cropped black moustache twitch as he retrieved some impatient answer, giving him the appearance of a smart kid who was uncomfortable with the bully's rough intimidations. "What do you want? Why have you come here?" asked Pierre.

"I think you know why, comrade."

"I know nothing."

Ilya laughed. He rubbed his stubby beard, stretched his neck. Maybe he was limbering up his jaws for some lengthy inquisition. "Andre has given you a copy of his pamphlet, *n'est ce pas?*"

"No. Who told you that?"

"It doesn't matter. I have ears. You see?" Ilya grabbed his left earlobe and pulled, as if demonstrating the obvious to a simpleton. His little grin was an annoyance, the expression of an overconfident man who doesn't know as much as he thinks he knows. But the countenance returned abruptly to serious scowl. "He must not publish it. You know that." It seemed that Ilya was about to display on the tabula of their dispute, what he thought to be a winning hand.

But Pierre Geras held his poker face. He had questions of his own. "What has happened to Zinovyev and Kamenev?" Now the Frenchman's riposte came forth, with spunk.

"You know, comrade. Why do you ask such questions? This is for the Party to decide."

"Ha!" Pierre, surprised at himself, looked around. His feigned amusement was unexpectedly loud.

Philip was napping, of course, a fly on the wall. No matter. Two men were talking three seats ahead. That's all. Still, his ears were tuned on their frequency, for some reason he could not surmise, dialed in like the RGD radio to BBC that Nathan had shown him back in London. But he could not understand; the night was dim, and the speech was French. The rumble of the wheels beneath their feet was a hypnotic cover of gray noise, a small subterfuge rattle beneath the narrowly careening railway of a vast, disjointing Continental rift. He could not comprehend the words of the two men, but the subdued urgency of their tone was vibrant, like the air before a thunderstorm.

"The Party—" continued Pierre. "The Party of uncle Joe? No longer the party of revolution. The party of Stalin. Where three were—now there is one!" Pierre's voice had morphed to a hoarse whisper. "And Bukharin? What of Nikolai? Where does the purging stop?"

"You should listen to our friend, Marchand. He can explain these necessities better than I can."

"Marchand is an egotistical fool, willing to do anything to keep the attention on himself. But no matter, Ilya, I did not ask for your explanation, nor his."

"The man is amazing. Do you know that the Republicans in Spain now have a hundred and thirty new planes—fighters and bombers, because Andre has convinced your government to send them, even though the British and these others are imposing their blockade?"

"I know about Andre Marchand. I have known him since before the war. But he has been deceived. His great power, given from Stalin like the gods, has blinded him to the real revolution. The people are cast aside while the Party turns more to the Fascist ways with every passing day. They are as bad as Mussolini himself, wanting to do to Spain what Mussolini has done to Abyssinia."

Ilya let out a long sigh. "Pierre, you are thinking backwards. It is Mussolini, and Hitler, who will smash Spain like Abyssinia, if the Republicans do not get real military support enough to drive Franco back to Morocco. There is nothing more important than this, and Marchand, more than anyone else, has convinced you French of that necessity. You must not forget that you are between Spain and the Nazis. Hitler will pluck you French like a chicken, from both sides, after Franco has been escorted into Madrid, Valencia, *and* Barcelona by the German Luftwaffe. And that is only the military half of it. The Anarchists—CNT and POUM, are too anarchistic to get the job done. As Marchand says, 'the Spanish anarchists are too anarchistic to carry off the victories that the Spanish Republic requires. There will be time for the revolution after Franco has been defeated."

But Pierre Geras was saying nothing, stupefied.

"These people have become useless, like Trotsky! Too busy stealing land from the kulaks to win a war!"

The thin man was still speechless. There was silence for a minute or more. Pierre seemed even more uncomfortable than before. Then he said, softly, "Every difference of opinion has become treason. This is not communism; it has become fascism."

After another quiet, Ilya said, in a low steady voice like a judge, "You intelligentsia are all alike—thinking and talking too much instead of winning the war against fascism. You are a Trotskyite, just like the traitor, Gigan, and that is why you will not give me the manuscript. I know he handed it to you in Paris. But you must turn it over to me now, or your sentence will be as severe as that given to Zynoviev and Kamenev."

But Pierre was not listening to Ilya Erhberg. Suddenly his eyes were fixed forward. Another heavy man was walking down the aisle from the front of the train-car. He was fat and red-faced, with an old-fashioned double-pointed beard. A ugly scowl covered his face; he appeared to be as unhappy as a snake in a closed room. The man's deliberate gait took him to the other two, and then past them. Then he turned around, said not a word. Pointing accusingly at Pierre Geras, he wasted no time or breath in making known what would happen next. Ilya grabbed Pierre's arm and began to twist, until the thin man was compelled to stand. The two disputants began walking toward the front, with the fat man following. In deliberate, calculated silence, they exited the train car.

Philip Morrow, he lay low.

But after a while, when the house lights had gone down, and the night had turned deathly quiet except for the dirging rails, and the crescent moon had sunk low into France's bosom, the curious American forsook the safety of his seat to find the toilet. As he passed the empty seats where the two communists had been, Philip glanced down at the floor, because he thought he had seen something clandestine earlier, just as Ilya Erhberg had intruded. Yes. A roll of papers with a rubber band around them, under the seat, against the wall, hidden almost, but not to his eyes, in darkness. He stooped, extended a trembling hand to the floor, retrieved the paper roll and walked as quietly, as unobtrusively as possible, back to his seat. Philip removed the rubber band, releasing a collection of papers that were obviously a typed manuscript. At the top of the first page, the title was plain to see:

Moscow Masquerade, *par* Andre Gigan

After a few minutes of French time had slipped quietly into the clickety-clack loco-driven night, Philip thought he would hazard a glimpse at the document that he had so stealthily procured a few minutes before, in the wake of the three men leaving the train-car. He didn't know why he was doing this. He—a tobacco salesman from the land of the free and home of the brave, minding his own business as his mother had taught him to do, now risking his own security and peace of mind to stick his insignificant hand into a dispute between three shadowy Europeans on a night train to Alsace, for what reason he did not know—he carefully removed the rubber band from the rolled-up papers.

Reading the French text was proving to be quite a challenge for Philip's laborious American mind, but he trudged into the first page, vaguely comprehending some introductory sentences about the author having just returned from a conference of Comintern writers that had assembled in

Moscow a few months ago. But just as he was encountering a indecipherable statement about the hand of Josef Stalin heavily laid upon those agitprop sessions, the upper range of Philip's peripheral vision was again invaded by the fat figure of the authoritative, pointy-bearded man who was now, for the second time in the last half-hour or so, striding down the aisle toward the rear of the train-car. With untamed, blonde eyebrows furrowed in impatient scowl, the red-faced man stopped at the seat where he had previously commandeered his two confused comrades into their hasty departure.

The big man's butt slid clumsily onto the vacated double-seat, and his shoulders promptly tilted downward on the left side. He was groping, it seemed, for something on the floor beneath the seat. Philip cringed and pretended to be reading a sales report in a leathered binder. The document, whatever it was, was of course none of his business. But there had been something ominous about the thin man's expression—it was an unholy fear—that was drawing him into the imbroglio, compelling him to take possession of the rolled-up document. Whether it was his own childish mischief or some deeper yearning, some more profound desire to reach beyond the comfortable, well-provisioned existence of a traveling salesman, and venture into the wider world—the danger-laden cosmos of sustained struggle from which this Continent seemed to have been borne—whether it was the mischief or the destiny thing, he did not know. But Philip had the feeling he was sticking his neck out, and possibly for no good reason. He was sticking his neck out of his own seat, and into the aisle, even across the aisle, to obtain a fallen object that didn't even belong to him. Surely the consequence of this insignificant act would not result in some dire fate, such as when Louis XVI stuck his neck out under the guillotine sometime back in the fraught history of this crazy country.

But now the fat man's distress, framed within his face by ruddy ire and impatient twitching, was reinforcing Philip's instinct to just hold on to what he had rather than risking further involvement by surrendering the roll to the mad man. The roll didn't seem to belong to the fellow anyway; surely it is the property of the thin man, from whom it would have been, by arm-twisting intimidation, taken, had he not managed to deposit the thing on the floor so that a brave itinerant traveling salesman could retrieve it, and thus protect the thin man from being apprehended with the dreaded document in his possession. When you get right down to it, Philip was holding onto the notion that he had caught a terrible glimpse into some enforced thievery now being perpetrated among contentious men, and that his momentary intervention would be somehow fatefully protective, or corrective. All of this could be, however, just the workings of his suddenly over-active mind, and he may be just, after all, a foolish busybody.

The mad man turned his head toward the aisle. He was surveying the passengers around him. His bulbous eyes, beneath the untamed eyebrows, were dull with what seemed an animal ruthlessness. Philip, presenting a façade of engagement behind his sales report, watched as the man systematically inspected each passenger in his vicinity, searching for signs of complicity in the disappearance of the roll. Then, without warning, he twitched his dog-eye directly at the preoccupied American.

Philip knew he'd been caught. For an instant, their eyes locked together, before he managed to lower them to the feigned perusal of some past sales report. His mind was now fearfully fixed on a certain entry:

British American Tobacco Company… $3,911 sales, February 1937

That had been a good month. But it wouldn't be any good to him now if the fat man had detected Philip's culpability in this impulsive purloining of a dangerous manuscript . The roll, now on the seat wedged between his butt and briefcase, felt suddenly like an extension of his vulnerable self. He felt he must act quickly to conceal it. *Why am I doing this?* Philip was the picture, so he thought, of innocent detachment as he set the leather binder on his lap, reached to his right, lifted the briefcase and opened it, then slid the report in and retrieved a newspaper he had been reading earlier. In the midst of this meaningless maneuver he managed to lift the roll of purloined papers from the seat and insert it gingerly into his briefcase while retrieving the newspaper. He snapped the briefcase shut, setting it down again between himself and the window. Then reaching inside his coat pocket, he pulled out his pack of Bullseyes. He noticed, with some alarm, his hands trembling as he pulled one cigarette out and lit it. His long exhale cast a whiff of smoke into the upper air of the train compartment, as the nicotine boosted his excitement, and the smoke carried a plume of innocence to cover his new, unfamiliar complicity in the fate of the civilized world.

The angry man got up. Pausing for a second, his survey of the immediate space was directed toward the front, but then he turned slowly to the rear and began walking. Once again, Philip's eyes and his were caught up on the same beam for an instant in time. But Philip could feel a steely resolve rising within himself now—a cold expression of disinterest as he stared straight ahead, just above the blue-haired matron seated in front of him. She was dozing, but he was far from dozing. The tobacco gas was streaming urgently through Philip's veins as he effortlessly presented a disinterested masquerade of passengerhood. The mad man passed his seat, dropping a quick glance at the black briefcase ensconced between Philip's body and the window. Then he exited the traincar. The wily American breathed a sigh of relief as another puff of smoke ascended into the dark atmosphere of France.

The dull thumpy repetition of locomotive wheels beneath floor was drumming a half-dream through Philip's consciousness—a dream of his bed back home in America—a flat feather-bed, soft but not too soft, with sheets, and a green wool army blanket and the owl outside hooting on a crispy cool spring night. The slumbery memory-apparition was dissolving in his mind as a man's voice penetrated the low-light of the traincar and registered, ". . .vous avez fait."

"Wha? . . .who?"

"*J'ai vu ce que vous avez fait.*"

"Me? What have I done?" Philip opened his eyes and rubbed them. A man was speaking to him, standing in the aisle looking down, with a black beret on his head. Philip had noticed the black beret before. It was. . . it had been on a man's head two seats ahead on the train car. Now the black beret was not positioned on a grey-haired head two seats in front of him, but now the beret sat atop the long, wrinkled face of a man with dark, sunken eyes who was speaking to him, saying something in French.

"Vous avez ramasse le manuscript," the man said.

"But, mais non. I. . .Je ne le voyais pas. Je n'ai pas le prendre," protested Philip, although he was lying, and he knew it. He knew he had taken it—the roll of papers that had fallen on the floor. He knew it was not his, but it was, nevertheless, in his briefcase. Why he had put it there he could not remember. It was just some . . .intuition, or instinct, or—

"The papers were intended for me, but you took them," said the man with the deepset eyes, deep eyes, intense. Almost a smile flickered on his lips.

Why is he speaking English?

"I need to sit here. Would you mind?" said the tall man.

Philip roused himself, sat up straight, slid toward the window. *He is saying something about the papers, the roll I picked up from the floor.* "What are you talking about?" asked Philip. But the man said nothing; he was looking ahead without expression. There was a mole on his right cheek. "Who are you?" Philip asked.

"Je m'appelle Charles Marais." The man turned his face directly upon Philip. "The question is: Who are *you?*"

But Philip held his silence. He retrieved a cigarette and lit it.

"Ah, may I have one of your American cigarettes, mon ami?"

Philip held the packet of Bullseyes in the man's direction. Monsieur Marais took one and set it between his lips; Philip lit the cigarette for him. The smoke curled up in a thick roll as Philip snapped his lighter shut.

The old man looked at Philip directly again. "You are an American, half-cocked, shooting from the hip. You don't know what you've gotten yourself into—picking up my roll of papers."

"*Your* papers?"

"Oui, monsieur. They were intended for me, but I was not able to receive them due to the intervention of those other two men, and then—you! Why, Monsieur, did you take the roll that was intended for me?"

This was a question for which Philip had no explanation. He still didn't quite know what had gotten into him. Instead, he asked, "Who are those men?"

"They are communists."

"Are you a communist?"

"Ha!" The man almost allowed a smile. His dark eyes twinkled with excitement. "No, my yankee doodle friend, I am not a communist. I am a Frenchman. There is a big difference."

"Oh, what is the difference?" This statement was an opportunity to evade, or postpone, further explanation of Philip's own impulsive act. Whatever it was that Philip now had in his briefcase seemed to be an important document of some kind. He felt as if he were holding an ace up his sleeve.

"The first thing is—what did you say your name is, monsieur?"

"Philip Morrow."

"Ah!" At this, Charles Marais did smile, having obtained the identity of this unexpected contender for possession of the manuscript. "A very good name, Philip. The first thing is: a Frenchman believes in God. A true son of France acknowledges that there are divine laws, written in heaven and given to men through his Church and the King. They are not—what is your English word—the laws are not arbitrary. They are not rules that men—such as the communists—have made up themselves and enforce with the power of the gun. Comprenez vous?"

"Oh, yes. I suppose so."

"And the second belief of the Frenchman is the sanctity of his family—his wife, children, his land. These are the good things that compel us to work hard, for the glory of God and la gloire de La France! A true son of France requires no meddling soviet to enslave him and make him work. *La joie de vivre est* to work the land, harvest the fruits of it, the fruit of the vine, the abundance of the earth. There is true order in this arrangement, with no chaotic social revolution to make of him a slave. The communists, and their socialist cousins, would rob us of this. They would usurp from us the divine privilege of serving God and La France."

Charles Marais snorted and blew his big nose into a handkerchief, but the disturbance was momentary. "However, my American friend, I am sad to report that the dignity and strength of La France has been corrupted, disabled. It has been carelessly laid upon a heathen alter for sacrifice, in this unholy alliance with the bloodletting Bolsheviks in Moscow."

"But doesn't Hitler, by rearming Germany, intend to put a stop to the Soviets?"

The old man had to think about that for a moment. "The National Socialists have got it right on some points, as compared to the communists. It is true that they have not subscribed to this Marxist spittle about the common people, the proletariat, administering the affairs of the state." Marais paused, blew smoke out. "The problem with them is that they are German." His jaw relaxed, in a kind of resignation, as if allowing a space for Philip's agreement. "The Germans should be rounded up into camps and made to remain there until they can be broken of their barbarism. But this may never happen."

The old man's face morphed from ire to gravity. "We French should have been the guardians at the gate. There is no civilization in Europe unless the French stand to defend the decency and order that comes through the Church and the ancient crown of Charles. We should never have given the Saar back to the Germans; now it has become the linchpin of their unauthorized rearmament, in blatant violation of Versailles."

"Excuse me, sir," Philip injected. "Did not the people of the Saar region— what is called the Rhineland—did they not vote, according to a plan predetermined by the Treaty of Versailles, to be returned to Germany?"

Charles Marais looked stunned for a moment, searching in his memory for a rationale. "Ah yes, my young friend," he replied, hesitating. "The League of Nations had determined that the people of the Rhineland should do such a thing, and yes, two years ago they voted to have their territory returned to German sovereignty. But ah . . . ah, this is the problem, you see, with democracy. The will of the people, as determined by elections, is not generally, a prescription for their true well-being. The people themselves are not equipped—they have not the wisdom—to make such determinations. The people in democracy will always vote for what they want, but rarely will they vote for what is truly in the their best interests. Such matters should be decided by the King and his Council."

"But France has no king, has had no king since 1793," Philip protested.

"Ah, yes, so true, my young friend, it is a sad state of affairs, but one that cannot be remedied."

"Remedied? How can such a thing as the execution of a king a hundred and fifty years ago be remedied?

"Restoration."

"How can such a thing happen, Monsieur Marais? Surely you are not advocating that the people of France restore the throne of Louis XVI and the house of Bourbon."

"Well, if this was possible," Marais was speculating, "we do know who those heirs would be. They can be readily located, and presented to the people of France."

Philip was amused.

Charles Marais was, for a moment, almost amused at this idea. "Actually, Monsieur Morrow, I understand the problems that would be inherent in such as development as this. There would be complications with the. . . ah, the legitimacy of the succession. So another candidate would have to be found."

"Another candidate? By what legitimate means would you, or any other royalist, present such a person in a way that would not be absolutely derided by the current leaders of France, the socialist politicians of the Third Republic?"

"There is a man waiting in the wings now, even now, to step into the restored authority of a King of France."

"Oh? Who is that?"

"I cannot tell you just now. But I can assure you that he is a great man, a man with the wisdom of Charlemagne, but strong, like Hercules, whose god-given anointing radiates in a way that is obvious to anyone who is in the same room with him."

"And you are not going to tell me who the ersatz King would be? Do you know him?

"I cannot tell you now."

"Perhaps his name is. . . Napolean?"

"Ha! You are funny, mon ami. You are funny, like so many Americans I have met, making jokes. But please. . . I must tell you. . . "The biggest mistake of the Third Republic has been our uncontested withdrawal from the Rhineland. In effect, the lily-livered socialists in Paris have handed the

Rhineland back to Hitler on an iron platter. The people of France will pay dearly for that. Believe me, I have watched this all my life, since before the war, when the Germans occupied it. Now they have taken it again--without firing a shot. Big mistake. My home is in Nancy, just down the road from the Saar and all that. I have watched it happen, and I have wept for France, and for all that is good and decent, which is now to be dragged down into Rhine mud by these Huns and their Bolshevik cousins, who are no better. Lenin and his blasphemous revolutionaries sold the Czar out to Germany in 1917, and they will do it again, unwittingly, no matter what they say. Stalin will kill off his best generals out of jealousy and paranoia before they can be sent to defeat the arrogant Prussian menace. That is what the document—the one you have apprehended, Stalin's foolish purge of his own household— that is what you have in your possession, and need to give to me, because I know what to do with it. Now the formerly fearless Russian bear has become a common murderer, enclosed in the ring to fight to the death the German savage. But let us not speak of that now. I have something you will enjoy."

He had a worn leather satchel. Opening the flap carefully, Marais retrieved two small crystal goblets and a bottle of red wine and set them on the padded seat between himself and Philip. Then he pulled out a rather large white napkin, wiped the insides of the two clear vessels. The cork, having been previously removed, slid out smoothly under the influence of his strong, slender hand, blueblood veins protruding. He poured the burgundy into each glass, half-full. The scarlet vintage was vibrating with the train.

"I propose a toast."

"Mais, oui," affirmed Philip, amazed at the uncommon ceremonial manner of Charles Marais' theatrics, and the suddenness of it all.

"To my new American friend, Philip, and to America, and to Lafayette and General Washington, and to France. Vive La France!"

After a plentiful sipping, Charles Marais recommenced. "All this trouble that is around us now—the Germans have stirred it up. But it started long ago. Marx was a German Jew, a troublemaker who thought he could, by writing a treatise on economics, rob the nobility of their precious heritage. He proposed, with his analytical German equivocation, to appropriate their lands and wealth and distribute it among the proletariat. Now his communist notions are being exposed to be, in the bloody hands of Stalin, nothing more than vain, but deadly, ideas, as manageable as smoke—pipe dreams of proletarian leadership on a printed page, deceptive and manipulative—no more humane than the atrocities of Robespierre were a hundred and fifty years ago."

Another long sip, and he looked intently at Philip, who was speechless. "Nothing could repair the fatal wound that the Jacobins inflicted upon the House of Bourbon and the good people of France—not even Napolean crowning himself emperor."

All was quiet as passengers slept in the low light of these wee hours, rocking gently in the cradle-like rhythm of the rails. All was quiet, but for the Frenchman's hoarse whisper. "Perhaps if he had submitted to the Holy Father—if Bonaparte had consented to be crowned by the Pope, with the blessing of the Church, the fate of France during the last century may have been fortuitous. But as a consequence of his presumptive arrogance, these Prussian butchers with their enslaved, decorated horsemen and their new, illegally manufactured airplanes, think they can run the world. But that is nothing new. Ever since Luther ripped the Church apart with his heresies, the Germans have found more and more inventive ways for making trouble continuously, scourging the Body of Christ and the Holy people anew, to shreds, as if civilization itself were an old garment to be discarded. May I have another cigarette?"

Philip obliged, *noblesse oblige.*.

Marais' rant had not yet run its full, plaintive course. " After King Louis was beheaded at the hand of the Jacobins—after that, the low people, the peasants, of France, led like sheep to the slaughter, had been deceived, you see, and manipulated by the angels of Enlightenment, the purveyors of enforced *egalite*, they had set themselves up for this fall. The Jacobins beheaded our King, threw him down, his head on the guillotine, executed him as if he were a common criminal. What anarchy was unleashed upon the world when such a thing was done! All decency, all order in France was doomed from that time on, unless we can ever—*Sacre Bleu!* restore it at some future time. Alas, we will not have the opportunity in these days, because the Germans are once again on the march of war! They have taken the Saar. Next they will be marching into Alsace and Lorraine. The women of Strasbourg will wail with grief and pain before the cock crows thrice."

The train stopped in Mulhouse, Alsace. A sleepy shuffling of passengers could be discerned in the dim gaslights, by anyone not slumbering, out on the platform in the station. It was four o'clock in the morning. One traveler exited the car in which they were riding, and two more entered. When the train began to roll again, after its speed had propelled them to the same

136

lulling lala sway as before, and the eyes of sleepy sojourners once again resumed their escape to remmy dreams, Charles Marais rose and, gathering the two crystal goblets and his satchel but leaving the empty burgundy bottle on the seat, he looked into Philip's weary eyes. Offering a soft smile, he said, "Your country and mine are like twin brothers separated in childhood a hundred and fifty years ago. I should like to speak more about this, of your Monsieur Franklin, and Jefferson, and General Washington. I wish that those reasonable leaders of your American revolution had been able to advise our Republican revolutionaries about the value of strong leadership that would not have been administered through the guillotine. Then, perhaps, the way that France has come since that time might have brought us to a more favorable position in the terrible chaos of this twentieth century."

Philip looked quizzically at the strange man now standing in the aisle. Feeling himself amused, he spoke to Charles Marais, "I would remind you, monsieur, that the men whose names you mention established a democratic republic. They did not make General Washington a king, nor an emperor, and that has made all the difference."

The old Frenchman smiled, and his eyes seemed to withdraw even deeper into the dark folds of his face. "I'll be back," he said, and with that simple declaration, began walking slowly through the aisle, until Philip saw Charles Marais exit the traincar at the front.

It was a misty morning outside when Philip was roused by the coming light. The rolling hills of Alsace began to manifest a suburban hodgepodge of cottages, homes, stores, churches, streets and early-bird pedestrians as the train rolled quietly into the city of Strasbourg. Philip checked his watch, the gold timepiece given to him years before by his grandfather Roby. 7:59. Philip sat up straight and thought about having a cup of coffee.

Two officials—a conductor and a gendarme—were walking down the aisle slowly, and stopping at each passenger. The gendarme spoke softly, though it seemed with some urgency, to each person and then moved on to the next, until they had delivered some instructions to each one the dozen or so riders in front of Philip.

When the two uniformed men, looking crisp, grey-haired, and, unlike the passengers, well-rested, reached Philip the gendarme looked at Philip and spoke. "Bonjour, monsieur. Je dois vous dire que l'un des passagers de ce train a rencontre une mort prematuree. Nous devons vous demander de repondre a quelques questions, s'il vous plait."

"How long will this take?" queried Philip.

The conductor responded, "Not long, monsieur, perhaps an hour. You are an American?"

"Yes, sir."

The conductor smiled. "I hope you are enjoying your travels in France, sir. Nevertheless, this incident—one of the passengers on this car—has been found dead. It is necessary that we ask you, and the others here, to remain at the train station for a few questions. These procedures must be followed, if we are to administer justice, and properly investigate into the man's unfortunate demise. Unfortunately, your presence will be required at the Strasbourg station. May I see your billet and your passport, s'il vous plaît?"

While Philip was retrieving his papers from his briefcase, another conductor squeezed past the other two men in the aisle. The conductor with whom Philip had been speaking asked the second conductor a question which Philip did not understand. "A la gare," was the answer given, while the gendarme moved past to address other passengers.

After a quick inspection of Philip's ticket and passport, the conductor said, "Please remain here until we stop at the Strasbourg station. Then I will accompany you and the other passengers of this car to a room in the station where a police inspector will have a few—only a few—questions for you, and then, monsieur, you will be free to go. I apologize for the delay."

"I was traveling with two other passengers until they obtained a sleeping berth in Lyon. I would like to speak to them."

"And who are those passengers?"

"Hannah and Lili Eschen."

"C'est bien. I will arrange for you to speak with them when we arrive, if not sooner."

As the two officials passed along, Philip remembered that he now had possession of a roll of papers which did not belong to him, which he had picked up from the floor, perhaps foolishly and for no reason, and he wondered what, if anything, he should do about this. *I should probably drop them back them under the seat where I found them.* But passengers were stirring, daylight was filling the car, and the two officials would certainly notice such a maneuver, so he decided to keep the roll in his briefcase. *Surely the dropped manuscript had nothing to do with the incident in question.. Surely not.*

A few minutes later, Lili entered the traincar, looking fresh and lovely. Tight, blondish-red curls on her head seemed to reflect morning sun from the window. Her lips were red with lipstick, and a rested smile, blooming with expectation of what the day might bring, contrasted the pale skin of her

138

face, making it appear magnificent. Above rosy cheeks her brown eyes shone with vitality. Philip, feeling tired, regretted that he had not been able to sleep in a bed last night, as Lili had done, but her refreshed countenance was a sight to behold. "Good morning, Philip!" she exclaimed.

"Bonjour, mademoiselle. Etes-vous heureux que nous sommes arrives a Strasbourg?"

"Oui. Would you like join us for breakfast?"

"Where will you have breakfast?"

"Hannah and I will be walking to the hotel. If all is well, and father and mother have gotten over the border as they had planned, we will see them there. We would be pleased to have you join us. I know they would like to meet you, and talk about America. You know we are hoping to go to London, and even over to the United States, if father can obtain the visas."

"I hope I can join you at the hotel, Lili. God knows I am hungry. Unfortunately, I am being delayed. A passenger who was riding on this car last night has died, and the French police are conducting an investigation. They asked the passengers of this car to remain in the station for questioning. What hotel is it?"

"It is the Hotel Albouee, on La Grande Rue, not far from the train station."

"I will find it and join you there as soon as I can."

Hannah came in, looking as chipper as her sister, but a little worried. "Hello, Philip," she said, with a thin smile. "Will you be joining us for breakfast?" She seemed to be in a hurry.

"Thank you. I hope to do that. Some passengers here have been detained. Lili will explain."

"Detained? What is the problem?"

"Somebody has died on the train. The police are asking questions."

"Oh? Who is that?"

"A man who was riding in this car. I don't know who he is."

"You didn't have anything to do with it, did you?" Hannah cracked a little smile.

"I hope not. I intend to see you at your hotel as soon as I can get there."

"Very well then. Let's get going, Lili. I hope you are not delayed for long."

"Me too, but don't wait for me. You should, God willing, enjoy breakfast with your parents this morning. Perhaps it is best this way, anyway. You probably have a lot of private things to talk about."

"Yes. Lili, let's go see if father and mother have any news about Heinrich."

The sisters retrieved their luggage and descended to the platform. Then they were off to La Grande Rue and Hotel Albouee.

Maybe a low buzz of impatience started to fill the space between the detained passengers of traincar #11. Then the gendarme returned, through the front door, accompanied by a handsome, gray-haired man in a gray suit with a necktie of French tricolor red, white and blue. The dapper detective addressed the fourteen passengers present, in French of course. Philip understood generally what the detective was saying, which was something like this:

"Once again, ladies and gentleman, we, the police of Strasbourg and Alsace, appreciate your patience and cooperation in this unfortunate turn of events, which has resulted in the death of a man who had been riding with you last night. I am Inspecteur Claude Clerbeau. I hope you understand and agree that, in order for truth to be determined in this matter, and so that justice can be done, it is necessary that some of us sacrifice a little time in the interests of discovery about what has happened. Please exit the car behind Lt. Pirot here. Then follow him to a room in the train station where our brief enquiry will be conducted. Then you will be free to go. I do apologize for the inconvenience. When you get to the waiting room, you will find coffee, tea and pastries that we have provided, so that hunger will not discomfort you and impede our hasty enquiry. Thank you. Now, Lt. Pirot. . ." Gesturing with his arm toward the gendarme, Inspecteur Clerbeau exited the car, descended the metal stair, stepped onto the platform and turned around to watch as the fourteen passengers vacated the train car in which they had spent the last twenty-four hours or so.

As Philip walked with this group along beside the train, toward the main hall of the station, suddenly the strange Frenchman, Charles Marais, slipped in beside him. He spoke in a very low voice, "Monsieur Morrow, you remember that I told you the manuscript had been intended for me. Can you pass it to me now?"

Philip continued walking. Casting a sideway glance at the tall man, he quickly resumed looking ahead, following the group, feeling like one in a flock of weary sheep. "No, sir. Although I enjoyed our visit, Mr. Marais, I still know nothing about who you are, or what your interest in this matter may be. Besides, I can only tell you that there is something wrong with this picture. The man who dropped these papers was being intimidated by the other two men, and I did not like the looks of them. The man who dropped these papers must have done so for good reason, and I have decided to return them to him if I can find out who he is and where he can be found."

"I am afraid, Philip, that will be impossible," Marais said, flatly.

"Difficult, perhaps. Impossible, no. Nothing is impossible. That's what we Americans are all about."

"This will be impossible because the man whose papers you recovered is the deceased man. He is the man about whom the Inspecteur will soon be asking you questions. This is your opportunity to dispose of that manuscript, right now, by turning it over to me. Then you will have no involvement with the dead man."

13

Expropriation

Philip could not think of anything to say, except, "I'll bet it was one, or both, of those two guys who were pressuring him—who killed him."

Philip's thoughts were accelerating as he felt an odd realization that his rubbery legs were carrying him; they were somehow conveying him along, within a stream of other travelers. The little flock of fourteen Car #11 passengers seemed to be slogging at a forward pace that his legs had not attained since a night and day ago. It had been a long ride from Perpignan. The bustle of Strasbourg *la gare* was enveloping his consciousness. Where in the world was he? He felt for a moment as if he was back in London. But the signs were all in French, and the people, all the moving people... *les Francais.*. . were not English, were not American. They were. . .a host of berets and moustaches and suits, lovely women with rosy complexions and wavy hair, and the smell of coffee, but then a whiff of lavender perfume from someone, almost narcotic with its exotic mystery.

A Degas poster on the wall, or something like it, and Philip looked aside again, where Charles Marais had been speaking to him a few minutes before, but the fleeting man of France was gone, nowhere to be seen. The woman with child who had been across the aisle on the train—she was where Marais had been. Then he saw the very dapper inspecteur who had given them directions. He was standing beside a double door, carefully surveying his fourteen charges as they passed into the cavernous main hall of Strasbourg *la gare* . The gendarme raised his arm high, stepped to the side, out of the traffic flow, searching dutifully with his upraised head to account for the fourteen passengers. He was counting them, and they were. . . fourteen.

After a moment of silent affirmation, the gendarme raised his arm again and gestured in a direction slightly ahead and to the left, then resumed their forward progress. After a minute or two of straggling through the throng, Lt. Pirot ushered his weary flock of respondents through a hallway, and into a room empty except for a few rows of wooden chairs. The weary troupe plopped themselves into the seats with a few vacancies remaining as their shuffle lapsed into silence.

Inspecteur Clerbeau, closing the door behind, announced, "S'il, vouz plait, Lt. Pirot will remain with you here, while I conduct the enquiry in a room just across the hall, each of you individually. Once again, *je suis navre* for the inconvenience." A woman in blue smock entered the room with a tray of stacked ceramic cups and a large coffee urn, which she set on a table at the far end of the room. "The order of my questioning will be according to the numbers on your billets, with the low numbers first, and progressing accordingly."

After a few eager caffe-seekers had preceded him, Philip was able to pour himself a cup of coffee, which he gratefully savored with a croissant, and then a cigarette for finish.

At 9:45, the room was about half-full of the passengers. The gendarme caught Philip's attention and summoned him out of the room. He crossed the hall, entered a small office where Inspecteur Clerbeau sat behind a wooden desk. Nothing was on the desktop except a telephone, a notepad, and a fountain pen. On the left side of the desk was another inspecteur, seated. Philip sat, facing the two men.

Inspector Clerbeau was looking down at his notepad, reading quickly. Looking up, he asked, in English, "You are Philip Morrow?" His large brown eyes, with wrinkles all around and bushy black eyebrows, were the embodiment of professional objectivity. Philip wondered how the eyebrows were so black beneath gray hair.

"Yes."

"And you are an American?"

"Yes."

"From what state?"

"North Carolina."

"And what brings you to France?"

"I am a sales representative for Brigham Tobacco Company."

"And you have come to Strasbourg to do business?"

"I have liberty to from my company to do business anywhere I go, but I have chosen to come here for. . .ah. . .for two reasons. One is, I am hoping to visit a battlefield in Belgium where. . .where my father died, in 1918."

"Ah! Your father was an American soldier in the war?"

"That's right."

Inspecteur Clerbeau leaned forward in his chair and looked intently at Philip. A little glisten was in his eyes. "I want you to know, Monsieur Morrow, that we, the people of France, deeply appreciate the sacrifice that you and your family have made in the defense of France." He paused.

"Merci," said Philip.

The detective's voice slowed, and softened. "I myself fought in the war. It was a terrible time for our country. . ." He leaned back against the chair, relaxing somewhat. ". . . a time of great testing for our nation."

"Indeed, sir, for the world," added Philip, hesitantly.

"Yes, and at that point in time—at the end—your father, and the Americans who fought with him, were a most welcome reinforcement to our effort. The Russians had almost pulled out entirely, due to the Bolsheviks taking over their government, or I should say, destroying it. *Mais* . . . I remember, vividly, when I heard that the Americans had come in at Dunkerque, our officers were noticeably relieved. I was an enlisted man."

"My father was an enlisted man as well. His name was Clint Morrow, of the 37th Division. He was killed October 30, 1918. When he was returned to our family, I was eight years old."

"I am sorry for your loss. It seems, Monsieur, that you have turned out well, in spite of the loss of your father at such an early age."

"I hope so, Inspecteur."

"And do you know where he was killed?"

"A place called Flanders Field, in Belgium"

"Ah, that could be one of several places."

"Yes, I have heard that, but I do intend to find his grave marker. I have a picture of it."

"That is good. It is helpful to have a specific destination." Inspecteur Clerbeau withdrew a card from a pocket inside his coat and handed it to Philip. "I offer to you my assistance in that effort." He looked aside, to the other detective. "Lt. Lambert, would you make a note of that, s'il vous plait.

"And so, Monsieur Morrow, what is your other reason?"

"Pardon me, other reason for what?"

"For traveling through Strasbourg, instead of, say, Paris. Most Americans would choose, in traveling from south to north in France, to pass through Paris."

"Yes, well, I suppose I will do that. All indications are that I should not deny such an opportunity, since I will be so near the capital city of France. Most likely, however, it will be after Belgium. As for Strasbourg, I chose this route because a friend in London asked me to meet some of his relatives, in Perpignan, down south, and accompany them back to England. As it turned out, however, their plans—two young ladies from Germany—had to include a trip to Strasbourg. They are hoping to be reunited with their parents here. Their parents have left Munich to come to France, and ultimately to America."

"Ah. They are refugees from Germany."

"I suppose you could call it that."

"Jews?"

"Yes, as a matter of fact."

"And you have been traveling on the train from Perpignan with these— the two German girls?"

Inspecteur Clerbeau looked perturbed. "What are their names?"

"Hannah and Lili Eschen. They were able to get a sleeper berth at Lyon."

The detective nodded slightly in the direction of his assistant, who made a note. "Thus, you were riding as a single passenger last night in Car #11."

"Yes."

The inspector paused. Then he stood. Philip could see the sixtyish man stretching his body somewhat. He began to walk around the room. "And you have. . . have had some success in sales during this visit to our country?"

"I did deliver a shipment of our cigarettes and smoking tobacco ."

"Ah, yes, and where was that delivery?"

"St. Jean de Luz."

"That is a long way from here."

"Yes, sir. It is."

Inspecteur Clerbeau's gray hair was combed back slick. The tri-color tie was a burst of color in the pale, institutional drab of this small, uneventful office. The other detective, sitting aside, was studying Philip's face. He smiled vaguely at Philip as Philip's eyes wandered around the room and then met Clerbeau's again. Now he was looking up at the man's face.

"Why is it that these relatives of your friend require your accompaniment?"

There was, really, no obvious answer to this question. In fact, Philip did not know why Itmar had recruited him for this expedition, and had provided some money for expenses. Maybe it was because of Philip being an American. But the northern leg of Philip's journey—to Strasbourg—had been a matter of choice, an impetuous decision that he had made while overlooking the waterfront in Perpignan as he talked to Lili."I . . .I . . ."Excuse me, Inspecteur, but what has this to do with your enquiry about a deceased man on the train?"

The detective walked over to his chair and sat again. He looked at his notes; he was studying them. Then he raised his objective eyes to Philip's and said, "Monsieur Morrow, there was a man, a citizen of France, who was riding with you and the other passengers on car number eleven last night. He boarded the train at Lyon, but he never deboarded that train as a live man, because during the course of his journey with you and the others between Lyon and Strasbourg, he was shot and killed, and his body was thrown from the train between Mulhouse and Strasbourg." Inspecteur Clerbeau paused, as if now would be the time for Philip to provide some shred of intelligence about this turn of events.

But Philip had nothing to say. He felt himself begin to sweat. It was time to smoke a cigarette; He pulled the pack of trusty Bullseyes from his inside coat pocket, withdrew one, and lit it.

"Do you know anything about this, Mr. Morrow?" asked the detective.

"No, sir."

The detective paused for a few seconds. "I must tell you that your answer is not consistent with the testimony of another passenger."

Philip felt himself, suddenly, a frog in water that may be beginning to boil. "What. . .which passenger was that?" he managed to ask. Philip could feel his voice quavering.

"It is not necessary that you know who this person is, Philip, but this passenger has identified you as the one who picked up, from the floor of the train-car, a document that had been dropped by the deceased."

"The two men were having an argument!" Philip blurted.

"The two men? Which two men?"

"They were—I don't know who they are—the thin man was being harassed by the other fellow, and then there was another man who came along. . .they were twisting his arm, and he left with them, but not, as it appeared to me, willingly."

"And the 'thin man'," Inspecteur Clerbeau arched his eyebrows. ". . .and the thin man left something behind, on the floor?"

"Yes." Philip conceded. He felt himself slumping in the wooden chair. *How in the world. . .?*

"And you picked it up?"

Oh, why the hell did I. . ."Yes," Philip murmered, with resignation.

"Why?"   The Inspecteur's countenance was, for the world, just like his grandfather's. *Why did you chop down the cherry tree?*

There was no answer to this question. "Je ne sais pas," said Philip. "Look. Whatever that document is, those two were stealing it from him."

"And how do you know that, my young American friend?" the Inspecteur shot back, sitting uprightly again in his seat.

"I don't, Inspecteur. But I do know they were twisting his arm. They were forcing him—"

"How do you know they were stealing it? Perhaps he had stolen the document from them!"

Philip felt himself collapsing back against the chair. He was on indefensible grounds. The whole thing was, in fact, not his business. He suddenly remembered his aunt Sylvie's frequent admonishment when he was growing up, '*mind your own business.*' Then he said, "It was just a. . .hunch."

"Hunch? mon ami. Qu'est-que ce? hunch?"

"It was—"

"Give it to me now," Inspecteur Clerbeau demanded, though gently. Suddenly his eyes turned agreeable, as if he knew, and Philip did too, that it was right thing to do. "It does not belong to you."

Which was true. And so he did. Philip slowly picked up his briefcase, inserted the key, opened it, and withdrew the rolled-up papers that he had stowed there in the middle of the night, while passengers slept and the recent egress of three mysterious men had provoked his insupportable curiosity. Hands trembling, he proffered the manuscript over the desk; Inspecteur Clerbeau took it. Slowly, while holding Philip's gaze in his steadfast brown eyes, he slid the rubber band off. Then he lowered his eyes to take a look at it.

Philip lit another cigarette. The other detective asked, "Would you like another cup of coffee, monsieur?"

"Sure," said Philip. Now what? He was remembering the name of the typewritten work, *Moscow Masquerade*, by Andre Gigan. He lit another Bullseye.

A few minutes passed, two, or many ten minutes. Lt. Lambert brought another coffee, which Philip gladly drank. He managed to distract himself with a visual inspection of a large poster on the wall—a photograph of a local landmark, the Palais Rohan. The photographic image presented a grandiose baroque façade with the L'Ill River in the foreground. Philip counted two rows of seventeen windows each in the building's exterior, with the same number of arched doorways at street level, beneath each window, and classically ornate French roofline above.

After a while, Inspector Clerbeau, though still looking intently at the papers, spoke, "Philip, what is your interest in this manuscript?"

"Sir, I have no interest in it. It was merely an item that I picked up from the floor, out of curiosity. Really, nothing more than that."

The inspector lowered the manuscript, inspected Philip's face carefully. "Really? Did you read any of it?"

"Un peu, monsieur. J'ai lu lentement Francais. Something about Russia, and Stalin arresting people."

"Indeed. Something like that. So we understand that you have no claim on this document. It is not yours, nor has it ever been yours."

"C'est vrai, monsieur."

Clerbeau straightened his posture. There was an air of finality in his movement. He tapped the pages on the desktop, aligning them; then he handed the manuscript to Lt. Lambert. "I have given you my card. I must insist that, should any other incidents or details of this manuscript arise, you should telephone, or telegraph me."

"Who was this man, the deceased?"

"His name is Pierre Geras; he is a writer with *L'Humanite* newspaper in Paris. The other two men you saw were, like him, members of the PCF—the communist part of France. The manuscript had been given to him by its author, Andre Gigan, who is a well-known writer of novels here." Clerbeau furrowed his eyebrows. "You said that the other two were intimidating him, is that correct?"

"Yes. They were threatening him, twisting his arm. At first, it was just Monsieur Geras and the one big, blonde fellow who sat beside him. It seemed he was saying some Russian, but I'm sure they were conversing in French, and having a disagreement about something. Then the fat man came along. It seemed as if he gave an order for them to leave the traincar."

"When the fat man walked in, did he approach from the front, or from the rear of the car?"

"From the front."

"And when they exited?"

"Also, to the front."

"And that was the last you saw of those three men?"

"A little while later, the fat man returned. He sat in the empty seat where they had been. I think he was looking for something. Then he left."

"In which direction did he leave?"

"To the rear."

"You are sure of that?"

"Yes. He passed very close to me. He looked at me. I was scared. For a moment, I though he knew what I had done. I thought he was going to say something to me about the roll of papers."

"So this was after you had picked up the papers?"

"Yes, very soon afterward."

"How much time had passed?"

"The fat man—he had a double-pointed beard—returned about ten minutes after I had picked up the papers, which I had picked up about a half-hour before that."

"The time, then, from when the three of them left until the fat man finally exited the last time was, what? forty minutes or so?"

"Yes. It was about that long, definitely less than an hour altogether."

Clerbeau said nothing for a minute or two, except to ask Lt. Lambert for the notes. Perusing them, he looked up and his eyes met Philip's directly. "And tell me, s'il vous plait, why you decided to pick up a roll of papers that did not belong to you?"

"There is no reason, sir," answered Philip, thinking this an honest response. Thinking better of it, he added, "I suppose I just felt sorry for the thin man—Monsieur Geras—because he was obviously being bullied by the other two. Later, I decided that, after discovering what the manuscript was, I may be able to trace it to the writer and determine to whom it should be returned, if such a thing were possible."

Inspecteur Clerbeau offered a minimal smile. "Not very likely, though, Monsieur Morrow. More probably, you would have kept it, if I had not demanded it from you, n'est-ce pas?"

"Well, Monsieur Inspecteur, we will never know what I might have done with the *Moscow Masquerade*, had you not appropriated it. What is it, anyway, that manuscript?"

"My guess is, Monsieur, you will know soon enough what is in it. I can tell you it is not a work of fiction. It appears that the author's intention is to publish it, and so, at that time, you can read what you had begun to read while on the train from Perpignan to Strasbourg, last night." Again, the flicker of a smile. "Meanwhile, please telephone or telegraph to me if I can be of any assistance in your continuing travels—that is, to locate the site where your father has been laid at the end—it was the *very* end—of the war. This is sad. Had he survived only another week or two, your father would have lived to hear the announcement of the Armistace. Once again, I must tell you that the people of France do hold dear the great sacrifice—what your President Lincoln has called the 'last full measure of devotion', which your father gave in the defense of France and her Allies."

"Merci," said Philip. This expression of appreciation was not something he had anticipated when boarding a train a thousand miles away, and he was feeling a little strange, and unsure of what was to come next. But following the two detectives' lead, Philip stood up, shook hands with Inspecteur Claude Clerbeau and his assistant."

"You are free to go, Monsieur Morrow. Please be careful of what you, ah . . . what you pick up, while in France. This is a dangerous place to be, just now. Lt. Lambert will show you out and release you from our enquiry. Thank you for your cooperation."

Three minutes later, Philip walked out from *la gare de* Strasbourg into a misty Alsace morning. His gaze landed on a large Gothic church edifice across the street, while his stomach was communicating emptiness.

"Philip!" he heard a woman's voice call, somewhere to his right. He turned, after reaching the sidewalk at the bottom of stone steps, and there was Lili. Her smiling face, gloriously framed in reddish curls, looked as beatific to him at this moment as she had hours ago on the train when their day had begun. She grabbed his hand gleefully. "Come with me. We have work to do."

"Work?"

They were in a crowd of people, moving to and fro, with cars on the street a few metres away, and buses, French voices, berets, crusty baguettes in bags of passersby, smiling girls, stern faces, military men, Gothic spires across the street pointing heavenward, unseen gargoyles grimacing at the spectres of what menace stalks beyond yon rippling Rhine, black uniforms, gray stone, cobblestone, brownstone cornerstone here, white stone there, pedestrian zone *de la gare*, whitewalled chateau structures with dark timbers embedded, sidewalks of stone and glass windows, leaded, steep roofs slanting skyward o'er horizontal beams, diagonal struts point to telegraphed streams, shop windows furnished with bourgeois dreams, flowers and vases, and fine fancy laces, church bells ringing, flower vendors they're singing, peonies and roses and pansies and posies, café on the wind and old wounds on the mend, while in the distance we see Alsatian ridges, where they're running and gunning and crossing the bridges, across the Rhine, in tick-tocking time, from Germany to France by meanders of chance, from Stuttgart to Strasbourg and back again in the dance, 'twixt Mainz and Metz, the sunrises and 'sets; it's all there on the street, thousands of feet, out here on the Rue, whence Strasbourg grew, from googles of history and gazillions of time, across the old Rhine, in massacres of metres and oodles of rhyme, a region so fine.

"Work?" He noticed her smile; she was stifling a laugh. "What is there to be done? Hey! Where's your hotel? I'm hungry. J'ai faim."

"We do not have a hotel. Our plans have changed."

"Did your Papa and Mama get out of Germany? Are they here?"

"They are here, mon frère. They are here!"

"Well then, where will you take me? I'm a yankee in Alsace, and I haven't a clue. What will we do?" Philip opened his arms wide, in an impetuous display, rare for his subdued southern persona, of enthusiasm. There was something positively inebriant about getting out of the train station after the marathon ride and question and answer session with Inspector Clerbeau.

"I will take you to a park down this way. . ." She gestured to her left. . . "near the river. My father is there in a car that our friends have provided for us." She had on a dark blue dress with a high white collar; little gold star-of-David earrings dangled from her ears. The sun sparkled out from behind a cloud. It was spring in Strasbourg. *Vous souhaitez vous rendre a Strasbourg. . . . If my French Mdm. Metz teacher could see me now!*

A few minutes later, after a stroll down a side street, they arrived at the corner of a very small, very green park, nestled at the edge of a churchyard. Lili's father was leaning against the driver side of a small, shiny gray Renault, which was parked at the curb beneath the overhang of a large oak. He was reading a book; when he saw the pair of youngsters approach, he closed the book and tossed it inside in the carseat, and straightened himself and greeted them. It was evident to Philip that the newness of their reunion as father and daughter was still ripe with joy and expectation. The man hugged his daughter affectionately, then stood back and looked at Philip, grinning.

"So you are the American!" The thin, balding man extended his hand, which Philip accepted as a very friendly greeting, and shook it with gusto. His brown eyes, through glasses, were bright with anticipation; his English was, like that of the two daughters, quite good, although with a thick German accent. "I am Hezekin Eschen, so pleased to meet you, the man who has accompanied my daughters on their long journey back to meet me again."

"Pleased to meet you, Herr Eschen. I am Philip Morrow."

"And what are your plans for a stay in Strasbourg, Mister Morrow?"

"Why, I have no plan sir. Your friend, Mr. Greeneglass of London, had asked me to secure a passage for your daughters back to London. But when we were in Perpignan, they had just received the good news that you would be able to leave Germany and meet them here, so—"

"So, here you are!"

"Yes, here I am, and I haven't a clue what to do. Do you have any suggestions?"

"I would suggest you spend some time with us. We have some friends who live in the country; they have a farm, a large house with plenty of room. We are staying there for a few days, until our travel papers can be put in order. And they have given me permission to bring you into their home for French hospitality! Est-ce bon?"

"Oui, Monsieur. Je serais honore de passer du temps avec vos amis."

Hezekin Eschen pulled keys from his pants pocket, walked to the rear of the Renault, opened the trunk. Philip dropped his suitcase and briefcase in. The father opened a back door for his daughter; she promptly seated herself. He gestured to the front passenger seat. "S'il vous plait, Monsieur Morrow, vous prenez le siege avant."

He drove the little car across two bridges, over train tracks, out of Strasbourg, and into the Alsace countryside in the direction that seemed, to Philip, to be southeast from the city. Herr Eschen began speaking to his new American friend almost immediately. "I am a happy man. I have lost much, but, you see, I have gained much more!"

"What, pray tell, what have you lost?" asked Philip.

"It appears that I have lost my business, a business that has taken my whole life to—qu'est-ce que c'est?—entwickeln."

Lili supplied his English word from the back seat. ". . .to develop, Papa; your whole life to develop. . ."

"Thank you, Lili. This has been my whole life, to develop."

"And what business is that?"

"I started in 1921 as a butcher, in Munich, *eine Metzgerei Eschen*. By 1932, my son, Heinrich, and another man—an experienced butcher, a good German—Hans Hallfreich, were running the shop. I found more profitable business in the cattle sales. Thank God we were able to prosper."

Philip was noticing, with pleasure, that the Alsatian country was a rolling hill topography, which very much reminded him of the piedmont region near his Appalachian home, back in the US. But the association was short-lived, as an unpleasant, much more recent, memory crossed his mind. "Heinrich—he is your son who, Hannah told me, has been arrested and put in prison. Is he not?"

Hezekin's eyes momentarily retreated from the driving focus; he turned to his passenger, with a face full of trouble, and almost spat it out, "The damned Gestapo have taken my son, my only son, Heinrich, to Dachau prison!"

Herr Eschen's sudden display of emotion took Philip by surprise. "I am so, I...sorry to hear it." Philip felt himself on unfamiliar turf; such things do not happen in America. "What...what is the charge?"

"Kosher killing."

"What?"

"The people of my country are going insane since Hitler took over, in 1933. There is, no longer, no respect for decent people, especially for us Jews. The Nazis have shredded the laws of Germany. They have torn our heritage of law and order, and decency, into little bits. Our good German ways are no more; they have—the way they do it is—"

Hezekin's eyes were filling with tears. Philip, unsure, extended his arm toward the stricken drive, placed his hand gently on his shoulder. "Please, Herr Eschen, it is not necessary that you—"

"The way they do it is—the Gestapo, and the *Sturmerpolizei*, the SS—make little regulations that drive us out of business; they make it impossible for us to do business. And they have imposed *Gleichschaltung* against us."

"That is 'boycott'," Lili inserted from the back seat.

"They have imposed boycott against us Jews, and that enables them to do whatever they please to put a stop to our—to our earning a living by the ways we have established over many years of hard work and—"

"They came in the night time, Philip," said Lili, from the back seat. "They came in the night time, because they had been watching us, and they knew that Heinrich and Hans were slaughtering cattle by the kosher ways, without a gunshot. They had forbidden that cows could be slaughtered with, by the knife, according to kosher practice, and they found the special knives that Heinrich was using, and then—right then and there—they took him away, and Hans too, though he is a Christian and not a Jew. They arrested them. It was January 19th. And they took them away; we have not seen them since that night—" Lili's voice, soft from the back seat faded to tearful sobbing.

"Where have they taken him?" asked Philip.

"To Dachau," replied her father. They have built a new prison there; it is especially for holding those. . ."

"Political prisoners," Lili inserted.

"Konzentrationslager," said Hezekin.

"They are special prisons for Jews, where they are concentrated in camps to do slave labor," said Lili.

Philip's American mind could not fathom it. "What is so special about you Jews that. . ."

Hezekin raised his voice: "From ancient times, God has called us out of slavery, and we will never, never submit to it on this earth—not from Pharoah, not from the Fuehrer!"

"What slavery are you talking about now, in 1937, with you a businessman, providing for your family?" Philip retorted.

The voice lowered. "Philip, the Nazis are building slave camps now!" His voice was tense with urgency, eyes flashing with offense. "The SS has built one at Dachau, and they have taken my son, my one and only son, and they have locked him in there with barbed wire all around the camp. What do you call that?"

"I've never heard of such a thing."

"Now you have, my friend. You are not in America now. This is the old world, the world from which your ancestors—Washington, Jefferson, Lincoln—the world of tragedy, and hope, from which they sprung, the world from which *their* ancestors fled!"

"If this is true—"

"It is true, my friend! This is happening, now, where I came from only two days ago. It is happening in my hometown, Munich, the place where I was born and raised and taught the Jewish faith, and my fathers before me. But my son will not be able to contribute to the great traditions of his fathers, because the Nazis have locked him at Dachau."

"Well, this—how did this happen in a civilized country like Germany? The land of Bach and Beethoven, the land of Luther? I just—I just almost can't believe it.

"What! You don't believe me?"

"It's not that I don't believe you, Hezekin, it's just so. . .absurd. It sounds like something out of a Frankenstein movie—Boris Karloff, or. . ."

"Dr. Frankenstein was a German, was he not?"

"Now this *is* getting ridiculous! Storybook stuff."

"Listen! I will explain something to you, my young American friend. If you do not believe me now, you will know soon enough that what I am telling you is true. Isn't it true, Lili?" He turned his head toward his daughter in the back seat, for support.

"It is true, papa, every word of it. Furthermore, Philip, as for the slavery thing—Pharoah and Fuehrer and all that—not only will we reject slavery, but the other peoples of the world will see, by our example, the way out of their own slavery."

"This is well-spoken, my daughter." Hezekin turned his face again toward Philip. His expressive eyes were pleading silently for Philip's acceptance.

Philip sighed, and there was a long silence. The Alsace hills were green all around them now, with morning sunshine that baptized their morning with something new and noble. Hezekin was guiding the little Renault through piedmont valleys; a rocky stream threaded through the field, flowing clear and clean through spring grass. Milk cows grazed on the hillsides.

"I'm just wondering, Hezekin, how in the hell could such a thing happen?"

Hezekin leaned back in his seat, relaxing from the previous tension of conviction. "It started, I am sad to say, in 1934, when Hitler took control of the German government. They made a bunch of laws against us. It started small, with little needles of regulations to make it more and more difficult for us to do business. First, they made it *verboten* for German citizens of the Reich to buy from Jewish merchants. If regular *volk* are caught buying from us Jews, they are publicly humiliated. Their names are posted on public billboards—*Sturmer* boards. They can even dismiss Germans from their jobs if they are caught buying from us. Those who are unemployed—and there are so many of them—will be cut off from the Reich dole and winter-relief, if they are caught dealing with Jews. This is called *Gleichschaltung*—it is boycott, in English.

"So your business as a butcher has gone down?"

"It is nothing, it is no more. They drove us out of business. It's what the communists call 'expropriation' when they do it in Russia, or now Spain. But here in Germany they just send the SS—a guard stands outside the door of almost every Jewish shop. Hitler rants against the communists because of their labor issues and expropriation of lands and assets, but his Nazi goons do the same thing in the name of the Third Reich. It is stealing, plain and simple. They have no respect for the law of Moses—'Thou shalt not steal— nor for any other law or tradition of human decency."

"Damn!"

"Young boys roam the streets, doing whatever they please to vandalize Jewish shops; they throw stones in the windows, breaking the glass. When the owner goes to replace the window, the SS guard calls it 'provocation.' Not the kid breaking the window, but the shopowner repairing it! That's provocation against the Reich."

"Did you just leave your business? Just walk away from it?"

"After they took Heinrich, I saw the writing on the wall, which I should have heeded long ago. By that time, a week or two ago, there was nothing much to leave. I could not even be admitted to the agricultural fairs any more, to buy or sell cows. Or, if I had chosen to, I could wait outside, separately as the dirty Jew, like they did in Leipzig three hundred years ago."

"So you just, locked the door and left?"

"That was when I put Hannah and Lili on a train to Genoa, Italy. And that was no easy feat—getting the papers for them so they could leave Germany. My wife, Hilda, and I decided it must be safer to get them out first, and thank God, that strategy worked, as you can see."

Lili spoke from the back seat. "Philip?"

"Yes?"

"When we met, at the restaurant in Perpignan, you may remember that Hannah and I had just gotten off the boat—it was a British ship—from Marseilles. But we had taken a German ship from Genoa to Marseilles. The French officials would not accept our German papers there, but the British allowed us on, and that's how we got to Perpignan. Thankfully, the officials there were not as strict about our papers."

"Well at least you managed to get here, my dear," said Hezekin to his daughter, looking at her in the rearview mirror. "It was a roundabout way, but now we are together in France, and we have freedom to make more travel arrangements." Hezekin glanced at Philip again. "That was the girls' ordeal. As for Hilda and me—I went to the bank. They had sequestered our account. We could not withdraw more that fifty marks; that was not enough to cover our expenses in obtaining exit visas from Germany, train tickets and other expenses."

"So what did you do to get over that hurdle?"

"Ha! Hurdle! That's what I like about you Americans. Everything is just a challenge to you, almost like a game—a hurdle to be jumped, a mountain to be climbed."

"Well, thank you, sir." Philip had never heard anything like this before, certainly not in England among the stuffy Brits. *It's been a long journey from Wechola County in North Carolina to the eastern extremes of France, standing in the shadow of this terrible thing called the Third Reich.*

"We got some help from outside. You know Itmar, in London, right?"

"Yes."

"Itmar, and others with him in London, and also in America, have sent money and personal contacts, which have made it possible for us to get out of Germany, although at the last, at the border we ran into one unexpected delay that we feared might be a 'hurdle'—ha!—that we might not be able to get over. So we paid a French Rhinelander to drive us across at night in a place where the guards would not stop us. And that is how we got here, yesterday. The group that has helped us—I believe they had started in Luxembourg—has a name, "La GourdeBoire.""

14

Provisions

In the middle of Joan Ravel's large dining table stood a fat vase of fresh white peonies. At the north end of the table, in the place soon to be occupied by her husband, Cartier, a bottle of Riesling awaited the group's imbibing. Next to the wine was a baguette, freshly baked that morning at the village bakery.

Joan's fourteen-year-old daughter, Cosette, had laid out twelve place settings around the table. This would be the first time, in the girl's memory, that all their dinnerware had been laid on the table at the same time in preparation for a meal. Next to each empty plate, Cosette had lovingly laid a fork, knife, and spoon upon a white napkin, and a glass. A small, thin-stemmed wine glass goblet was also provided for each guest, although these vessels were of three types that had been retrieved from the upper recesses of their kitchen cupboards.

Philip Morrow stood near the table, catching snippets of the French being spoken by *Directeur* Donald Satie, of the LaGrange village *ecole*. Skillfully including the hapless American in his lively pre-dinner conversation, the principal was talking to his friend, M. Henri Leblanc, a grower of superb sprouts, onions, mustard and squash, prepared delicacies which would very soon be passed in warm dishes from hand to hand around Joan's well-appointed table. The men were analyzing Alsace political developments. Their respective wives, Freida and Sandi, were already seated, speaking happily of children and other important matters.

At the south end of the table would be Joan Ravel's place. The next seat around the corner Cosette had been instructed to set for herself. Her status as eldest child would be inexorably acknowledged at this meal's sharing, while her two siblings and the other children would share a table nearby in the kitchen, to be administered by the Leblanc's eldest daughter, Maxine, who being a year younger than Cosette, felt honored to accept dinner responsibilities for the other seven juveniles present.

The other four seats at the table's east side would be occupied by the Eschens: Hezekin, Helene, Hannah and Lili. This family, having managed to free themselves from the meddlesome oppressions of the Munich Gestapo, would be, as it were, the guests of honor. A disturbing absence of their son, Heinrich, and the recent deprivations in Germany that had provoked his imprisonment, would surely be a matter for some solemn explanation during the meal. Apart from that worrisome weight, there nevertheless seemed to prevail a mutedly celebratory aspect to this supper; at least the other four Eschens were here, safe on the French side of the Rhine.

The last rays of this day's bright sun were slanting through the Ravels' dining room window, refracting a luminous coral glow over the peony blossoms. Cosette and Joan were busily positioning casseroles, salad bowls, viands and other deliciositees wherever space could still be found on Joan's table. Now that provisions had been set in place, Cartier Ravel, the cattle rancher whose beef and chicken would be the main courses, came in. Tinkling the empty glass with his fork, he addressed the company of guests who had gathered in his dining room, "Laissez-nous manger, mes amis!"

Cartier prayed to the Provider in French; Hezeken gave thanks in Hebrew; then they sat down to share the meal. The host broke bread and passed it around for all. Joan hovered around the table, half-filling each goblet with wine. Cosette poured water in their glasses. Maxine and the other children were dismissed to the kitchen table.

Cartier, a solid man, a man of the earth, knew well the active mind of his learned friend, who was seated at his right hand. He turned to the school principal and said, "Donald, is there something you'd like to say?"

Donald Satie, somewhat surprised but nevertheless accustomed to this role, spoke. "Well *merci, mon ami*, for hosting us. And we do want to welcome these friends from Germany, the Eschens." He raised his arms in a gesture of magnanimous greeting. "We hope that our receiving you here in Alsace, in this household, can, in some small way, assuage the pain you must be feeling now. I myself have only just now met you, Hezekin." He smiled gently and nodded to the guest seated opposite him. "But Cartier has told us of the rude circumstances of your departure from your home in Munich. We pray for the deliverance of your son. May the Lord bring Heinrich out of the captivity that Nazi cruelties have devised against him!" He sipped the wine. The fire in Donald's eyes flickered, then subsided as he looked directly across at Philip. "And to you, Philip, we welcome you as well, and celebrate your family back in the United States, of whom you told me earlier. And we mourn the passing of your grandfather, who had given his son—your father—in the defense of France, during the war. We thank you for the sacrifice your family has made on our behalf."

Philip nodded dutifully. He felt strangely as if he were in a ceremony, like graduation back in Chapel Hill, but somehow laden with greater gravitas.

Donald Satie continued. "But I cannot help wondering about this unseemly coincidence—the presence of this family who have just now fled German oppression. . ." His eyes darted to the Eschens, then back to Philip. ". . .while you are here with us today, a young man whose childhood was deprived of fatherhood, because your father's life had been snuffed out on the battlefield by. . .by that same aggression—that same Prussian belligerence—that has compelled the Eschens—Hezekin, Helene, Hannah, and Lili—to this place of sanctuary in France."

Philip could see that the schoolmaster's eloquence was a wield that he tenderly utilized, by some implacable consensus, among this small group of friends—this assembly of whatever sort—nurtured within a spring-greening valley of the Vosges. Proactively, the group's benevolence was reaching across the table through the words of *Le Directeur* Satie.

"So, while we welcome you, we cannot neglect to raise the question: what is it that we can do to help you?" Donald took a gulp of wine, then his first bite of salad. He had done his work of shephardic initiation.

"Thank you for asking, Monsieur," said Hezekin, without hesitation. But then a torrent of distress came forth from lips. "Our intention, ultimately, is to go to America. But at this moment in time, we are torn between many hard choices that we must make. The first is: what is to be done about Heinrich? Indeed, what **can** be done? Is there anything that can be done from this remote position? Should we go forward and establish a new life, completely leaving our many years of accrued worth? Should we go on to New York, where relatives are preparing a way for us? Would we, then, be abandoning our son to a fate, in Dachau, worse than death, or even. . ."

Tears were flowing from the dark eyes. His face constricted with the tribulation of it all; a dark, stitched spot of yarmulke suddenly bespoke the ancient distress of his tribe, as the bewildered cell of Christians beheld Hezekin, weeping for his only son. The man lowered his head in grievous resignation.

Is this a time for feasting, or fasting?

After a moment, Hezekin recovered his composure. "Please, please, *mes amis*. . .we are so grateful for you. We do not wish to. . ."

Helene intervened. "We were not expecting such generosity as you have shown here. We crossed the border—we. . .we had no idea of what awaited us. Itmar had given us your name, Herr Ravel, in a coded telegram, and here we are. Please, let us celebrate our arrival in France! Let us eat, with thanksgiving. The sun is setting on this beautiful day, this day of our deliverance to a bountiful table. The sunset. . . *Sunrise, sunset, swiftly through the years, one season following another, laden with happiness. . .and tears!*"

Like a violin string stretched across the bridge of time, rendering some rare vibrato of tenderness that struck now upon their resonant souls, a note of empathetic enquiry sounded forth. Sandi Leblanc, sitting across the table, a woman whose attentions were continually attuned to affairs of the heart and issues of the spirit, asked carefully, slowly, "What is it, Madame, that you and your family must find—what is it that would require crossing the ocean, going all the way to America—to find? Surely you will not have to travel so far for peace of mind?"

Helene wiped the tears from her cheek. "What we seek, Madame Leblanc, is a young man, a good man in the very flower of his youth; but he is locked inside Dachau prison—our son, Heinrich. And now it is so very hard to decide what is to be done. Should we stay or go?"

"Even if you must go. . .somewhere. . .must it be to America? Why not wait here, here in Alsace. You are close here, close enough to respond quickly, if Heinrich were to be released. If you were all the way to the United States, your help for him would be almost impossible."

"Our travel visas here are good only for two weeks. But we have relations in New York—they are our people, Jews like us—who are working on our behalf. They are even willing to deposit thousands of US dollars in the banks for us, and send affidavits to endorse for our immigration, so that we can obtain visas to enter the United States and start a new life there."

The host, M. Ravel, at the head of the table, inserted, "Peut-etre . . . your temporary visas here can be extended. We may be able to find some help for you with that. Although there is no consulate in Strasbourg, we do know some people who have political responsibilities. Other refugees, like you, have come from Germany and have been able, with a little time, to make better arrangements, to stay in France. Now that you have gotten out, you should slow down and get your bearings, form a strategy to establish communication with Heinrich, if that is possible; there may be more resources here in Alsace than you realize. You really do need to stay close to Germany, Hezekin." Cartier looked directly into the man's face, then at his wife. "You do need to stay nearby until Heinrich is released, or at least until you have heard some definite news, or until this whole damned Nazi thing blows over."

Henri Leblanc then spoke excitedly, "The Third Reich is not going to go away! They will inflict their German hatefulness on Jews and some others as long as they can! They will not stop until they are forced to stop. Hitler and Goebbels have railed against the Jews since the beginning, even since '33. It was their intention all along to rob you of your business and then run you out of Germany. But our leaders, Petain or—we need another Clemenceau, or Poincare, maybe that young man, DeGaulle—somebody needs to rise up and intervene *la-bas*. Ever since Hitler waltzed into the Saar last year, with no resistance whatsoever from us, those Nazi brutes who salute and follow his every command without question have been frothing at the mouth to run the Jews out of Germany. That is what the Gestapo is assigned to do, and the Third Reich will not cease its campaign against the Jews—especially the prosperous ones such as you."

"But do not despair!" said Henri's wife. "You have come to the right place. We can help you. We'll give you sanctuary as long as we can."

Helene looked carefully at Sandi; she constructed a slow response. "I appreciate your willingness to help, Madame Leblanc, but you do not know what you are saying. Consorting with Jews brings a whirlwind of trouble."

"But now you are no longer in Germany; this is France, where all citizens are the same, according the law," Sandi retorted, tenderly.

"Perhaps so, but we are not French citizens. Now that the Third Reich of Hitler has rejected us, it seems that we are stateless; we have no citizenship, although we, and our children, were born in Germany, in Bavaria. We have now no citizenship except with our Jewish people." Helene's words hung momentarily upon a silence, beyond any further comment of their stunned dinner company.

"It has always been so," were Hezekin's words, intoned gravely, and sadly laid out upon their hearing, a remnant, as it were, sewn into the tattered fabric of this present time. Hezekin's dark eyes seemed to hang within his face like deepset phylacteries. ". . . since the time of the Maccabees, when Antiochus the Greek, and Pompey, the Roman, put an end to Eretz Israel."

"Harriet Tubman," Hannah broke in.

"Harriet who? What are you talking about?"

"Tubman. Harriet Tubman," the young woman repeated. ". . . an American Negro woman who escaped slavery about a hundred years ago. She went to the north, to the free states of America, where the practice of slavery had been outlawed. She started an organization for her people to escape the cotton plantations in the south, and go up to the free states in the north, where they could begin a new life."

"The Underground Railroad," said Philip. "How did you know about that?" he asked, looking with surprised interest across and down the table at Hannah.

"I've been reading the Encyclopedia Britannica," she replied. "It just occurred to me that, in our predicament here, our family is like those slaves who had escaped before the American civil war. "The Negroes were, like us now, a stateless people. They had been sold into slavery in Africa, and shipped across the Atlantic in terrible ships, where they were forced to pick cotton for plantation owners for many generations, until Harriet Tubman escaped and set up secret itineraries for their escape."

"But you are not like Negro slaves. You are prosperous Jews," objected Donald, gently.

"Not any more, we're not, Monsieur Satie," Hannah answered. "This is the enormity of it—of the changes that the Third Reich has imposed. "All that my father and mother have worked for—and our grandparents before them—has been robbed, a little bit at a time, from us!—including my brother. And now the Nazis have built a slave camp, where they intend to concentrate us Jews—Heinrich is not the only one—and force us into doing work to build up the *wehrmacht*, so Hitler can exact vengeance against us, and not only against us 'prosperous' Jews, but against you, too, you French people, and the British, who imposed the treaty of Versailles on Germany after the war."

"Excuse me, Hannah," Philip interjected, ". . . not to change the subject, of course, but you, ah, you say you read about the Underground Railroad and Harriet Tubman in the Encyclopedia Britannica. Where did you find the encyclopedia?"

"We have an Encyclopedia Britannica. Or—we **had** one. It must belong to someone else now, whoever has expropriated our home, or maybe the

Gestapo have taken it by now, and burned it. They do burn books, the Nazis do."

"I found the encyclopedia in a pawn shop in Munich, near our own shop. I bought it for our children a few years ago, although it is old, 1921, I think," explained Helene. "Philip, I attribute our daughters' English proficiency largely to their reading in that collection. It has been a valuable learning resource, especially in the last few years, as the Nazis have been attempting to rewrite history to agree with their aryan program."

"Aryan program?" asked Donald.

"The Nuremberg laws. The Reichstag passed them a few years ago. Germans are now forbidden to marry Jews, or even do business with us."

"Why?"

"These laws legislate racial purity; they are designed to breed pure German stock, whatever that is. It has something to do with, I believe, blond hair, fair skin, and certain facial characteristics, and a certain way of thinking and acting—something like 'following orders.' Germans are being bred like cattle to develop this strain of super-aryans, who will rule Deutschland with an iron hand under the sign of the swastika," Hezekin explained.

"And the swastika—where the hell did that come from anyway? It's such a strange-looking emblem," said Cartier.

"It comes from Asia," answered Hezekin.

"India," added Donald. "It is a very old emblem, originally Hindu, but having different ancient symbolism for Buddhists and the Chinese."

"What does it mean?" asked Philip.

Donald answered, "It's nothing so terrible, really. I think it stands for a few quite positive concepts in the far east, like goodness and peace."

"So why the hell have the Nazis taken it as their symbol?" queried Cartier. "One would have thought they'd adopt something that is native to Germany, like. . ."

". . .like the cross," Donald surmised.

"Yes, like the cross. Why didn't they just use a regular cross, instead of . . . a crooked one." Cartier continued. "That would be consistent with German history, the Holy Roman Empire and—"

"I can assure you, Monsieur Ravel," Helene inserted, "that the Nazi party has nothing to do with the cross of Christ, or even with, for that matter, the Christian Church."

"Isn't the church a part of their program—the Fatherland and the Church and being good Germans?"

"They would want you to think so." Hezekin said, his voice slightly raised to emphasize the point. "These National Socialists who are running Germany now have nothing to do with true Christianity—and I know you people consider yourselves a part of that tradition—but in fact their only association with the Church is their intention to use the institutional Church, if they can, and manipulate it to their own ends. However, there are a few Christian pastors in Germany who have spoken—quite bravely, I might add—against what the Nazis have done in their attempts to make the Church an arm of the Nazi political machine. I have heard that Hitler himself has tried to strong-arm his way into the councils of Christian leadership in Germany. But there are a few who can see through his godless rhetoric and pagan agenda: men like Dietrich Bonhoeffer, and Herr Niemoller, in Berlin."

"We have noticed," added Helene, "in fact, Monsieur Ravel, that, back home in Munich, some of the very few Germans who were willing to help us, at their own peril, are Christians whose faith is strong enough to resist the hateful Nazi pogrom. They can see through its facade of false aryan propriety; they can disregard the reprobate *zeitgeist* that seems to be compelling gullible people to act against us Jews."

"People are like sheep," observed Cartier. "They will go wherever they are led, especially if they are Germans."

"Not all people can be led astray like sheep," protested Henri. "My Huguenot ancestors are a testimony to that. We are people of conscience; we have no need for a government in Berlin, or Paris, for that matter, to instruct us in the way we should think, or believe, or pray." He paused and, seeming to finish with his point, cast a glance around the dinner table in search of a *piece de resistance* of a different genre. With a more elemental appetite in mind than the desire to identify cross-cultural contentions, Henri pointed to a dish and requested, "Please pass me that casserole. My compliments, Joan, to you on your excellent cuisine. I am praying that there will still be some of it in the dish for others, after I have taken another helping."

They laughed.

Donald responded in kind. "I will pass this casserole dish to you, Henri, mon ami, if you will kindly pass the beef platter in this direction," He lifted the dish and passed it along; then as his eyes settled on the platter being placed into his hands, the wise *Ecole Directeur* resumed, "But I fear, my dear Henri, that the truth of this phrase—that men are like sheep and can be easily led in wrong directions—is altogether too true, in the case of our German neighbors. I have heard very little about these pastors of good conscience that Herr Eschen mentions. My reading of the news from Deutschland is that, for the most part, there are far more Germans who have subscribed to the Nazi program instead of, say, mounting any significant resistance to it. I daresay it is because so many had been unemployed for so long, during those years before '34. But now the Nazis have began putting the *volkish* proletariat to work again in rebuilding what they think is some magical Prussian birthright, German military superiority. Now the good Germans are intimidated by their nationally inbred yearning for security and order, and they are doing what they're ordered to do."

"Order?" Henri erupted. "From the Eschens' report here, what is happening is *anything but* a return to order. It is nothing like the security that Germans' have obsessed about since before the last war. They are turning the world upside down."

"But only for the Jews," said Hezekin. "The obsession with security and order certainly is a characteristic of our German temperament; it is nothing new. But Adolf Hitler is using that desire, along with resentment of you French and the British, as leverage for the Nazi program. He has deviously convinced the people that somehow their future welfare depends on abrogating the Versailles restrictions and, by the way, also ridding the nation of us Jews. This too is nothing new under the sun. We have always been a scapegoat in eastern Europe. Whenever times turn bad, some fanatic group always comes out of the clockwork to blame us, because we are different, and because, perhaps, we have figured out a few things about how to handle money. So there is a willingness in the people to rearrange society, but at the expense of us followers of Moses. They will turn the world upside down, all the while believing that a nationwide pogrom will produce order when all the Juden are expelled from their midst. And that is why we are here, as exiles, with you now, sharing this delicious meal. Perhaps someday we will enjoy such a meal as this in Jerusalem. לנדיבות אותך יברך שאלוהים ייתכן היום כאן שמוצג".

"More likely in New York, than Jerusalem," said Helene.

"But America is so very far away—a whole ocean away—and that is after you've gone clear across France," said Sandi. It would seem that to build a new life here would be much simpler. You need not sail half a world away to find some place of security."

"Have you not heard that the United States is called a new world?" Hannah chimed in. In that country, the old ways do not even exist. Our

166

relatives have prospered greatly there, and they have provided an opening for us, if we are willing to enter into it."

"Do you think that is possible?"

"What?"

"A new world."

"A world in which somehow, some group of contentious people doesn't pin the blame for all the world's misery on us Jews?"

"Yes. It is possible."

"I don't think so."

"I believe it."

"Don't believe it, not in this world."

"In America!"

"Ha!" Henri Leblanc laughed. We tried that already, here in France. Napolean himself couldn't even dissuade the most egalitarian society in the world that all citoyens –your people included—have the same rights as anyone else."

"We haven't done such a bad job of it," M. Satie interjected. "Jews in France are better situated than anywhere else in Europe. Why, in Paris, they practically run the place!"

"I wouldn't be so sure of that. Wait and see what happens when those Germans take us over and nimrod their Nuremberg laws down our throats," Henri said.

"That will never happen, Henri!" Hostess Joan piped in.

"You watch and see! Hitler and his gang of dragonnades are up to no good, and when their guns and tanks—now being manufactured in violation of Versailles—are ready, they will not stop at the Rhine. I don't think our M. Blum will be able to muster the strength to stop them, Maginot line or otherwise," Henri parried.

"This is why we are looking for America," said Hezekin, quietly. "No offense to you Les Francaise. With what we have been through these last four years, I am ready to take a chance on a new world, no matter how unlikely is the prospect of a universal egalite and fraternite for all men. Certainly, any possibility of a better life is greater in the United States than anywhere on this continent. What's more is, my cousin Leonard, who lives in New York, attests to this."

"It is true," Helene followed, "that such an arrangement as Leonard can establish for us comes at a dear price. He has already paid at least two thousand dollars to the US State Department on our behalf, all of which we will repay when this is over. So, in a sense, we are buying, or will be buying, our way into America." She smiled, an explanatory expression. "So you see, the die is already, in a sense, cast. Our Leonard has already invested so much into our application there, it would be foolish for us not to follow up on his generosity. We see this as the provision of G_d."

"So to flee to the United States is what you will choose, and this is better than, say, Jerusalem?" asked M. Satie.

Hezekin raised his eyebrows, surprised at the question. Slowly and considerately, he answered. "To leave Germany and emigrate to Palestine would be like. . . like jumping from a frying pan into the fire."

"But is Jerusalem not the holy city, the ancient home of Jewish people?"

"It is that, mon ami, but not for the Eschen family at this time. At some future time, perhaps, more likely generations from now. There are many impediments that now prevent such a thing."

"So much for 'next year in Jerusalem.' eh Hezekin?" Donald smiled.

Hezekin returned the smile, with a shrug, his hands raised and opened slightly.

"There are other Jews who think otherwise, who think that the time for your return to Israel is ripening."

"They are free to think as they please, and those who have adopted the strategies of M. Herzl, G_d rest his soul, are free to do according to what they believe is best. The Mufti of Jerusalem—he is an ally with Hitler—will contend fiercely with those of us who pursue that course. But as for me and my family—we have had enough of such tribulations as would be required to initiate and defend such a project. We have lost one son to the beast; we will not risk now, our daughters being laid upon the altar of history."

"If you only knew, M. Satie, what we have endured, you would understand," Helene added.

"Oh I do understand," said the schoolmaster. "And we do understand. I have read about the Maccabees; I have read, in our Scriptures, about Hayman, and Esther, and Hezekiah and Nehemiah. We understand a little of what is at work here. That is why our sister, Sandi here. . ." Donald gestured toward the bright-eyed lady two chairs to his right. "She has suggested that there could be a more, ah, agreeable accommodation for you here in Alsace than you may surmise."

"This is too close, monsieur, too close to Germany. Perhaps we can rest here for a short while, but the heat of Nazi burnings—it is almost as if I can still feel it—is too intense. . . just a few miles over there." She pointed, with her thumb, to the east, behind herself. I fear that what now is the firebrand of Hitler's hatred for us will one day soon be a raging fire."

In the midst of all this, the young American who sat at this table did not know what to make of it all. For some reason—he knew not what—he thought of his father, laid in the cold ground somewhere, many, many miles north of here, in Belgium. And his father's shadow, a presence he discerned as if it were some silhouette in front of bright sunlight in his own four-year-old memory, seemed suddenly to be darkening the space behind him. Philip turned to look. But the presence was not his father; it was not Clint Morrow. There was a young girl, Cosette, eldest daughter of this household, standing there to refill his wine glass. Her fourteen-year-old eyes sparkled in the dusky light as they met his. She smiled. Philip hadn't known that he would ever venture this far across France, almost into the dusking dark of Deutschland dread.

15

Exhibitionismes

In Paris, a very public preview was being foreshadowed on the world stage. Mars, the Roman god of war, was busily directing a rehearsal for his newest production; soon an infamous cast of international players would enact the updated version of an ancient bloody tragedy. The elaborate set was under construction in a well-chosen cosmopolitan venue, in the very shadow of the Eiffel tower. High above Parisian gaity and earthy impressionist passions, on the edges of a ceremonial field, two Titans of Modern Ideology stood, poised for an encounter of epic proportions.

Towering pheonix-like above the banks of the River Seine, two newly-erected stone structures dominated the skyline of the *Exposition Internationale des Arts et Techniques dans la Vie Moderne* of 1937. Clad with grandiose architectural bravado, the German monolith faced directly across *Le Champ de Mars*, overlooking a more fluidic, statutary monument that the Russians had built on the other side of the field. These two giants were preparing for an elaborately-staged theatre production yet to come. Soon their curtains of bellicose bluster would be drawn back, and a death-struggle of unprecedented scale would be unleashed upon the world. Nevertheless, their monumental confrontation would prove to be, alas, only a nazified rerun of the earlier conflagration that had erupted twenty-five years earlier. The war that would soon be waged between these giants would, in the long run, desecrate and cripple the same damned nations that had suffered through 1914-18.

But who knew, or understood, the terrible encore that was about to take place?

There was, at least, one man who understood what was happening; he had a premonition of what gruesome events were waiting in the wings. And he painted it.

Pablo Picasso's large mural painting, soon to be on display at the lowly Spanish pavilion, gave an odd picture of the total war strategy that German luftwaffe bomber planes had recently inflicted on a Spanish village. The bloodshed of Basquish peasants was hardly dry in Viscayan soil when the artist had seen reports of the bombers' ferocious mutilation of simple human existence. The Guernica atrocity had happened only a month before, on April 26, on the north coast of Spain. Picasso's presciently surreal rendering of it hung unceremoniously in what appeared to be an insignificant background corner of this internationally staged Paris Exhibition. People gawked, but didn't know what to make of it. Somehow the dark mood that the mural provoked did not fit in with lighter art-deco themes that were rampant throughout the Exhibition.

Dwarfed by the German and Russian megaliths that towered above it, Pablo's *Guernica* painting in the Spanish pavillion seemed darkly mysterious, an enigma.

Capping the German tower was a great bronze eagle. Lofty aspirations of German power and authority were thus on display for all the world to consider. Across the way, illusions of a different kind were set in stone atop the Russian monument, in the form of a sculpted couple of comrades, one man and one woman, whose zealous forward postures bespoke dialectic dreams of communist progress to be realized in the union of the Soviets.

The world could not yet comprehend what Stalin's paranoid purges were even now inflicting behind the scenes in that stillborn Republic up north.

Into this splendid exhibit of stony European hegemonies Philip Morrow wandered, clueless. He had come to Paris to accompany the Eschens in their appeal for visas at the American embassy, and to render whatever assistance his simple American citizenship might provide.

But first, there would be a rendezvous with Itmar, the man who had initiated this roundabout expedition to spirit the Eschens away from Germany. Now it seemed that the refugee family, with Philip's hapless accompaniment, had been drawn into a kind of French suspension between two tyranical poles. On this bright Tuesday afternoon, Philip was standing on a bridge over the River Seine, looking westward into the afternoon sun. The Pont d'Iena was busy with pedestrians who had come to see the Exposition's unveiling. In front of him to the left, sculpted high atop the USSR pavilion, two windswept Soviet workers appeared to be striding confidently across the Parisian skyline, as if they intended to lead French citoyens, and perhaps the rest of the world with them, far beyond their café-cultured socialist ambiguities into some glorious Communist paradisiac of the proletariat yet to come.

On his right, a swastika-clad eagle had been enthroned even higher than the Soviets in Parisian airspace. Nazified Germanic hands had lifted the predatory icon's brassy visage to a lofty perch, upon the monumental aerie from which blitzy swoops of conquest could yet be designed.

Philip turned slowly to his left. His vision skirted beneath the bridge. Glassy ripples of the ancient blue-green Seine whispered their enlightened illusions into the cooling afternoon air. The passersby were mumbling all around, sipping carelessly their *aperitifs* of festivity. Looking now to the darker east, on the River's other side, he saw that great graceful steel spire of Gustave Eiffel's dream; it stood, as it had since 1889, still manifesting French pride, and memorializing from now 'til kingdom come the world's first bold venture into cold hearts of industrial steel.

At the River's edge now on his right, the blocky British pavilion had been plopped down like some preposterous Wimbledon cricket wicket, its muraled wallpaper architecture declaring the mercantile power of proper non-intervention in nothing of consequence at all except sporting leisure. Over to the left, on the other side of the grassy Champs de Mars, the Belgian construct roundly agreed with their English cousins' safe mediocrity. Both of these nations were conceding their bourgeois wonders to the lofty blusters of Russia and Germany.

In the shadows of these giants lurked a latent charge of the still-unfinished Spanish pavilion, a wallflower among fox-trotting titans. Cloaked in featureless squared modernity, it nevertheless would expose, for all the world to gasp, an open wound in Europe's thin-skinned peace, an explosive depiction of Europe's smoke-filled future, which, unveiled as a work of trendy surreal art, and hanging as a painted opus consistent with the Exposition's purposeful artish themes, yet silently screaming as if it were some nightmarish disturbance of oil on canvas which had been hastily and stealthily composed under Pablo's deliberate cubist hand, based upon the news reports from Guernica that the Andalusian artist had seen after April

26. He must have been having a bad dream when he painted it—a surreal dream—the handwriting, as it were, on the wall. *Mene mene tekel U Luftwaffen.*

"Meet me at the Exposition at 5 o'clock. I'll be on the bridge, the Pont d'Iena, near where it crosses to the Left Bank. The British pavilion will be on your right," Itmar had said on the telephone when Philip had called him from the hotel. Philip looked at his watch; it said 5 o'clock. He lit a cigarette. A few minutes later, as slanting sunlight glistened on the Seine, a familiar voice that Philip heard was not the tailor from London, but a crisp German lilt from lips of the young woman he had so recently met.

"What are you thinking of?" Lili Eschen asked, approaching from behind.

"This is a city on the edge," he replied.

"On the edge of what?"

"I don't know yet; I can't figure it out." A water-bird began yipping as it perched nearby on the concrete rail. A child reached up to it, but the bird flew upward across the River. It landed on the Russian statue, where young comrade and comradette were joining hands.

"This city is on the edge of Germany," she said.

"But the border is hundreds of miles away."

"Paris is closer than you think, to Berlin."

Philip considered this. Then he pointed beyond the Russian edifice, to the west, and said, "Over there, between us and where the sun will set, is Versailles, where the treaty was agreed to and signed after the war. The treaty should ensure peace and security, *n'est que ce pas?*"

"That doesn't mean a thing to Adolf Hitler." Her eyes, stern with the memory of where they had just come from, were cast down upon the Seine. "Germans know. That treaty means nothing to the Nazis."

"Do they? Do Germans know?"

"Some of them do, though they will not say it. There is a lot they will not say. We have neighbors in Munich who will not say that they have done business with my father for many years. Instead, they pretend to not know us. These last few months when we were at home, near the shop, when I would walk on the streets, I felt at times that I must have some horrible sign on my head, something like a mark of shame, a big. . . yellow patch of . . . *verboten*, or something . . . Even people my own age would act as if they had never known me. What makes people do such things? What compels them to change their attitude toward others whom they have known all their lives, people they grew up with?"

"They must be scared as hell of the Nazis."

"Nazi police; they call them Gestapo." Lili's expression turned sour. She had been casually surveying the busy scene of pedestrians and pavilions around them, but suddenly her gaze fixed upon the German pavilion. Philip turned to look at it. "That monument over there—the obscene monolith with the swastika on top of it—it upsets me," she explained, speaking deliberately, precisely.

"I can understand that, Lili, since your brother is still in prison there."

"I don't want to be here, Philip. Is there somewhere else we can go?"

"Where would you like to go?"

"I. . . I mean, this is Paris! Why are we standing here beneath that monstrosity?"

"Okay. Just say where is a better place, and I will go there with you."

"There is a church that I have for a long time wanted to see, not because it is a church, but because the stained glass there is said to be the most exquisite in the world. It is the Saint-Chapelle."

"Where is it?"

"I do not know exactly. I, too, have never been here before. I do know that it is very near the church of Notre Dame, and I think it is on an island in the Seine."

"Let's find it together; we'll make an expedition of it. I have a guide book here; I have been reading some of it. But, of course, Lili, . . . this will have to wait. I am expecting to see your father's friend, Itmar, here. He had told me on the telephone he would meet me here at five o'clock. But now it is 5:30."

"Oh, I know what that is about. Father has arranged a meeting for us tomorrow at the American embassy."

"I wonder if there are some preparations that your family should make before that meeting."

"Surely not. What can we do in Paris? All we have is left behind, in Munich. And if there are still details to arrange, I am sure my father is working on it. He has been talking on the telephone and sending telegrams all day, it seems, since we arrived. That's why I had to get away. This is Paris!" Munich is so. . .so shameful, in comparison. I don't want to ever go back there."

"What if Heinrich is found? What if they release him?"

"That would be very good, of course. But I know—father and mother have already said—we will not risk going back there to get him. It is sad to say, but, my brother is on his own now, although I do pray for him every day." Then her head turned up, hand raised and she began to wave. "Oh look, there is Hannah." She pointed toward the British pavilion, where her sister was standing on a stairway. "She will know what is being done. Hannah always knows what our plans are." She waved broadly at her sister again. After a few seconds, Hannah acknowledged, waving back. "She wants us to go over there."

Philip looked up from his guidebook. "Okay." He waved at Hannah. "It says here that the Saint-Chapelle is at the Palais de Justice, on the Ile de la Cite, near the Pont de St. Michel."

Lili gently took his hand. "That's good. Let's go see Hannah. She knows what Father and Mother will be planning." Lili smiled whimsically, cocked her head in their new direction. Consternation over the German pavilion had passed into the thick Parisian air. Her brown eyes glinted, squinting as she looked at him with the afternoon sun at his back. As they began to walk, Lili's hand dropped to her side again, but the momentary touch conveyed all the tenderness of a baby's breath, and Philip's world changed from whatever it had been to wonder. He walked beside her, and slightly behind. The tight, red-blonde curls on her head fascinated him more than anything. He wanted to take her to the Saint-Chapelle, or wherever she wanted to go.

Philip hesitated. He found himself wanting to linger on the bridge, with just the two of them amongst the crowd. There was no need to seek out the others. Such an afternoon—in the slanting sun, the golden light of Paris.

She grabbed his hand again. "Come on, silly."

He was loving every minute of it as the firm grip of her soft hand compelled him, threading them through these stylish Europeans, along the edge of the bridge-rail, with all the while the Eiffel tower looming ahead, getting larger and larger. Then there was a wide walkway to the right, and Hannah had sauntered up the steps to join them in an open area in front of the British pavilion.

"Mother and Father would like us to meet them at the hotel for dinner at 6:30," Hannah announced. "If we walk from here now, we will be just in time, or if we take the Metro we will be early, and have some time to freshen up."

"This is such a lovely evening, Hannah. We should walk along the River. No need to be in a hurry." Lili's sweet, high voice had a plea in it.

And so they did, ambling along the Quai d'Orsay in the cool of the bright, spring evening, two German girls wandering in a newfound *Liberte*, and one young American company-man, wondering just how he had come to be in this place. Less than two weeks ago he had been minding his own business, working accounts for Brigham in the stodgy old city of London. Then he had watched a man die and a few minutes later had met a Jewish tailor, who somehow had persuaded him to travel to France, so that now he was strolling along the Seine with two lovely fleeing fräuleins—one in particular, the younger one with the curly hair—hair the color of, in a muted sort of Ashkenazi way, the sun now dipping below *la rive droit* behind them, between the Eiffel they had just come from and the Arc de Triomphe that he was noticing in the distance. And he was aware that now the arc of his life was somehow bending in a new direction.

She walks with her hands clasped behind her back, and a sort of rhythm, a little glide with each step, like she's pondering something pleasant or imagining herself on ice skates.

As they were approaching the Pont de l'Alma, Philip stopped abruptly. "Wait a minute. I was supposed to meet Itmar Greeneglass back there, at the Pont d'Iena., at the Exhibition. How could I forget about it?"

"It is no matter, Philip. Itmar has been delayed," said Hannah, as they halted by the bridge.

"Oh. What is the delay?" he asked.

"I don't know. We will hear more about it from Father when we arrive at the hotel," said Hannah. She shrugged her shoulders.

"Has your father talked to him? I talked to Itmar on the telephone, at about mid-morning. He had just gotten off the boat at Calais, said he would meet me at the British Pavilion."

"Well, mon ami, you met me instead, at the British Pavilion. Don't worry. We will see him in a little while at the hotel, and have dinner there. Aren't you hungry?"

"And what hotel is it?" They had checked in late last night, and he had taken a small room of his own. It was not on the same floor as the Eschens' suite.

"The Hotel d'Orleans. It is just a couple of kilometers from here. When we get to Ecole des Beaux Arts, we'll walk a few blocks south to Rue Jacob, and all will be well. We will have wine, and good French food, and Itmar will tell us what our next step away from the Third Reich will be."

"Well okay then. *C'est bien.*" They resumed the stroll, approaching the obelisk at the Place de La Concorde across the River on their left. A breeze began to blow. A strange breeze. It blew all the way from long ago, but not from far away. This sudden brisky wind came from north; it whistled along the wide expanse of La Place de La Concorde, but it was not coming from now; it was coming from long ago. The air of France had been stirring more forcefully, more wrathfully, and picking up speed from somewhere, no, not from somewhere, but from some time, some other time it was, time a time o time oh what a time it was, a time of discontent a time of overthrow a time of long ago. A time of bloody revolutionary change, a wind of anarchy and terror that had blown across this place, before Napolean had snapped a bridle onto all that French zeal in 1804, and before a constitutional monarchy had named the place *Concorde* in 1830—before all that—in 1794, just before the innocence of France had begun to splatter away, dripping onto smooth-cut stones beneath a Sainted *Guillotine* red with blood; t'was then, when the reign of Bourbon Kings had fallen at the reign of Terror, the place was called Revolution: *La Place de la Revolution*. It was a wind from 1789, and from

---1794---

"You'll soon follow me!" screamed Georges Danton, at Robespierre, as he was being hauled up to the scaffold at the center of **La Place de La Revolution***. His desperate, prophetic proclamation still carried faintly on the wind of this place, though none could hear it, except those whose search for history had taught them to detect and mysteriously remember the sound of it, the sound of the wind that now silently licked those smooth-cut stones beneath auto tires and striding shoes of Parisians and Frenchmen and their curious guests from around the upheaving world of 1937. There was something in the air, something in the stones—the blood of innocent men and women crying out from the ground, across La Place de La Concorde, across space and across time.*

Goerges Danton had given his life to the Revolution. Now the Revolution was demanding his life—every last moment of it, every last red drop of it—while his former friend, now his accuser—Maximilien Robespierre, impeccable purveyor of justice, ruthless dispenser of Nature's moral principles , self-appointed spokesman for the Supreme Being, pure fount of enlightened reason, Reason that he had said would make the Republic immortal!—sat silently in a home nearby, unable to hear Danton's prophecy being hurled through the insurrectionary wind at him.

"You'll soon follow me!" Danton shouted on April 5, 1794.

But then, alas!, on July 28, 1794, Robespierre himself, the incorruptible enforcer of revolutionary purity, did indeed follow his former comrade Georges Danton to the guillotine, after being condemned by his former co-revolutionaries for opposing the people of La France, even as Georges had been condemned. And then Maximilien, whose Reason and Principles were as pure as the royal blood of kings and queens, was trundled like the Queen, the very same Queen that his Committee had convicted, in utter humiliation, while enduring not only the taunts of the rabble but also the miserable pain of a gunshot wound, from the Conciergerie, and all this had happened in 1794,in spite of the fact that:

Maximilien Robespierre had observed, after attempting to extract new Republican religion from old bones of dead men and new blood of headless women, after the wind of their spirits had expired or blown away into the blue sky, sky blue like color of Max's vest beneath the frock coat as he strove to bridge the gap between La Revolution and the **Ancien Regime**, *not to mention the gap between a Supreme Being and the fickle, violent meanderings of a sans-culotte mob—after all this: Merciless Max strove religiously, oh so meticulously, to reconcile, by implementation of the bang-bang silverhammer-like sharpened steel blade, these anarchic forces of mob destructivity with the vengeful gods of Nature's ungodly chaos, somehow coercing them into a Reasonable course of action by which the people of France might proclaim for themselves and for all mankind hereafter a heavenly Republic on earth, to, once and for all, establish* **la liberte, egalite, et fraternite**.

---1937---

"Room 105, North Tower?" Hezekin Eschen asked the hotel clerk.

"No shower, monsieur," said the clerk, raising his voice slightly to be heard. "There is no shower in room 105. If you wish to have a shower, the cost will be five francs more, for the small suite at the end of the hall, room 111."

"I will take that suite please, number 111," said Hezekin. "If you please . . . to make the arrangements." The family had checked in hurriedly, late, the night before, and accepted a small room in which the two daughters and their parents were cramped and without privacy.

"Where is Mr. Greeneglass?" asked Lili, gently tugging her father's sleeve. She, Hannah and Philip had just walked into the Hotel d'Orleans.

Hezekin looked quizzically at his daughter. "That is something we need to talk about. But first, we are moving to a better room. Please collect your bags and take them to room 111, at the end of the hall."

"But have you heard from him?"

"No. Do as I said. We are going to settle into room 111. Then we will have dinner and talk about it."

"Where will we have dinner?"

"I do not know, Lili. Ask your mother. She is in the room, the room we had last night, 122, packing so that we can move. Please go and help her? Make yourself useful instead asking so many questions."

"I found a restaurant where we can have dinner. It is just up the street, on the corner at Rue Bonaparte. They say it is reasonably priced."

"Tell your mother."

A few minutes later Lili had located her mother, who had commissioned the assistance of a bellhop to move their luggage. They were unpacking in room 111 when she suggested the nearby restaurant for dinner.

"What is the name of it?" asked Helene.

"Le Pre aux Clercs."

"Is it kosher?"

"Well, no. . . I, I don't know. We can inquire when we. . .this is France. We are not in Germany now. I am sure there will be no difficulty in finding kosher food."

"Perhaps, and for that reason, I have already made arrangements for us to meet some people for dinner who can assure that the food is acceptable."

"Oh, mother. . . who are they?"

"Raymond Berrot, a friend of Itmar. I have talked to him on the telephone. He and his wife, and their daughter have agreed to meet us. They live here in Paris. They will be coming here in a few minutes in their car. Monsieur Berrot has selected a restaurant for our dinner."

"This man is a friend of Itmar?"

"I think so, yes, or he is an associate of some kind. Itmar mentioned his name to me in relation to an organization."

"What organization? and. . .where is Itmar, anyway?"

"I don't know where Itmar is. We have not heard from him since I spoke to him on the telephone this morning. He had just arrived at Calais, and was waiting for the train."

"He said he would meet us here this afternoon, or perhaps somewhere else. He was not sure."

"And you still have not heard from him?"

"Perhaps Monsieur Berrot knows where he is."

"I certainly hope so. It seems a little strange to be meeting these people without Itmar being there."

"The world itself is strange, Lili. We need to prepare ourselves. From now on, it seems we will be crossing one unfamiliar bridge after another, to arrive at a destination that is yet to be determined."

"And what is the organization that Itmar mentioned?"

"He called it the. . .some letters. . .ICA, I think it was."

"What does that stand for?"

"I don't remember. Monsieur Berrot mentioned the name."

"Jewish Colonization Association," said Hezekin, who had just walked into the room.

"What does the 'I' stand for, Father?"

"I suppose it stands for Israel. Itmar has spoken of this before, but I never paid much attention, until now. He has been a member of it for a long time. It is based in London, and it is for people just like us."

"Jews, like us."

"Jews who are looking for a way out."

"A way out of Germany."

"Yes, my dear Lili, but not just Germany. I think the ICA has worked in Russia, and a few other places, Lithuania."

"We should have listened to what Itmar had to say about this ICA, before they took Heinrich," said Helene, her voice trailing into bitter disappointment, and her eyes bequeathing tears.

"Oh, mama." Lili wrapped arms around her mother, rocking her in a slow embrace. After a few moments, while still holding Helene, Lili turned her eyes to her father. "Monsieur Berrot's daughter, what is her name?"

Her mother responded. "Her name is Helene." She gently pried herself away from Lili's tenderness, walked to the window and sat on a cabinet-seat beneath the window. She looked out at Rue Jacob below. It was dark now, but stirrings of conversation on the sidewalk below, and traffic, could be heard through the open window.

"Helene, like yours?"

"Yes."

"I wonder how old she is."

"I think she is about your age, or a little older. She is a violinist, studying at the Sorbonne."

"Ah, when will they be here?"

"Soon. Seven o'clock."

"Can Philip come with us?"

"Oh yes," said Mother. "I have already invited him. Philip is our resident expert on America. I am hoping he will accompany us to the Embassy tomorrow morning. He may be able to help us get through the application process for obtaining visas."

"Do we have an appointment?"

"No. The woman I spoke to on the telephone—a Mrs. Deegan—said they do not make appointments for new applicants. She said to come after nine o'clock. She is the receptionist, and will direct us to the proper official."

"Mother, where is the American Embassy?"

"It is on the Place de La Concorde, at the far end of it."

"Oh, I wanted to walk over there this afternoon. We were walking along the River, on this side, and went by it. I wanted to walk over the bridge to see the obelisk, but Hannah said we did not have time enough to go there."

"We will go there in the morning, first thing. And I hope we will find a good reception at the American Embassy."

"Are you sure we will go America? I thought Itmar would be making arrangements for us to go to London."

"We may travel through London. I do believe that Itmar would like to have us in London, in his synagogue there, and we already have transit visas for London. We shall see how it develops. But cousin Herschel, in New York, has already acquired some professional associations for your father there. He may have even obtained a job for your father, at a deli in a place called the Lower East Side."

Hannah walked into the room. "The Berrots are here. They have a car, but I do not think there is room for all of us to ride in it."

"Oh, mother, Philip and I will meet you at the restaurant."

"You do not even know where the restaurant is."

"It is not far from here, mother. Madame Berrot has said that the walk to it is only half an hour or so. We will have to wait a while for our food anyway. And she said that their daughter, Helene, would accompany us there. She dines at Les Deux Magots occasionally anyway."

"So you would like to walk with Helene, and Lili and Philip?"

"Oh, yes, Mother." She offered a big smile. It will be fun. You will ride comfortably in the back seat, and visit with Monsieur and Madame Berrot, while we walk to Les Deux Magots, and Helene introduces us to the Latin Quarter."

"I suppose, with the car, that is our only choice," said Mother.

"Now we have a guide for Paris!" Lili exclaimed.

But when Lili met their "guide" a few minutes later, her evening's celebratory prospects became strangely obscured. It was because of a visual presence, a sight of some prophetic realm. She saw, or thought she saw, a small thing hanging surreally, ghostly, on Helene's left shoulder—a stitchy yellow hallucination—of implacable identity, about the size of a person's hand. It appeared angular and sharp, although from Lili's vantage, unfocused—a starry, post-impressionist spectre of indeterminate distress. But then momentarily it was gone, leaving the clueless fräulein confused.

But then the spell was dispensed when tall mademoiselle, her brown-haired head slightly bowed, parted her lips to offer a smile and a greeting. "Bonsoir, je suis Helene Berrot. Comment ca va?" she said, with perfectly normal Gallic courtesy. Her brown, doe-eyed simplicity bespoke kindness, and the stitchy yellow illusion disappeared, if ever it was even there.

Lili's unexpected visual made her feel disoriented; she could feel her head wagging, in an involuntary sort of denial, though she had nothing to deny. "Je. . .je. . .ca va bien," she must have mumbled.

16

Babylon

Itmar Greeneglass had been waiting outside the train station in Calais for ten minutes when his plans were rather interrupted..

He was expecting, based on arrangements he had made while still in England, to be picked up at the curb by an ICA contact person, a man named Jacob Bruchis. He had never met Jacob, although they had corresponded, beginning a few weeks ago, by letters, and on the telephone twice. Mr. Bruchis had described himself as heavy-set, with black curly hair. He would be driving a blue Citroen.

A clocktower across the way was chiming twelve low gongs to announce noon when a blue Renault drove up and stopped at the curb in front of Itmar. A tall man with slick, dark hair got out from the back seat, driver's side. He walked quickly around the back of the car and approached Itmar, extending his hand in what appeared to be a helpful gesture. "I can help you with that suitcase, Monsieur Greeneglass."

Itmar looked carefully at the man; then he stooped to get a view of the driver. Neither man resembled the self-description that Jacob had provided. "Who are you?" asked Itmar, in an authoritative voice.

"I am Victor. I am here to help you." He had a deep voice, but eyes unable to convince.

"Victor who?"

"Victor Doriot. You may be seated in the front seat, if you prefer." He opened the front door of the Renault.

"No thank you. I will wait here," said Itmar, resolutely. His expectations about Mr. Bruchis' welcome were not being met.

"It is no trouble, monsieur. We will be happy to take you." The man straightened himself, and smiled.

"Who sent you?"

"Mr. Bruchis sent us, sir," said the driver, in a Flemish accent.

Itmar bent slightly, to get a view of the driver's face. He was a pale man, with blonde hair. His hands looked large, and freckled, on the steering wheel. "Where is he?" demanded Itmar. "I was expecting to be picked up by Mr. Bruchis himself."

"He has been delayed," said the driver.

"I am sorry to disappoint you, sir. I must decline your offer. Thank you, and I wish you a good day." Itmar clutched his briefcase in the left hand and small suitcase in the right, turned on his heel and began walking away.

Glancing over his shoulder once or twice, he moved quickly back to the station. Reaching the steps in front, Itmar's last glance to the street revealed that the car had gone away. Entering the cavernous depot again, he was left wondering what to make of this dubious reception that had culminated in his refusal to be transported. Had he made a mistake?

Could this envoy have been a legitimate effort by Jacob, having been actually delayed, to retrieve him according to their pre-arranged schedule? Had his crossing the Channel, thus forsaking the peace and security of merry old England, infected him with an Englishman's distrust for the unpredictable ambiguities of *La France*? Had this new encounter with Continental uncertainties provoked within him a visitation from the ghost of Paranoia? These questions were racing through Itmar's mind while he vacantly watched French people, so fetchingly dressed and coiffed, going to and from in the station, and for a moment he could hardly remember where he was or why he had crossed over to this god-forsaken Frankish nation to deliver, probably to no avail, his ancient people from their latest imbroglio in the belly of the heathen beast. . . from Teuton hinterlands beyond French borders, in Bavaria or Berlin or Bergen-Belsen or wherever the hell they were coming from.

And he suddenly remembered the terrible dream he had had last night, of a freight-train out of control, colliding headlong into a stranded caboose, blasting the little red car aside, smashing it to smithereens as if it were a child's plaything, and then the huffy engine with its heavy load barreling forward, belching steam, hellbound, as if nothing had happened.

But now he found himself holding a telephone.

184

"Monsieur, il n'y a aucune reponse a ce numero," came the operator's voice through the earpiece. But Itmar didn't hear her; he was distracted. Hanging on the edge of their seats, in front of him, two lovers were affectionately, very lovingly, saying their goodbyes as the man prepared to depart to the *quai* outside.

I left Miriam and my children for this? "What? Repitez s'il vous plait."

"Il n'y a aucune reponse, Monsieur," she said, patiently.

What now? "Merci." He hung the earpiece and looked around. *I've got to get out of here.* But where to? *Paris. Go to Paris. Rendezvous with the Eschens, and with Philip. They are waiting for you anyway. You have transit visas for England that they will need. You have information from New York.* But what about Jacob? I've got to talk to Jacob. We've got to make plans. We must exchange information. I have visas for his people. *Where the hell is Jacob?* Call Jacob when you get to Paris, and arrange to meet later, on the return trip. *Why will he not answer to telephone? Who were those men outside who tried to get me?* Surely I have made a mistake in sending them away. Will they come back? How will I know if they return?

Dazed, Itmar walked outside again. Clouds were gathering. In the distance, lightning flashed. He felt a drop of rain. No blue Renault. No blue Citroen.

A few minutes later, "Un billet pour Paris s'il vous plait, Monsieur," he requested, and paid for it.

"Le depart du train dans quarante-cinq minutes, Monsieur. Nombre a trios voies."

"Merci." Itmar wandered into the restaurant, ordered a glass of burgundy, a small Caesar salad and a baguette. *Perhaps Jacob will show up here while I am waiting.* He seated himself near the door, with a view into the waiting room. Rain was falling outside. He could feel the cool, damp breeze blowing in through the main entry.

Forty minutes later, he was standing at Track 3, awaiting the Paris train. The rain had ceased, although the clouds persisted. Drops of water were rolling slowly down from everywhere. His position at Track 3 was remote, with three tracks separating him from the main depot. Sitting on a wooden bench with briefcase and suitcase next to him, Itmar was idly watching a man on the far side, three tracks away, whose clothes were entirely black, like the damned blackshirts in London, with black military hat that displayed an unfamiliar insignia, something like a cross, but not exactly a religious symbol, when suddenly a darker figure passed directly in front of him in a flurry of motion and before he knew what was happening the man had grabbed his briefcase and was escaping with it, running at full speed. Having no time to think, Itmar leaped to his feet and began pursuit, leaving the suitcase, and probably the train due to arrive in seven minutes, behind.

The dark man made an abrupt turn left, disappearing into a stairway. Itmar, shaken and furious, was falling behind, running a full five or six seconds after him. Itmar darted into the stairway, down to a landing halfway, turning ninety degrees and descending further to a pedestrian crosspoint. On the right was a lighted tunnel leading under the tracks. To the left was a train yard with more tracks, a few random carriages at the ends, and straight ahead of him four pairs of tracks, punctuated with gravel, smelling of diesel, at the far end of which was the running man, and Itmar's briefcase in his hand. The thief made an abrupt right turn just beyond a caboose attached to what appeared to be an intact freight train. Itmar continued his pursuit, although he was falling further behind, as the man's pace was much speedier than what Itmar could muster. After catching a glimpse of the intruder's profile, Itmar seemed quite sure it was the man who had emerged from the back seat of the Renault at the curb in front of the Calais station at noon.

When he reached the caboose and train where the dark man had changed direction, Itmar careened likewise and persisted in his chase, beginning now to exhaust himself and feeling his lungs protest in painful, ill-prepared response to the demands of such panic-driven rigor. And although his lungs were crying for relief, his heart was working overtime. After a fifty-or-so meter torture run alongside the freight cars at his full speed, he had to stop before the pain in his lungs became unbearable. He halted, gasping, bent over, yearning for recovery from the unexpected ordeal. After a minute's panting or so, he straightened himself, looked ahead. As far as the eye could see, a train was on each side of him extending to some indeterminable point and he was worn out, busted, broken, bleeding where his hand had struck some metal object and then a noise came from behind and he turned and there were two of them, one in brown the other in black and he saw something moving at his head from the side, then the sudden thuddy impact, smell of trouble in his nostrils and taste of blood.

Itmar awoke in the darkness, his head splitting in pain. He could feel beneath him a bed of old, flattened filthy straw, and he was immersed in the smells of manure and blood. Two thin, vertical slivers of faint night sky were visible on his left side, and everything was vibrating with the rattly rhythm of the cattle train as it moved along track into the French nocturnal darkness, although *Clair de lune* it was not.

```
```

"This is not new. Germans have always been cruel and oppressive like that," said Helene Berrot, as they strolled on Rue Bonaparte. Hannah and Lili were explaining to her why they had fled from their home in Germany.

"But we are Germans too," objected Hannah.

"You are Jews, like us," was Helene's retort. "There is a big difference between a Jew and a German."

"Permettez-moi de vous poser une question, Helene," Hannah requested.

"Allez-y. Je suis a l'ecoute."

"Etes-vous francais?"

"Oui."

"So, mon ami, you can be French and Jewish at the same time?" Hannah asked, with a wry smile.

"Oui."

"And I cannot be German and Jewish at the same time?"

"You do not want to be. German is not something you want to be."

"I was born in Germany, in 1912. What does that make me?" Hannah asked.

Helene guided them into a right turn as they came to Boulevard Saint-Germain, and she said, "It makes you a Jewish girl born in Germany in 1912, but your citizenship is in your people, not the country of your birth. You are like . . . Esther, in Persia. You are like Daniel in Babylon. It is good that you have left Germany; it is for the best that your family will settle somewhere else, and I do recommend France."

Hannah was laughing, but through a tear or two. "Why would I want to do that? Are we to wander into a wider world, where Germany is forsaken, dismissed as a haven—or, a hell—for Jew-hating goyim to have a field day? No! My brother is, has been, the target of their Gestapo sport. We cannot just write off our Heinrich! We cannot leave him for. . ." Her strange laughter had been but brief; it had been snuffed out by deeper rumblings. "We cannot leave him for dead."

But they had left. Heinrich was still there, his status, living or dead, still unknown. That was the cold hard truth of it. The Eschens had seen the writing on the wall, and had decidedly fled, so that the four of them would not be taken by a similar fate, whatever that was.

"I am not trying to insult you, Hannah. I am serious when I say that there is something wrong with Germany, something wrong. . .in the land of your birth. The Germans—they glorify violence; they are prideful, and yet they are morosely melancholy, brooding and moody as they try to assert themselves above everybody else in Europe. Germans are no better than the rest of us."

"You, then, are allowed to be French—to identify with France, while I must reject my birthright as a citizen of Germany?"

"Why would you want to retain any German identity with all that is happening there?—and the injustice with which your family has been mistreated. It is a pogrom, plain and simple. Here in France, we. . .we have a constitution that assures all people equal citizenship. That is the legal difference. There are other differences, cultural ones. *La France* does not persecute Jewish people, or any other people. I am sorry to make such a comparison with your country, but it is the truth, and the sooner you can overcome this . . .this grief, or whatever it is, about leaving Germany, the better off you and your family will be." Helene halted and looked directly into Hannah's eyes; she offered a gentle smile. "Honestly, I do not wish to insult you. You are in France now; you can make a new beginning."

Hannah was considering all that Helene had said. "All I can say at this point is that Germany was not like this until the Nazis took over the government four years ago."

"You are both right," Philip interjected. They had stopped at the restaurant, and the two girls, at a sudden loss to find agreement, were intent on what the American had to say. "The Germans have always been, generally, contentious and militaristic. But since the Nazis have taken over, there is something much deeper—much more oppressive going on there, in the country of your birth, Hannah." He looked at her carefully. "I can see this whole ordeal of emigration has been hard for you." Philip glanced at Helene, intending to evoke some empathy from her. "This family, Helene, has endured terrible loss—a traumatic displacement, and much confusion—and, tears. Many tears they have shed since leaving Munich, which was home for Hannah and Lili, all their lives."

Lili, slightly apart, was willing to be distracted; she was looking through glass into the foyer of *Les Deux Magots*, and could see, mounted high on a column inside, the two Chinese figurines that had contributed to the restaurant's reputation as a gathering point for free-thinking people of the world. The place was crowded, inside and out.

"We are to meet my parents here," said Helene.

"C'est bien," said Philip. "Nous ne sommes pas presses. C'est une belle soiree a Paris."

Helene understood the need to soften her assessment of the Eschens' predicament. "Ecoutez, s'il vous plait. I can see that my own French pride has distorted what I am trying to say. This is no time for me to be judgmental. I am, you see, a student at the Sorbonne. Just this morning, I was practicing a Beethoven string quartet with my colleagues. I should not neglect there is a great contribution from Germany in music—Bach, and Schubert, and not only that—in literature, Goethe, and Schiller, and in science."

"Not all Germans are so terrible. There are bad people everywhere in the world. God know we have some real doozies of wickedness back in the US," said Philip.

"Oh? Who is so bad in the USA?" Helene asked him.

"Well, there is. . .Al Capone, John Dillinger, and . . ." Philip pulled out his packet of Bullseyes and lit one. "Care for a smoke?"

While the older two girls declined, Lili said, "I would like one," while her sister frowned. Lili retrieved, rather awkwardly, a cigarette from Philip's proffered packet.

"This is how I make my living, by the way," said Philip.

"Oh, I will have one, s'il vous plait," Helene said.

"Sure," he offered.

"Well that is one bad thing about America," chided Hannah. ". . .all the cigarettes you send over here."

"All over the world—right, Hannah. Cigarettes are all over the world, but they are not all American, not even half of them, and we do get our share of the business." He smiled the salesman's smile, slightly less authentic than his previous inputs to their cameraderie.

"I do like the smell of pipe tobacco," Hannah conceded.

"We sell plenty of that too."

"Cigarettes were invented in America, weren't they?"

Philip laughed heartily. "Ha! No way—why, men rolling herbs and leaves up to smoke 'em is probably as old as Methuselah. But we Americans did invent the mass production of them. In fact, the first cigarette manufacturing machines were cranked up in my home state of North Carolina over fifty years ago. My company devised it—well, not my company exactly. Teddy Roosevelt busted up Mr. Duke's tobacco trust in 1908, I think it was. The manufacture of cigarettes was first developed for profit by the grandfather of the man I work for."

"And who do you work for?" asked Helene.

"The company, mademoiselle, that made that Bullseye you're enjoying—Brigham Tobacco Company of North Carolina, USA. As I said, the company has been busted up by the Feds because it got too big for its britches—"

"Too big for britches?" Lili interjected, laughing.

"Uh, too big for—it was a monopoly. Americans don't like anyone taking control over an entire industry, or an entire. . . anything, for that matter. . . the government. We could never have, for instance, a Hitler, or a Mussolini. Americans just don't put up with that kind of tyranny." He looked at Hannah with a curious intensity. "You and your family should come to America," he said to her. "You might just forget about all this European. . . trouble." He offered a jocular smile, an innocent sort of American awshucks shrug.

Hannah was studying him. Lili said, "I think we should go to America." She laughed.

"Father and Mother may decide that we should go to Palestine," said Hannah.

"You do not want to go there," Helene asserted. "There is as much trouble there as in Germany now. My parents know people who have gone there recently, not only from Germany, but from France, as well, and Russia. Lots of Russian Jews are moving there. But last year the Arabs rioted because so many of us are going into Palestine. So many, that they are exceeding the quotas that the British will allow."

"You could be safe in America," said Philip.

"Or, Father and Mother may choose England. That's where our cousin Itmar lives. He is a tailor in London, with many associations, not only with Jews, but also among prosperous British gentlemen, and their companies," Hannah explained.

"I don't think we will be settling in England," said Lili, with a buoyant sort of confidence.

"Oh, why not?" her sister queried.

"I don't know, exactly. . .England is old and rusty, like . . .like Germany. But the United States is the future."

"Land of the free, and home of the brave," Philip added, smiling, a lighthearted advocacy.

At that moment, a shiny gray Peugeot stopped at the curb in front of them. Helene, recognizing the car as her father's, walked to their car-window, with the other three behind. She began speaking with her mother. The Eschen parents were in the back seat, and so their daughters peered in, watching their faces as they listened to what Madame Berrot was saying. She placed a considerable sum of francs into her daughter's hand, with some instructions.

"Helene, take this and go inside the restaurant. Have dinner, and enjoy yourselves. We will meet you later at the hotel."

"Will you not be having dinner with us? Surely you are hungry. It is almost nine o'clock."

But something was wrong. Helene could see it in her mother's eyes, and in her father's also, as she glanced furtively at him. Something was disturbing them. "It is necessary that we make other arrangements for dinner," said her mother, looking so worried.

"What is it Mama? What is the matter? What. . . where is Monsieur Greeneglass?"

"We are going to fetch him now. He called the hotel just as the Eschens were preparing to leave."

"But where is he? Has something happened?"

"He will be alright. We are going to the Metro now to get him."

"The Metro? Which station?"

"He is at La Gare Sevres-Babylone, waiting now for us."

Monsieur Berrot, in the driver seat, leaned toward his daughter at the passenger window. "Helene, Itmar is waiting for us now; we must go, and we will explain later. It is too much to explain now."

"But why was he delayed? Why would he be—"

"His train from Calais came in at Drancy. It was not. . . ah,. he managed to get on the Metro and get to Sevres-Babylon."

"It was not—what?" Helene's curiosity was unrelenting.

"It was not a passenger train. Helene, step back to the curb. We will explain later when we get back to the hotel. Comprens tu?"

Helene reluctantly complied with her father's uncharacteristically blunt command. The Peugeot eased into Saint-Germain traffic. She peered after her parents' car as it pulled away, heading west toward La Gare Sevres-Babylone to retrieve their English friend. *Pourquoi* this sudden change of plans, and the trouble in their parents' faces she did not know. "At least he has made it to Paris," she mumbled.

"What?" Hannah barked. "Has something happened?"

"The Metro is just up this boulevard, a kilometer away. Monsieur Greeneglass is there. But it doesn't make sense. Why would he have arrived at the Drancy station, and 'not on a passenger train'?"

The four young people prepared to enter the restaurant and, at last, have dinner, although the cloud of tension accompanying this news was diminishing their appetite somewhat. "I'll get us a bottle of Burgundy," said Philip, a little too brightly.

A while later, they were sitting at two small tables in the restaurant, swilling wine, awaiting food. Lili sat across from Philip. His attention was divided between her youthful face, framed in golden curls, aglow with curious beauty, and a framed picture on the wall , which was behind and to the left of her seat. It was an impressionist painting, a dappled smattering of what appeared to be a swathe of red poppies in a field of green, beneath blue sky. Distantly high on the horizon, a single, rounded tree was silhouetted against the clear, bright heavens with a few billowing white cumulus clouds strewn randomly above. The small figure of a person stood near, but apart from, the tree, with arms slightly upraised. Near to the person, but up in the air, the artist had brush-stroked the miniscule suggestion of a high yellow kite, which seemed to be nearer in the artist's perspective than the figure who had released it.

Seeing this artwork on the wall reminded Philip of a poem he had encountered in a magazine before leaving the States, and he wanted to remember the poem but he couldn't, so he pulled out his little notebook and wrote one of his own:

> In Flanders Field Roby Morrow was laid low,
> his voluntary body being compelled to go
> beneath the stinging swathe
> of a German bullet's whistling path;
> that rifl'd wrath had wrought its fatal woe,
> nineteen years ago.

At age eight, Philip's grandmother had told him of his father's distant death, somewhere over there, over there, in a place called Flanders Field. He could remember the memorial service in their hometown Baptist church back home. His mother, clothed in black, was weeping, though she held one hand of his younger sister, with her other hand tightly clutching his. His older brother stood on the other side of him, apart and irate.

Perhaps it was the memory of his father's fatal Flanders date with a bullet that was now compelling him thus far into such an unchartable European odyssey. In a roundabout way, he had been steadily sojourning, since entering France way down south just below the border with Spain, northward toward a battlefield in Belgium where Pa had given his last full measure of devotion.

Philip was wondering what improvements that war's legacy had enforced upon this terrible, torn-up world since that day of his father's demise in 1918. But out of the corner of his eyee he saw Itmar Greeneglass, oddly disfigured, enter the restaurant, accompanied by the Eschens and the Berrots.

Itmar's left eye was swollen, ugly and blackened. His left jaw was swathed in a white bandage, and another bandage clung to the top of his head where his yarmulke belonged. His grey suit, sans tie, and disheveled as if he had just retrieved it from a suitcase, was not what a London tailor would be expected to wear in a Paris café.

Philip stood and greeted with a handshake the man who had convinced him to come to France on a very unusual errand. But as they clasped hands, Itmar drew him into a tight, enduring hug. Philip could almost feel, in his embrace, a release of some tension or angst that must have accumulated during Itmar's as-yet-unexplained ordeal.

While everybody was standing and greeting, an alert waiter moved tables into a suitable arrangement so that the eight of them could dine together. The waiter then spread one long, white tablecloth on the assembled surface and began distributing glasses and silverware. While this was being done, Itmar wasted no time in choosing a spot on the wall-seat by sliding himself, somewhat painfully. on the long cushion, into a position at the middle of the table. Then after waving off a host of questions from the three youngsters who had not gone to retrieve him at la gare, he breathed a heavy sigh and said:

"As you may have surmised, crossing the Channel has proven to be almost fatal for me. God only knows what perils await us should we ever attempt to cross the Rhine."

This was a curious thing to say. "Are you. . . are you intending to cross the Rhine?" asked Philip.

A hint of a smile crossed Itmar's swollen lips, He glanced at Hezekin, as if he had already answered such a question. "No. I have no such plans at this time. But of course, Philip, our friends here. . ." He nodded lightly toward the Eschens. ". . . have just come from there, the far side of the Rhine. And Heinrich, whose condition is still unknown, has not managed to, as was mentioned, 'cross the Rhine.' For all we know, he has not even been able to cross the barbed fence of Dachau prison. Furthermore, since my reception at Calais was met—not by the ICA person I was expecting—but by two unidentified criminals who grabbed my briefcase and then hit me over the head and threw me onto a cattle train, this may be a painfully bad omen that whatever malignancy has taken hold of Germany may now be extending into La France."

The waiter, stretching in unwaiterly fashion across the table, set a goblet in front of Itmar and poured it half-full of the Burgundy. Itmar promptly raised his. Announcing, "La chaim!" he took a healthy gulp. "Excuse me for not waiting for you, but this is the first moment of anything like normalcy that I have had since putting my feet on this Continent however many-odd hours or days ago, and I am grateful to be alive and to be able to celebrate it with you." Eyeing Philip through the glass, he then took another gulp. "Mazel tov!"

"Have you been able to telephone your wife?" asked Helene Eschen.

"I did manage to send Miriam a telegram when I got to Drancy. Then she telephoned me at Le Bourget. Of course she was upset when I told her that I had been assaulted, but we had anticipated that eventually something like this might happen, since I have become more involved with this refugee work—it has become a flood!—of our people from Germany. Nevertheless," he waved his hand casually—"she reported that our children, Oliver and Emma, are well. Their tender lives have not been affected adversely by what I have gotten into, and hopefully never will. But who knows what snares this world is casting out to possibly entrap these young ones. May it never happen to them what—whatever it is—that has become of Heinrich. I am sorry to mention it, but. . ."

"You are doing a good work," said Raymond Berrot. "And it is a work that someone needs to take on. But it is quite troubling that you had only been here in France for an hour or two when your life was almost snuffed out. Whatever malignancy has overtaken Germany—it is apparently taking hold here."

By this time everyone had a little wine and Jacques was taking food orders. Philip was perplexedly peering across the table at the disfigured, uncharacteristically disheveled tailor, whom he had only met a few weeks ago. *Whatever it is that is happening in Europe now. . .* "Dare I ask, Itmar, what happens next?" he said, looking directly into Itmar's burdened, though zealous, eyes.

"Tomorrow we go to the American Embassy, as you and Hezekin and Helene had planned to do," he declared with unexpected simplicity, as if his near-fatal skirmish with dark assailants in a French train-yard were of no consequence. "I had not expected to accompany you there, because, had things worked out as planned, I would still be in Calais, meeting with Jacob.

But I would like to go there with you, and if possible, even meet Ambassador Bullit."

"And what is it, Monsieur Greeneglass, that you hope to accomplish there?" Raymond Berrot asked.

"I do believe that the Eschens here were intending to complete their applications for American visas. Is that still your plan, Hezekin?"

"Yes."

Philip, studying Hezekin's face, inserted, "So you have decided not to go to England?"

"It seems that, in the circumstances, our destination is not something that we can determine. Whichever country will first open the door for us—Britain or the US—we will go there. Although we will be passing through London, using our travel visas, it is more likely our destination will become the US, because we have people in New York working on our behalf. They have, in fact, deposited money for us at the State Department in Washington. I'm assuming that the Embassy staff here in Paris will confirm that deposit tomorrow."

Itmar said, "And, although I would be happy to see you reside in England, Hezekin, it is common knowledge in London that there are far more immigrants coming from Germany than we Brits can properly accommodate. We can't even keep our own people employed. We've had damn near bloody riots in East London these last few months, with the labor unions up against the blackshirts out in the very streets—at each others' throats if the Home Office would allow to cross each others' barricades. The whole East end could blow up at any minute. I daresay the Eschens would be better off in the long run to go to America. The yanks have a lot more room to expand than we do."

We've heard all this before. A thought suddenly crossed Philip's mind. "Itmar, may I ask you?"

"What?"

"What was it that was in the briefcase that was stolen from you?"

"Oh, Philip. You don't want to know."

"I asked, didn't I?"

Itmar let out a heavy sigh, and Philip could discern his pain, down low, probably in the ribs. "Names, Philip, names," he said, wincing.

"That doesn't sound good."

"It's not good. Many of our contact people on this side are now in jeopardy."

"Who do think those two that assaulted you are? Do you have any idea?"

"Actually, Philip, I think it was the same two who had earlier tried to trick me into getting into their car in front of la gare. They presented themselves as having been sent by Jacob Bruchis. But the little bit of what they did and said in that minute or two put red flags in my mind. First of all, I was expecting Jacob himself. He had assured me he would not be sending someone to get me."

"So you talked to them?"

"I did, very briefly. One of them might have been a Frenchman, but I'm quite sure the other—the driver—was Dutch, or perhaps Flemish."

"And now these men have a list of all the people with whom you would be meeting in France?"

"So it seems, Philip, so it seems." This last reminder of the danger now probably imposed on Itmar's French connections made him visibly nervous. "Oh, Jacques," he called to the waiter, raising his glass, "I'll have some more of this."

"You have no clue, then, who they are?" asked Monsieur Berrot?

"Itmar shrugged his shoulders. His bright, brown eyes laden with heavy brows expressed something between alarm and untempered recklessness. "I don't know. Fascists. They are everywhere now!, all over the Continent since Hitler absconded the German government from its own people. Everywhere—Franco attacking his own government from Morocco, Mussolini muscling into power in Rome, and then attacking Abyssinia. And I know they're all over England. The communists and the fascists are practically fighting each other for public displays of labor support. The working blokes in London are just grist for their mills. In France, behind the woodwork—you know they're here, Monsieur Berrot—the *Doriotistes*, *Action Francaise*, *Croix de Feu*. Maybe those guys that beat me are Action Francaise, sent to intercept me. Who knows? The Nazis are probably so organized now all over, they can probably just make telephone calls to their henchman in whatever country, anywhere between Gibraltar and Berlin, and dispatch them to intercept whatever unsuspecting Jews or Socialists, or even democrats who are trying to force a breach in their wehrmacht fortress."

"The Bolshevists are doing the same thing from the other side, from Moscow. You know that, don't you?" Raymond responded.

"Tell me about it!" Itmar erupted. "The Communists are what's got the bluebloods, and the businessmen, in Britain all up in arms. Half of them are ready to shred the Versailles treaty, thinking that Hitler will build a wall between them and the Russians, who seem to have their eyes on Poland and the Czech Republic."

"Ah, but if they only knew! the sinister nature behind what Hitler and the Nazis are doing in their own country, they would not be so willing to lend support to them," said Hezekin.

"They don't care. All they are interested in is their damned money, and their trade routes. Why do you suppose they looked the other way while Mussolini blustered his way into Ethiopia? They don't want the Africans, or the Arabs, getting any ideas about administering the Suez. They would rather let Il Duce be the big kid on the block down there in the straits of Suez, because he is European, and even though he's a greasy Italian, they still speak the same European language of money and state power. No, the money men in London don't want the colonials getting ideas about independence or control of the Indian Ocean. The bankers! The Bank of England is lending money to the Third Reich, because Stalin's soviets aren't even interested in money—or they don't seem to be—Stalin's goons are drunk on power, while capitalists in London are drunk on money!"

Jacques was serving food around the table now. But the salad with Roquefort had no effect on Itmar's discourse, now becoming a rant.

"Let me tell you something. I have a friend—that is to say, I **had** a dear friend, Paul Wallris, now deceased—who had partnered with one of the bluebloods, Lord Afton—to run an international shipping company. They were delivering goods all over the world, in both directions, British manufactured goods going out, and colonial commodities coming back in. My friend Paul, a good man who had worked his way up to ownership from the docks, was allowing his own ships to send humanitarian aid—food, fuel and clothes—to the peasants in Spain because Franco was trying to starve them out and the Madrid government couldn't do any damn thing right. But then my friend Paul up and died—Philip was there when it happened, and that was the day we met—Paul collapsed right on the street the day King George was crowned, and as soon his wife and daughters had laid him in the ground, Afton cut off the aid to the working people of Spain, and the MPs in Westminster assisted him with their so-called non-intervention blockade. But then—even after Hitler sent his new, under-the-Versailles-radar planes with their incendiary thermite bombs to drop hell-on-earth on the Basque village of Guernica, so the Luftwaffe could have a practice run before tuning up their sights to assault a more important target—Prague, or London, or even right here in Paris. . ."

17

Pearl

Cyrus, the Pershing rifleman, had spoken boldly to his friend and fellow-soldier, Clint Morrow, as they crouched ankle deep in Scheldt River mud during the Great War, back in October 1918. He told Roby that the damned Germans had camped along the Marne, only forty miles from Paris, long enough, and that now the time had come to drive their kraut asses back through the Hindenberg line and back across the Meuse River and the Belgian border and the German border beyond that. And so that's what the Allied armies, with much blood, sweat, tears, and bombs and bullets, had done.

But it was a terribly dear campaign, because Cyrus and Clint and thousands of other American boys and Frenchmen and British soldiers had expended not only their blood sweat and tears in the forests of France and the fields of Flanders and God-only-knows what other entrenched battlefields, but they had ultimately paid the dearest price of all. They had secured the victory with their own last full measure of devotion, and so now in 1937 the two of them and all the other fallen doughboys were forever reposed in the cold, mudded fields of Europe.

This is what Philip thought of when Itmar told him that there was a very precious delivery to be made, and he requested that Philip deliver it, but that he would have to go up north to the city of Lille to do it. And so Philip had thought of his father and his father's combat buddy Cyrus because they were laying in the earth in Flanders field, from whence they had never returned, somewhere in Belgium, just beyond the French city of Lille, where Itmar was now asking him to go.

"What is this 'precious' item to be delivered?" Philip asked Itmar as the two of them were sitting in the lobby of the Hotel d'Orleans.

"This pearl was taken from the home of a French family in 1917, and you will be returning it to the rightful owner," replied Itmar, in a low voice. He carefully opened a small, black ringbox to reveal a rather large, pinkish pearl. As Philip gazed at the lustrous orb, thinking that it was such a strange object to behold unexpectedly in a Paris hotel lobby, he found himself laughing.

"Well, uh, whose is it?" asked Philip.

"It was stolen from a woman named Magda Bruchis, who was then living here in Paris. But since she has died, you will return it, if you choose to do so, to her son, a man named Jacob Bruchis. He is the one with whom I was to rendezvous at Calais if I had not been assaulted there."

"And you said he is in Lille?"

"Yes. He lives there."

"Have you been able to contact him at all?"

"No. My last communication with him was by telegram a few days ago when I was still in London. We had agreed that he would meet me outside the train station in Calais, but then these other men were there instead, claiming to have been sent by him."

"Why would those men have done that?"

"Well apparently, Philip, because they wanted to beat the hell out of me. I don't know why they didn't just finish me off. When I woke up inside a moving cattle car, and it was night, and. . .I . . . I don't know. I think their rough treatment of me must have been interrupted. Maybe they had to stow me somewhere so they would not be discovered in the act. But the result is that I landed here prematurely. Of course, I had intended to join you here, but not before tending to a few matters up there in Calais, this delivery to Jacob being one of them. So, since I know you are headed in that direction— you're planning to take the ferry to Dover, and then on to London—right?"

"Yes, eventually, but I have assured the Eschens that I would accompany them to the American embassy tomorrow, to be an advocate for them, when they apply for a visa there."

"I see. What time is that? Do they have an appointment?"

"Two o'clock. But beyond that, Itmar, I am in no hurry to get back to London. I have rather enjoyed spending time with the Eschens, getting to know them and . . ."

"One in particular, eh? the younger sister, Lili." A smile turned the corners of Itmar's lips upward. The corners of his brown eyes wrinkled with a mischievous glee.

Philip felt himself returning the smile. He shrugged.

"What about your business, your accounts and so forth?"

"Yes, well, it is about time that I should get back to working. I did arrange with my company for a few weeks of leave. But that's another thing—my sales manager has asked me to call on two companies while I am here in Paris. That's another two items on my list before leaving here, so it may be a few more days before I head north. And then there's the Belgian leg of my trip. I cannot pass so close to Belgium without finding the battlefield where my father was killed in 1918."

"Of course. Where is that?"

"A place called Flanders Field."

"Yes. Sure. That's as it should be. There is no hurry with the pearl. The pearl can wait. Jacob's family has been without it for almost twenty years now. A few more days will be of no consequence."

"How did it come into your possession?"

"It was in a trunk, in the attic of my flat, when I bought the shop on Haymarket seven years ago. There were some family pictures—ah! there's Raymond Berrot"— Itmar raised his arm and motioned to Monsieur Berrot, who had just entered the large lobby from the desk area."

The Frenchman approached them. With no seat available, he smiled and issued an invitation. "Can I interest you gentlemen in a nightcap?"

"Righto! I can't think of anything better than that to cap off such a day as this," Itmar replied as he rose from the chair.

"The bar is just over here." Raymond Berrot was a well-dressed, middle-aged man in a light gray, double-breasted suit. A dark blue silk handkerchief in the coat pocket matched his tie. There was an air of authority about him. As vice-president of a large chemical company, he was accustomed to hatching strategies for business development among the captains of French industry. And yet beneath his confident bearing, an alert sensitivity shone from bright eyes and a ready smile. As they took three comfortably padded seats at a small table, he requested three cognacs from the barman.

When they were seated, Raymond wasted no time in resuming the explanation that had begun earlier at the restaurant. "France is in dire straits," he said. He leaned back and peered, squinting slightly, at the expectant faces of the two younger men. "Our nation is being torn apart by political extremists while, at the same time, we have run out of money."

Itmar and Philip, curious, though not surprised at his blunt assessment, just sat, waiting to hear what was behind this grim news. A waiter brought cognac. Philip offered a cigar to the Frenchman. Itmar accepted a cigar, which Philip lit for him, then lit his own and inhaled the fresh smoke.

"On top of that, gentlemen," Monsieur Berrot continued, "the Germans, under Nazi authority, are turning alarmingly bellicose again. Even as they defy the Versailles agreement by undertaking a massive new program of armaments production, they seem to be systematically dispensing with the ordered legacy of legitimate German law, and replacing it with their own— which, which, by all accounts, originates mostly from the disturbed mind of Chancellor Hitler. The SS-designed constriction of Herr Eschen's business in Munich, which we heard about earlier, is not the first account I have heard of such *de facto* expropriations. Now pressure is being brought to bear, and appropriately so, upon the French government to respond in kind with new, updated defensive armaments of our own. But the Socialist government is incapable of an effective response." Raymond's sharp, urgent tone had gradually supplanted the thoughtful demeanor with which he had begun speaking. His formerly cheerful eyes had narrowed and intensified with a carefully bridled alarm. "And if that is not enough to bode some terrible trouble in the making for France, coming out of the East, the republican government of Spain on the other side of us is collapsing, just like the Socialist government here, with internal dissension and the fully-blown military revolt that Franco and his army are conducting against their own people from Morocco."

Itmar's response was as a lava-flow of heated, irate gravity. "The non-intervention pact is destroying any effective resistance to counter the fascist offensive. Every day that goes by it gets worse. Look at what happened at Guernica last month—German airplanes bombed the hell out of the place in broad daylight while both Parliaments sat around pretending their best strategy is not to get involved. And it is common knowledge that Mussolini has his fascist gladiators fighting alongside the Falangists. They'll run roughshod over the Spanish before it's all over with, as they are doing now to the Abyssinians. Both the Germans and the Italians are openly flaunting their disregard of the Versailles and Locarno treaties, and blatantly ignoring the damned non-intervention pact, while lawmakers and diplomats in London and Paris fret over the Russians because they're communists. Even worse, the banks provide credit for the German government to rebuild their illegal war machines so they will erect a wall of security against the Bolsheviks."

Itmar took a deep breath and shook his head disparagingly. "My friend Paul Wallris was trying to send supplies to the Spanish before he died, but the damned British navy were blockading the port of Bilbao, turning our own merchant ships away after threatening to fire on them!"

"It's not just a simple matter, Itmar, taking sides in this. I don't have any sympathy for the Socialist Republicans who are trying to govern Spain now. And what is worse about that situation is the Communists, with many of their leaders from Moscow, are moving in to occupy the power vacuum that develops in Madrid and Barcelona. In some ways, the French Socialists are making the same mess of things here in Paris—and my friend Leon Blum is the leader of them—but every day that goes by indicates that their disorganized mayhem could actually be the lesser evil when compared to what the Italian fascists and Hitler's Nazis are gearing up to do. If they were ever able to join forces with the French Right, France would be in serious trouble. The *Croix de Feu* and *Action Francais* are already making serious trouble, running in packs and clashing with the leftists in the street. A couple of months ago in Clichy, six people were killed in a mob confrontation between the two groups, because the leftists were out in the streets to protest fiscal retrenchment and Blum's canceling public works projects."

"Surely the French government can pluck up some resolve—some remnant of Napoleanic strength, or something—to put a stop to this," said Itmar, frustrated.

"Don't count on it, mon ami." Raymond reached over to Itmar, who now had his hands on his head in grief, and placed a hand on his shoulder. "Don't forget, it is our French government who initiated the non-intervention pact. Our Premier, Leon Blum, whose pacifist inclination and moderate, peacekeeping disposition has, for a while, neutralized the communist wing of the Socialist party. If they could, those leftists would have rushed to Madrid's aid with planes and artillery. In fact, they almost got away with a shipment right after the war broke out last summer. But the Conservatives in London, along with his own Socialist moderates, convinced Blum to take the non-intervention position; otherwise this Spanish thing might drag the whole damned continent into war." Raymond Berrot sighed. Itmar sat up again, but said nothing, seemingly exhausted by Raymond's report on the French predicament.

Raymond sipped the cognac. Then, slowing his explanation a bit, and softening the voice, he continued. "We cannot **afford** a war right now. This is the worst time to have to fight the Germans again. The French Treasury has been bled dry, to the point of near bankruptcy, by the French Chamber's social experiments. The Socialists' legislation package was calculated, it seems, to put money into the pockets of the labor unions and the proletarian citizenry of France. A week after Blum took leadership last summer, which was, unfortunately, almost exactly the same time that Franco attacked his own country and started the war down there, the biggest labor unions went on strike here in France. I think they were trying to force Blum's hand right away, because they knew that their support had enabled him to take the Premiership. While the Rightists were still in a kind of shock that the Leftists had managed to assemble a Popular Front coalition to win a majority, the Socialists rammed through their long-awaited reforms—the forty-hour week for workers, two-week-paid vacations, and of course wage increases."

"Tell me about it," Philip interjected, fascinated.

The distinguished Frenchman let go a sudden smile, his neatly cropped moustache bristling with enthusiasm for the informed report that was being issued. He paused, sipped at the cognac goblet, and peered curiously at Philip. "Your President has proven to be quite an inspiration for our Premier. Leon Blum speaks highly of him. Mr. Roosevelt, who took office in '33, has been a far more suitable role model for leadership than Herr Hitler, who also assumed office that same year. But the New Deal has demonstrated some accomplishments that, I fear, Monsieur Blum and our French people will never realize. The leaders of French industry, my company included, reacted to the government's social reforms—most of my friends call them 'experiments'—with alarm. Investors in France have, it seems, withdrawn their support from our industries. The sitdown strikes with which French labor greeted their Premier's accession to power were answered with what my friend Joel Colton calls 'sitdown strikes of capital.' "

"I have seen in the papers that Mr. Blum pleads with the investors to return their capital to circulation, so that confidence in French industry and business will not be eroded."

"That is exactly right, mon jeune ami. Confidence is very important, as you know, being a salesman, in business. But the political unrest, economic stagnation, and all this . . . ah, tension surrounding the Spanish war and the German war economy. . . these things make it hard for French investors to remain loyal to the nation's best efforts toward productivity, and even, I daresay, our very survival. While the Communists and the Socialists march in the streets and rail about the 'two-hundred families' who control France, those well-endowed backers and financiers of French industry have sought, and found, safer employments for their capital."

"And what might those be?" asked Philip, amazed at his own ability to comprehend the torrent of information this Vice-president of a French chemical company was explaining to him.

Raymond Berrot laughed. "Mais. . . your country, mon jeune ami, the United States of America. . . and Switzerland, and, well. . .they convert their francs into gold and then purchase foreign stocks and currencies. And why not? If France falls apart, and bankrupts itself, while the proletariat mob storms the 'bastille' of the Bank of France, and they erect barricades in the streets with frenzied chants to tear down the 'bastille' of all these supposed privileges that Capitalists are heir to—if France is thus weakened by so much internal dissension and, God forbid, civil war! as the Spanish anarchists have provoked—then the Germans will have a field on French soil if they ever do cross the Rhine with their tanks and their Luftwaffe-strewn thermite incendiary bombs." Raymond Berrot stopped, rather suddenly. He leaned back in the padded chair, relaxing.

Then he continued. "But of course. . .they do not understand. They do not know what Hitler and Mussolini are up to. They are not paying attention. Why should they? They are working people, only trying to make a living by gathering the crumbs that fall, so to speak, beneath King Louie's table. They do not know." He chuckled. "Oh, that is unkind. I am only making a joke here, a sad joke, to lighten the burden of my French soul during these perilous times in which we live. They are very wise people, in their own way; most all of them are . All citoyens of France must find some way, somehow, to prosper and to grow, to raise their children, and enjoy the wine of our vineyards and the fat of our land. Times. . . as they say in your country, are hard." He offered a muted smile that seemed to express as much pathos as it did joy.

They all lapsed into deep thought. After a long pause, it seemed that Itmar still had nothing to say. Maybe, Philip thought, he was starting to fall asleep. "I wonder what will happen," Philip mused.

Raymond Berrot, a captain of French chemicals, allowed a few more moments of silence before spoke again, softly. "What is so sad, Philip. . .I am a Jew, like my friend Leon Blum. In the fascist press, here in France, it was written, and I myself saw it, that Leon Blum, and the Jews in general, are responsible for the disorder and disintegration that is going on in France and elsewhere."

"Who said that?"

"Oh, it was. . .I think it was Charles Marais, or one of those guys. There are a whole bunch of them these days: French fascists, the *Cagoule*, the 'hooded ones', paramilitary *ligues*, monarchists, Catholic extremists, papists, who want to take us back to the days of Napolean, I suppose, and *la gloire de la France.*"

"Do you think any of these Rightist groups would offer support to the Nazis and the Italian fascists?"

"Good question. Some of them are adamantly French, nationalistic and arrogant, with their sense of importance rooted in their Frenchness. They carry an animosity for all things Prussian or German, which goes back for generations, encompassing the disputes over the Rhineland, and Alsace and Lorraine and so forth. But, on the other hand, I think many of them—probably most of them these days—have their zeal and their extremism rooted ideologically—in their hunger for authoritarian leadership and societal order. They are vehement in their opposition to the anarchy and mayhem with which the syndicalists, the anarchists, and even the communists, strive to provoke a kind of perpetual revolution."

"They don't want to see the working classes take over the means of production and establish a dictatorship of the proletariat. Correct?"

"Exactly. That's Marxist stuff. These fascists—and that name originated in Italy, by the way—*fascisti* are, I think, a bunch of sticks bundled together. They are absolutely opposed to the communists. They blame the Bolsheviks, who revolutionized Russia when they forced the Czar out of power in 1917 and then murdered his family at Ekaterinburg. The fascists hold the Bolsheviks, who were later called the Communists under Lenin and now Stalin, responsible for just about every ill and evil of modern government that you can think of."

"Which of these two—the fascists or the communists—makes more sense to you, Monsieur Berrot?"

The dignified Frenchman thought, carefully, for a moment. "Neither. I am a chemist. I investigate the outcome of interaction between electrons and protons. I manage research to discover the productive applications of both the creative and the destructive properties of the material world. I administer a company that develops profitable uses for those outcomes."

"Electrons and protons. Hmmm," Philip mused. "Creative and destructive properties. . .what then, of good and evil, Monsieur Berrot?"

"We have yet to see the worst and best of both," replied the Frenchman.

Philip glanced at Itmar; he had fallen asleep in his chair.

18

Le Pont Neuf

The next morning, Philip awoke at the sound of an insistent knock on the hotel room door. He glanced at his watch. 8:55. Rousing himself and springing to the door, he opened it and was pleasantly struck by the sight of Lili's smiling face. "Bonjour!" she declared. A nearby window at the end of the hall was illuminating her with morning sunshine; it rendered the curly ends of her brown hair in a rosy transluscence. "Please, let's take a walk . I need to go across the river and see the St. Chapelle."

Philip rubbed his eyes. "Well, ok, I'd love to go with you. You seem to have. . . an itinerary in mind?"

"Yes. I've been wanting to come here for a long time. I mean. . .we can go wherever you want to; I've just got one destination that is. . .I've been admiring the Rayonnant ceiling at l'eglise St. Chappelle, and the stained glass, in an architectural book at the library in Munich." Her face was radiant with expectation of what wanderings the day could bring. "You should see the place. There is nothing like it in Gothic old Germany."

Philip felt as if he was still awakening, maybe dreaming, basking in the sudden apparition of her innocent, ashkenazi beauty. Her brown eyes flashed with delight, and he couldn't help noticing the perfectly diminutive body beneath a pink cashmere sweater. She had tied a wispy gray silk scarf around the swannish neck; underneath it was a taut string of small white pearls. A matching gray cotton skirt provided elegant simplicity on her hips.

"Don't you have an appointment at the American embassy?"

"That's not until two o'clock. But the day is yet young," she was convincing him, ". . .and sunny. *Paris au printemps!* I know my parents have asked you to accompany us to the embassy, although. . . now they're talking about going to Palestine instead of America."

"What?" Philip rubbed his eyes again.

"Mother said that last night after dinner, father met with someone who told him that kosher butchers are needed in Palestine, and that help is available for us to relocate there."

Philip stepped gently into the hallway, lightly brushing gently Lili's cashmered shoulder as he stepped over to the window, bright with sunshine. Squinting, he peered down into Rue Bonaparte, three floors below. Pointing to a tree that was growing by the sidewalk across the street, he said, "Give me a few minutes; I'll meet you by that tree in twenty minutes." He looked at his watch. "So, under that tree at about 9:20. We'll find a place for breakfast and then take a walk to the Ile de la Cite to see the St. Chapelle, and the Palais de Justice, which is right next to it. Ca va bien?"

"Oui, monsieur." She was chuckling. "Je vais vous y rencontrer a neuf a vingt." With that assent, she turned on her heel and walked back down the hall. After a few steps, the princess turned her lovely head, smiled and offered a little wave as she moved toward the elevator.

A little while later, they were walking in the sunshine on the street toward the river. "What's this you say about going to Palestine?"

"My parents are meeting a man this morning to talk about going there."

"Who is he?"

"Robert. . .something. Mr. Greeneglass asked my father to telephone him last night. And so they are going to discuss. . . mother said there were opportunities in Palestine for my father, since he is a *shochet*, a kosher butcher, before he was a delicatessen owner, before he was a cattle dealer."

"Do you know where, in Palestine?"

"I heard a little of what father said on the telephone. He mentioned Haifa—that's on the coast, and ah . . .*Rishon le Zion*. Some foundation has bought a parcel of land there, and they have drilled a well for water."

"Oh? What foundation is that?"

"It is, ah. . .*Mikveh* Israel, I think, or something like that." She halted and stooped down to study a pigeon that had been waddling around on the sidewalk just ahead of their gait. Reaching forward to touch the iridescent little gray bird, she almost made contact before it leaped up into the air, flapped a meter or so ahead of them, and resumed its sidewalk vigil for crumbs, or whatever it is that pigeons await in their patient, persistent, perennial pursuit of food.

"What do you think it would be like, to go and live there in Palestine after growing up in Munich?" he asked, watching her as she watched the bird make its escape.

Lili let out a low, nervous laugh, and raised her eyebrows. "Ha! Are you kidding? I don't think it—the place sounds like a wasteland . . . probably not my cup of tea. I think I'd rather have my tea. . ." She affected an English accent. ". . . in London, thank you very much." She laughed again, more easily this time.

"Or New York. What about New York? Isn't that where your parents have already established some contacts?"

"Oh, sure." She tugged gently at his sleeve, eyes flashing with mirth. "Let me wake up on a bright morning like this, and see Lady Liberty, lifting high her torch, just outside the cabin window. She began singing, "Oh, give me a home where the buffalo roam, and the deer and the antelope play. . ." Her amusement now uninhibited, Lili lifted her arm in imitation of the colossal statue in New York harbor and held an imaginary torch aloft.

Philip found himself laughing with her, trying to think of a clever follow-up quip for the levity. Her German accent singing of buffalo was a hoot. "The buffalo and the antelope are a long way from New York, you know."

"Oh sure. The further I go into America, the happier I'll be. The furthest I can get from Deutschland, the more liberty I will see. O look. Here's a café!" With no premeditation, she scooted just inside a wrought iron rail and promptly plopped herself into a metal chair beside a small table for two. "Je suis prêt pour le café maintenant. N'etes-vous pas?"

Philip sat in the chair opposite, feeling himself brim with her ebullience. "Well, you . . . how did you know about the 'home where the buffalo roam'?"

"We saw a motion picture, Hannah and I. It was about your American cowboys. . . Gene Autrey. He was singing that song. Je l'aime. J'adore cette chanson. J'aime l'idee d'etre libre. I love the idea of being free in wide open spaces." She was looking directly into his eyes with a sort of veiled eruption of joy, but underneath the flashing eyes Philip thought he could discern some faint melancholy, a muted mourning that she was striving to pass o'er.

The waiter, in crisp black pants and starched white shirt, approached quickly and stood next to them with an empty tray in his hands. "Bonjour, monsieur," he said to Philip. "Mademoiselle. Que voudriez-vous cette belle matinee?"

"Café au lait et des beignets pour moi, s'il vous plait," she said

"La meme chose." he said.

Philip looked around and realized they were sitting in a wonderful spot. With several other café-sipping patrons seated around them in cozy way-station nonchalance, the steady stream of passersby provided a constant presence of busily aimless activity. Across the street, the stately entrance to L'Ecole des Beaux Arts provided a classic sort of statuesque regality. At either side of the open gateway, the heads of two noteworthy artists' had been sculpted and set high upon pedestals. Their stony vigil must assure that art is thriving in perpetuity, in the city of Paris. Within these gates any passerby can partake of it. *Citoyens* from every proletarian village—all representatives of universal brotherhood—could be ushered herein to experience the montage of cross-cultural images and ideas by which Paris entertained itself. Here they celebrate eternal expression. Philip imagined that one of those stately silent busts might be the sculpted head of Renoir, or Monet, or. . .Van Gogh?

After a little while, Lili said softly, "This place is so different from Munich. There must be something wrong. . ." Her voice had descended into a low lament. "I wonder if Heinrich is still alive."

With no warning, her crying began to trickle out; it was the cry of Lili, weeping for her brother at Dachau. Her anguish was sounding an echo across time, a renewed evocation of the cry of Rachel, weeping for her children. It was a millennial lament, intoned at the base of some uncrossable wall. There was a wall somewhere. . . in the sought-after realms of justice, in the hoped-for pales of deliverance; it was a protective wall that had been bloodily, violently, and tragically breached, but not totally torn down. It must be some Mosaic rampart of righteousness that could never quite be completed to its rightful height, an ill-repaired ancient wall still standing upon their long-lost benchmark of hope, and still inspiring some last, almost-full measure of devotion. Lili was wailing at that broken wall.

Philip was looking at a picture on the café wall; he was trying not to look at Lili. Feeling alien, he did not know how to comfort her, as if he were peering into a world he could not enter, wishing to assuage a grief of which he should not partake. Then Sylvie, his sister, entered his mind. He had not been there for her two weeks ago when their grandfather, who had raised them as his own, had died. The brother Philip had not been there to embrace the sister, nor to comfort her. But this was his chance. He felt that this moment was somehow a recovered opportunity to rectify his absence during his own family's recent grieving. While he was not able to provide for Sylvie, he could now comfort another grieving woman.

Lili's tears were rolling down reddened cheeks without restraint. Their moist warmth penetrated her shirt. Though he be gentile, or genteel, or gentle, he must do something to let Lili know that she need not suffer this episode of regret alone. She need not endure the grief, or the guilt she perhaps felt at having left her brother behind, without his support. Moving his chair next to hers, mustering his confidence, he put his arms around the forlorn fräulein.

All Philip had to do now was hold on; he could feel the balming influence of his embrace upon her. She was shaking. In order to steady himself for what would seem to be her slow recomposure, He adjusted posture, finding a little comfort for himself in this supportive position. This was indeed the thing to do—to shelter another human being from the storm of humiliation that had overtaken her family in Germany, maybe even initiating some protection for her to persevere through whatever would be the next storm to blitz across that border.

A cathartic satisfaction seized him. His wandering eyes settled again upon a picture on the wall. After gazing at it blankedly for a moment, Philip noticed it was a painting of a man on a horse—a king with crown upon his head. A new-style composition it was, not painted in the classical mode, but rather applied in splotchy dapples and sharp, ridgified strokes. A little too edgy to be impressionist, it had the stark visual intrusion of the surreal, but there was no element of irreverence in it—it could be an image in a church, having no disturbing Daliesque images, until Philip noticed that the horse had a human face.

That seemed a little strange.

Philip's discovery of this detail in the painting was interrupted, however, as he felt the movement of Lili's head upon his shoulder. She lifted her head, then gazed out in the direction of the street. Not looking yet at him, she sipped from the coffee cup and seemed to resign herself to some new direction. Then she righted herself, and turned to him with eyes wide, tearful but drying. She was released from the burden.

A rueful smile flashed across her lips. "Marchon un peu plus," she said.

"Okay," Philip replied. He was glad of this. Withdrawing a few francs from his wallet, he left them on the table; they stood, and resumed their walk toward the Seine and the Sainte Chapelle. In the distance, visible beyond the end of Rue Bonaparte and the River, a plume of smoke was rising from some northern arrondissement of Paris.

Lili was calm now, but seemed a little preoccupied. After a while, she said, "Edmond Rougond—I've been trying to think of his name—he's the man who is speaking to my father this morning about possibly going to Palestine."

"How do you feel about that?"

"I'm confused. Monsieur Rougond, according to what my mother has said about him, makes it sound as if Palestine is the Promised Land."

Philip laughed. "Ha! Well it is, isn't it? according to the book of Exodus in the Bible."

"Yes, but we've already been through this—my people, that is. It didn't work out, which is why we were all—my family—born in Germany, instead of, say, Haifa, where M. Rougond says we should go."

"What does your father say about that prospect?"

"He's thinking seriously about going there, which worries me."

"You don't want to take a chance on the Promised Land?"

"It could turn out very well for us, with such a new beginning, in the land of our forefathers. There is something very satisfying about the thought of it. But, on the other hand, the Arabs, who have lived there for generations, are trying hard to prevent us Jews from moving in. Mother said that, last year, they were rioting, trying to upset the British, and persuade them to cut off Jewish immigration."

They rounded a corner, to the right, and were strolling along a cobblestone quai by the River. Lilac blossoms wafted on the breeze down to the water, floating and lazily drifting. The faraway smoke plume, noticed earlier, seemed to have billowed larger, dispersing in the upper atmosphere as a gray swathe that vanished westwardly in powder-blue sky. High clouds were moving in; the sun was not as bright as when they had started from the hotel.

"The Monsieur Rougond—who is he?"

"He lectures at the Sorbonne. I think he is a physicist."

"Is he a Zionist?"

"Well, yes, Papa did say that. . . he is a Zionist."

"And how does your father know him?"

"My father does not really know him, but he is a friend of M. Berrot, with whom we dined last night."

"I talked with M. Berrot last night after our dinner; he is a very knowledgeable man, but he didn't say anything about going to Palestine."

"Well, no, there is no reason for the French to be moving there. Mr. Rougond says this is an opportune time for us German Jews to emigrate there, because they are saying—and it is true—that, as bad as things are in Germany now, they will still get even worse for us. So settling a new homeland in Palestine may be our only real choice, according to the Zionists. Mr. Rougond says they want to have enough Jews there to populate a new. . .a new Zion." She laughed.

"What about you? Do you want to become a Zionist too?"

"No, not really. I think London sounds like a great place to live, according to Mr. Greeneglass."

"What about Hannah? Has she expressed an opinion about where you should go?"

"Ha! She's crazy. Sometimes I think her Zionist friends have convinced her we should go to Palestine. But at other times, I can persuade her that we would do better to go to California!"

"Oh, what is so good about California?"

"Well, Philip, you ought to know. . . you're an American. They make movies there! Fred Astaire and Ginger Rogers are teaching everybody there how to dance, and there are orange trees at the end of every street. Haven't you heard?" She was laughing again.

"I've heard that the place is filling up with Okies who are looking for work," he responded.

"Okies?"

"Farmers and their families from Oklahoma and Kansas, two states in the middle of the USA where a drought has blown dust all over their farms, so badly they can't even grow crops there any more. They call it the Dust Bowl. When the dust drives those farmers out of their homes and lands, they all go to California, the so-called land of fruits and nuts, or milk and honey. There are thousands of Okies in temporary camps now, trying to find work. But even in California, there aren't enough orange trees, nor any other crops, to keep them all employed."

"I'm sorry to hear that. I suppose times are hard everywhere these days— even in America. But papa deals in cattle; surely there is plenty of land for grazing cattle in California, or somewhere over there. Hannah has a friend of a friend, from, I think, Reckendorf, not far from Munich. She knows a banker in San Francisco who, she says, would loan Papa money to set up his kosher business in San Francisco."

"Is that so?" Philip laughed with mild skepticism. "I wish I knew a banker in San Francisco. Who is this banker?"

"Ah. . . a Mister Heilman, or Hellman, or, something like that. Hannah may be stretching the truth a bit. She reads so much, she can't keep it all straight in her mind, between what is real and what she has constructed in her mind, based on all her reading. But one thing I know about her is, she would have us go to California in a heartbeat if it were her choice to make."

They were approaching a bridge on the left, the Pont Neuf. A man was selling fruit from a cart at the corner, next to a low wall by the Seine.

"How about some apples, Lili?, or . . . these pears look perfect."

"Mais oui, ils ne semblent parfaits."

Philip bought an apple and a pear for each of them. Lili dropped her apple into her handbag, which was slung across her shoulder. She grabbed the other apple from his hand and deposited it in her bag for safekeeping. Then she giggled, stepping back and leaning forward, as juice dripped copiously from the ripe pear when she bit into it. "Oh look!" she exclaimed, pointing to another cart on the opposite corner, "C'est un libraire. Voyons ce qu'il a." With no immediate traffic, she trundled across Rue Dauphine to inspect the bookseller's offerings.

Philip was impressed with the vendor's books. Their bindings were of the highest quality, and generally in very good condition, though it was obvious most of them were quite old. Lili settled on a third edition of Les Misérables. After perusing it for a few minutes, she purchased the book and slipped it into her handbook. Philip noticed, and purchased, a small, dog-eared Les Droits de l'Homme, the classic political pamphlet of Thomas Paine, whose incendiary ideas had been distributed widely during both the American and French revolutions.

They were about to walk away when Lili suddenly stopped herself, looking again at the book rows. "Is that what I think it is?" She picked up a worn brown volume, opened it to the title page. "C'est ca! This is Herzl's Der Judenstaat. Philip, we would not see this being sold on the streets in Munich, and yet it is written in German. Speaking of Zionism, this is where it all started. How fortunate!. She handed the vendor a payment and stepped aside to inspect her discovery.

"I have heard of this book, although it is now forbidden in Germany. Theodor Herzl wrote it forty years ago. Listen to this." She read aloud slowly, translating from the German: " 'The Jewish question persists wherever Jews live in appreciable numbers. Whenever it does not exist, it is brought in, together with Jewish immigrants. We are naturally drawn into those places where we are not persecuted, and our appearance there gives rise to persecution. This is the case, and will inevitably be so, everywhere, even in highly civilized countries—see, for instance, France—so long as the Jewish question is not solved on the political level.' "

Philip was considering what Lili had just read aloud, while she continued surveying the book. "So maybe you should, Lili. . ."

"Should what?"

"Move to Palestine, and help to start a Judenstaat there."

"Ha! Easily said, my friend. The possibilities for that happening get bleaker every day. The Arabs are revolting, and the British are fed up with us Jews. I think maybe Hannah is right. We should just move to California, where our people can make a brand new start, without the baggage of two thousand years of anti-Semitism."

"So you think there's a banker in San Francisco who will give your father a loan to get started in business?"

"Well, it makes sense, doesn't it? There are no pogroms in California, no Nazis, no Arabs, only some Mexicans, a few golddiggers, and a bunch of Americans who can do business with anybody because that's the way you Americans do everything in your land of the free and home of the brave."

"You don't feel a sacred obligation to reclaim the Promised Land for the children of Israel?"

"Oh, let the Russians do it."

"The Russians? What are you talking about?"

"The Russian Jews. They are the ones who've had the most trouble; they've had more pogroms than anybody. And they are poor; they are peasants, with no choices. Palestine will only be an improvement for them."

"But Lili. What is happening in your country now is a pogrom. Don't you see that? It is a pogrom on a massive scale."

She stopped suddenly. They were in the middle of the bridge now. Turning to view the Seine upstream, her levity seemed to slip away like the water below them. Her eyes focused on a distant tower that stood on the Isle in the river. Beneath them, a pair of ducks passed, floating on the current under the bridge. It had gotten cloudy. "I am sick of hearing about it; I am sick from waiting to hear news about Heinrich. I am sick of it all. Just put me on a boat to America. We cannot stand going to Palestine, where all this tribulation started, and where it will surely end badly. I just want to disappear into . . .California will do. Any place but Europe or Palestine. Let the desperate Russians go to Jerusalem, and let them run the Muslims off of the Temple Mount, with their bloody hammers and their sickles and their bloody balalaikas. Let them tear down the world so they can build their Temple. I just want a simple life. . ." Lili's tirade had slowly diminished to what was now a lament, a dirge. I just want the life of. . ."

"Of what, Lili?" Her hands were spread out upon the stone rail-wall. He gingerly took her right hand with his left. He wanted her to turn toward toward him, but she stood unmoved, looking away, upstream.

"Let them build the Temple. All I want is the life of . . . Shirley Temple," she said.

Gently, he reached up and touched her cheek with his right hand. The tears were welling in her eyes again. "You're kidding me. Right? Shirley Temple?"

Lili extended one foot onto the low stone ledge of the bridge rail. She had positioned herself on a half-circular bastion of the Pont Neuf. Arching her foot, she lifted her thin frame a few inches, as if seeking a better view of upriver Paris. With face turned toward Philip on her left, she smiled mischievously at him and launched into what seemed to be a pronouncement of some kind. "No. She's a mere child, but she has the power to go around the world and, with her innocence and good will, persuade men who are at war with one another to lay down their weapons and make peace," Lili explained.

Philip was chuckling. "You're talking about fairytale stuff. Hollywood dreams! But this. . . this is the real world out here, Lili. The world is what it is. Men make war. Remember the other night in Perpignan; we were talking to Plia about her husband, now imprisoned by his own government because he made a few misjudgments, or some such while defending that same government of Spain. All the while, the war there rages on. That is. . . that is reality. The Shirley Temple thing is just. . . it's just pipe dreams that some screenwriters in Hollywood created. It's not real! Shirley Temple is just a young girl's dream, and. . .well, you are young, and impressionable. You've got to understand that about America. I mean, this is something I've noticed since I got here in Europe about a year ago. It's a whole different world in the country that I come from; we really don't have a clue about what is going on over here in the old world. This Europe, this, well, France itself. . .Germany. It's almost like a different planet. And Shirley Temple is just. . ." He was shaking his head and chortling at her naiveté. "You can't take this Hollywood stuff too seriously. I mean, your brother is locked up back in Germany. That's reality."

She looked at him with a kind of fierce resolve, but a hint of the smile was still on her lips. "I can dream, can't I? No law against that, no SS *verboten* on dreaming, hoping. . ."

"Sure." He touched her hand tenderly. He could see that her trepidation was showing again. Underneath, she was in a kind of ongoing agony due to Heinrich's unexplained imprisonment. But there was, in her escapism, an odd kind of reality. Maybe it was a deep manifestation of some survivalist hope, as if hope itself were, on some higher level, a greater reality than the world's enmity that had provoked it. "Sure, you can dream. I suppose we all do."

She touched him on the cheek. She looked at him in a way he had never seen before. He felt as if he knew for the first time ever the true meaning of life, new life, here, perched upon a bridge over the Seine in the month of May, somewhere in 1937. He was about to attempt a kiss, but then peripheral vision revealed a sisterly countenance in the near distance, striding dutifully toward them. "Here comes Hannah," he said.

"Now, now, children, let's get on with it," Hannah admonished, with an amused sort of vigilance. It almost seemed rude, but Philip could not tell. She stopped abruptly, then stepped on the low ledge lookout bastion, next to her sister.

"Get on with what?" asked Lili, impudently.

"With . . . going to, wherever you're going. You are not allowed to make us late for the appointment at the American embassy, at one o'clock."

"We certainly will not make you late, or anybody late," Lili affirmed. "But it doesn't depend on us anyway."

Philip smiled broadly at Hannah. "I wouldn't, for the world, miss an appointment with my consulate, and I surely would not deter you or any member of your family from such a meeting. I would like nothing better than to see you all come to America, land of the free and home of the brave." His gaze upon her was an amused challenge, battle of the sexes with sister Lili as the prize, but not really, not yet. Nevertheless, he felt himself unnerved at Hannah's untimely interruption. Just like a big sister.

"Well, what are you dilly-dallying around for? Loitering on a bridge. Where are you going—better get on with it." She was projecting a curious smile in this faux urgency.

"How do you know about about 'dilly-dallying?'" he queried her.

"I heard it in a Shirley Temple movie," explained Hannah, looking him squarely in the eye. He knew she was telling the truth, but it seemed a little uncanny. It seemed Shirley's filmed adventure had been influence on both these fräuleins.

Lili was amused.

"I bet Lili was telling you about her Shirley Temple dream, ya?"

Philip was quite surprised. "Well, yes, as a matter of fact. . ."

She was telling you, probably, how the childish Miss Temple had, in her mind, replaced the meaning of the word—Temple—with this starry-eyed notion of making peace with the world, when what we persecuted Jews really should be doing is rebuilding our true Temple in Eretz Israel, the land of our fathers and mothers."

Whoa!

"Where did that come from?" asked Philip.

"Where did what come from?" Hannah retorted.

"The idea of going to . . . it's Palestine, and rebuilding the Temple."

Hannah lowered her eyes down toward the flowing river. A boat with a party of four haut-fashioned Parisians was passing. Laughter could be heard as their craft glided underneath the bridge. She lapsed into a slower, more circumspect tone. "I don't know really, know, Philip, about the Temple part. That may never happen, according to what I've read about the Temple Mount itself, and how the British have allowed the Muslims their run of the place. But of course it will never happen unless we ourselves go there and make it happen." She turned and looked directly into his eyes. She was challenging him on a deeper level. It was not just about her sister Lili, or about America or anything else; her stealthy bravado was rooted in a purpose much older and more substantial than merely choosing a place to live.

Philip was stunned. "Well, if this is your intent, Hannah, then why would you be so concerned about a scheduled meeting at the American consulate?"

"Ha! Thou art wiser than thy gentile demeanor would indicate." She was not mocking him, just bantering, just testing his resilience. "These associations, Philip—the American, the British, the Palestinian—they are closely connected. Realistically, I do not think your country wants to admit us displaced Jews. They've already turned away a boatload or two. I think it much more likely that between your government and the British, they will find a way for us to make a new beginning in Israel."

"Oh?" He was considering her scenario, and watching a flock of geese as they noisily descended to the waters. "Aren't the British now reversing their policy about Jewish immigrations to, uh, to Palestine?"

"That is true, unfortunately, but the English, and you Americans, are having problems of their own. There are not enough jobs to keep natural citizens properly employed. You think either country is going to admit a multitude of homeless Jews with this Depression going on? And. . ." She looked at him with a curiously persuasive smile. ". . .since you, and the English are more reasonable than Nazis—and surely more compassionate— I'm betting your politicians will find a way to help us make our Zionist inclinations a reality. Your leaders understand, I believe, that we will never be a well-adjusted presence in the world until—and the so-called Jewish problem will never be solved until—we can be allowed, and assisted," She lifted an index finger for emphasis. " To return to the land of our heritage."

"You think so, eh?"

"I think so."

Lili was inspecting the title page of her new, old *Les Miserables*.

"Hmm. . .but tell me, Hannah. Is your analysis. . . did you, ah . . . it sounds to me like your thinking about this is a little more developed than just, you know—and I'm not questioning your intelligence, or your judgment, or anything—what you might be thinking on your own."

"Well, Philip, that is true. What I am telling you is based, partly, on the ideas and research of Dr. Chaim Weizmann, in a book that he published twenty years ago, before the war."

"I see, and what book is that?"

"Zionism and the Jewish Future is the name of it."

Lili closed the cover of her book. She put her hand on Philip's again, and spoke to him, "You see, Philip, although I have my Shirley Temple dreams, my sister has her dreams too—Zionist dreams."

Hannah's eyes flashed with a zealous flare. "My aspirations, dear sister, are not the mere inventions of American cinema. They are more than nineteen hundred years old. Do I have to remind you? Every seder that we can remember has ended with the prayer of 'Next year in Jerusalem!'"

Lili was watching the geese on the water. Her nonchalance registered a kind of sibling impudence. She called out to the geese, mimicking them, 'honk! honk!'

"Oh, Lili! you are so immature," said Hannah.

Philip, feeling a little out of place, wanted to interrupt the sisterly posturing. He caught Hannah's eyes, said to her. "I think you're correct. We need to get on with it. We were about to visit the Sainte Chapelle, and the Palais de Justice. Let's go."

Hannah was still looking at her sister with a disdain that only a family tie could explain. "Furthermore, my hopes for Israel are not mine alone, and they are not without very substantial financial resources. Mr. Weizmann's Zionist organization is backed up by funds from the Baron Edmond de Rothschild. There is plenty enough money to make this hope for Zionism become a reality!"

Lili hopped down from her perch on the bastion ledge, striding past her sister. "Mais, c'est bien. Assez de bavardage. Allons!" she declared, appropriating for herself the initiative to move forward from their present position on the middle of the bridge. "Allons a la Conciergerie."

Hannah addressed her sister's back, as Lili was moving assertively along the bridge walkway toward L'ile de la Cite. Raising her voice, Hannah called, "I thought you were going to the Sainte Chapelle."

"Il n'a pas d'importance ou nous allons. Allons a la Conciergerie." She turned around to face them. "I understand you, Hannah. You would probably prefer to see a prison than a church. So let's go. You want to get on with it. Allons!"

Philip and Hannah looked at each other. He shrugged; she grinned. Hannah said, "She is so fickle!" And so they followed her off the bridge.

They crossed the Pont Neuf and traversed the narrow, downriver point-end of the Ile de la Cite, near where both Le *Conciergerie* and *L'eglise Sainte Chapelle* were located, separated only by the complex *Le Palais de Justice*. Lili's impetuous leadership took them across the westward, point of the island, past the statue, on their left, of a horse-mounted King Henri IV.

That king had narrowly escaped death in 1572 when the Catholics of Paris went on a rampage against their Protestant Huguenot kinsmen. Having survived that infamous St. Bartholomew's Day massacre, the good Henri, whose worldly identity was curiously suspended in religious purgatory between Catholicism and the Protestant faith upon which his mother had raised him, then managed to somehow—whether by Providence, or by God's immeasurable grace, or some combination thereof—go on to reign o'er the then-unruly French people. His royal leadership and legacy was controversial, insofar as he had sought to tread a delicate middle path between the established power structure of the Catholic Church and the emerging upstart Huguenots, who had been led down a heretical Protestant path by the infamous John Calvin long sometime around 1530 or '40. Nevertheless, Henri's trailblazing, unprecedented precedent of attempted religious reconciliation and royally tolerant kingship had later been rendered to stony perpetuity in the form of a very impressive statue of him riding victoriously on a horse. Lili, Hannah, and Philip fixed their attention briefly on it as they proceeded across the little island, which was the oldest part of Paris and truthfully the very heart of this great City of sometimes bloody strife, sometimes regal peace, sometimes a great notion and other times tradition-busting art or revolutionary ideas or just downright decadence.

Now Lili resumed her indecipherable trek, with her footsteps silently directing Hannah and Philip, along a course that brought them eastward along the north edge of the island, traipsing the Quai de l'Horlage in the long shadow of Le Conciergerie.

The *Conciergerie* had been a mega-prison of ill-repute and untold cruelties during the most disruptive, the most pivotal, period of modern French history. From one brightened corner of the dark recesses of this monstrous building the Queen of France, Marie Antoinette, had been brought forth, 16 October, 1793, after Robespierre's Revolutionary Tribunal had condemned her to death and then had ordered her beautiful, aristocratic hair to be cut off in anticipation of her privileged, aristocratic head being sliced away by the guillotine after she was humiliated among the jeering Parisian mob as they trundled the disgraced queen along the Seine from Palais de Justice to Place de La Revolution (now called Place de La Concorde) for her ill-fated appointment with the executioner. . .

This Conciergerie prison was, from olden times, appended to the Palais de Justice, seat of French *legalité* and judicious pronouncements since the legendary 13th century reign of King Louis IX, also known in certain Roman-leaning ecclesiastical institutions as Saint Louis. But in the 500 years between the anointed, most Catholic King Louis IX, and La Revolution of 1789-94, when Jacobin revolutionaries replaced bloodletting religious factions and their inbred *Ancien Regime* with newly-rationalized, highly enlightened cadres of hair-splitting doctrinaire *Humanite*, many profound changes had taken place in France.

In the post-Revolutionary Reign of Terror of 1794, Robespierre's Committee for Public Safety had met in the Palais de Justice and issued death sentences on most of those unfortunate nobility who been apprehended. Furthermore, as if that were not sufficient enough "justice" to put the fear of Man into the general populace, The Committee also imposed the same fatal verdicts on many a misguided patriot from within their own Gerondin or Jacobin ranks. Most of the miserable defendants, while awaiting or enduring their swift justice, had been housed in the Conciergerie.

But the place had been cleaned up and rededicated for gentler purposes, so that now the once-dreaded hellhole of French Terror appeared as any other masonified institution in the City of Light. Now Lili, Hannah, and Philip walked in the shadow of Conciergerie with no thought of the horrors that had been inflicted there in former ages, except insofar as what Hannah could remember from her sparse reading of French history.

As the three young people arrived on the corner of Quai de l-Horlage at Rue de Palais, and thus the end of their long walk beneath the Conciergerie, Philip asked Hannah, "Do you really want to live in Palestine?"

She answered, "Yes, I really want to live in Israel."

"And you really think that's better than living in New York or London?"

"I do." She turned to Lili and said. "Here is where we part, for now. I am going to the Louvre. If you are going to the Sainte Chapelle,, please do not forget to leave there in time to get to the American Embassy on Place de La Concorde at one o'clock."

"Didn't mother make our appointment there for two o'clock?"

"Ah, yes, you are correct. It is set for two. I am sorry I told you wrong."

"Why did you do that, Hannah?"

"Look, I am sorry. I wasn't thinking." She was backing away, toward the Pont Au Change, to cross the north part of the Seine onto the Rive droite. "Nous allons repondre a deux heures, d'accord?"

"Yes, Hannah," Lili affirmed, with irritation in her voice. ". . .a deux heures."

Hannah turned and walked away. Philip and Lili turned the other way, southward on Boulevard de Palais, toward the middle of the Ile and the entrance to the Palais de Justice complex, within which they would find the St. Chapelle. "She doesn't want me to go to the St. Chapelle," Lili said as they started to walk again.

"Oh? Porquois?"

"The main reason is it is a Christian church, not a synagogue. But it is not an ordinary chapel. King Louis IX had it built, beginning in 1242, for his personal devotions, and to house some precious relics from the Holy Land. King Louis is revered by most Catholics as the greatest king that ever ruled France, and a holy man, so he is called Saint Louis. There's nothing too terribly wrong with that, I suppose, but the problem is that he consented to the Pope's demands and allowed some terrible things to happen. Actually, there were many kings among European royalty who have allowed terrible things to be done us Jews. In the year 1244, while the St. Chapelle was being built, Louis allowed the fanatical Catholics to confiscate all the copies of the Talmud that they could find in Paris. After an ecclesiastical court condemned the reading of the Talmud, the priests burned twenty-four cartloads of them. It probably happened right in here somewhere, very close to where we stand."

They had arrived at the very tall, imposing gate of the Palais de Justice. Behind the gold tipped wrought iron bars of the fence and the elaborately wrought, gilted capitol of the gate itself, the Palais stood, thirty or so meters away, a stately, classically French institutional building with rounded and mansard roof lines above four high stories of stone walls with large windows.

"Behind the palace and to its left, you can see the steeple of the St. Chapelle," Lili said, pointing upward to it. "As you will soon see, it is, on the inside, probably the most beautiful building that men have ever built anywhere. Although Louis may have been just as intolerant toward the Jews as all the other Catholic kings of that time, he sure did build a masterpiece during the six years that the St. Chapelle was being constructed. And although I may overlook his intolerance, Hannah does not. But it has been this way for as long as we can remember."

19

La Lumière

An indestructible life was being celebrated.

Melzec, master artisan in the court of King Louis IX, had cultivated a flair for orchestrating light. His work was in glass. He understood that, by the training of light's fragile refractions through stained glass, past could be translated into present, and present into future. With glass, the artist could present a story much more colorful, and with far greater longevity, than any man could tell.

In May of the year of our Lord 1247, Melzec was up to his eyes in elevated labor, very busy with his chosen craft. The master definitely had his work cut out for him, insofar as his apprentices had completed their task of cutting the glass pieces. After being assembled, these pieces would comprise the breaking of bread at Emmaus, an meal that, according to the Gospel, the Lord himself had served to a few of his disciples only a day or two after Resurrection. Now Melzec's apprentices were arranging the cuttings on a work table. After being joined together with lead strips, the individual cutouts would together form a brilliant representation of the Catholic Church's defining moment.

Melzec picked up the bread piece, and the wine piece, to inspect them.

The light of a bright spring day was streaming through large unfilled window openings between the slender, stone-stacked stanchions of the Sainte-Chapelle. The artist held gold-hued bread piece and burgundy wine piece up to the light of day. Squintingat their edges with a trained eye, he confirmed that the proper grozing had been applied, and that the glass pieces were ready for insertion into lead channels that were now being cut to length. The crafted glass fragments were shining just as he intended. Melzec gave approval, and assembly of the Emmaus panel was completed. Later that day, the reinforced window was hoisted up the scaffold and set in place, to become a sacred component of the passion of Christ window.

And so the great Sainte Chapelle refractory of light had been tenderly, lovingly prepared for its saintly place among the landmarks of Paris. The enlightened circumspection through which succeeding generations would experience its visual splendor would render the sanctuary timeless, presenting no dogmatic stubbornness, portraying no ecclesiastical dead weight, but simply radiating incomparable beauty. Perhaps 'twas this undeniable otherworldliness that had somehow prompted a merciful withdrawal when the revolutionary mob had thrashed and burned its way through the City of Light in 1789. No pearls before swine in this case.

As Abraham, long ago, had put the kings of Elam and Goiim in their grave places, so King Louis would soon take upon himself the mantle of *marechal* might, and thus attempt to deliver the Holy Land and Jerusalem from its Muslim and Mongol occupiers. However, in order to make sufficiently spiritual preparation, Louis had commissioned the construction of the Sainte-Chapelle. It would be a place to express his personal devotion and service to God. Not to mention that it would also house some old relics that had been redeemed from a Venetian merchant after Louis' cousin, Baldwin, the bankrupted emperor of Byzantium, had hocked them. Whatever the authenticity of the relics, and whatever might be their arcane power to legitimatize his authority among the sycophants and the masses, the King of France had secured those precious artifacts and had built a sufficiently beautiful shrine for their safekeeping.

All relicry aside, however, now Philip was standing in the Saint-Chapelle, appreciating Melzec's masterful legacy, and thinking how lovely it is. Lili, caught up in her own Judaic thoughts, had wandered toward the middle of the south wall, where she was squinting in the bright sunshine to see the glass-clad story of Esther. The room was full of people, and filled with the low murmur of respectful humans in a sacred setting. Then he heard, to his right side, a man speak quietly to him. The English was clear, with a slow French accent. "Quite a revelation, *n'est-ce pas?*"

He was an old man, with bushy white eyebrows. His eyes were shining with exultation, face smiling unabashedly. Wearing an impeccable dark blue suit, white shirt, red silk tie with gold fleur-de-lis clasp, he stood straight, with hands clasped behind his back, rocking slightly on his heels. The gentleman lowered his eyes from the window. Directing his mirthy gaze at Philip, he asked "Hello. My name is Mel. What's yours?".

"Philip Morrow."

"Ah, Philip. That is a good name. King Louis, who built this chapel and dedicated it in 1248, was succeeded by his son, Philip. But you are an American, yes?"

"Yes."

"And what part of the vast American continent do you hail from?"

"I am from the state of North Carolina; it is on the east coast."

"Ah, yes. I have heard of it. The first Declaration, to declare independence from George III of England was promulgated in North Carolina."

"That is true, sir. The Mecklenburg Declaration, in 1775. Not many people have heard of it."

"I have studied the revolutionary movements of that period. You know, your revolution in the United States is closely linked with ours, which came about thirteen years later. Your American legacy, however, has proven to be, *je pense que*, more orderly than ours has, and more, ah, rational."

"I suppose it has. Your politics here is very different from ours. I can see that."

"How so?"

"Your politics are, I think, more extreme on both ends, the liberal and conservative ends, than what we have in the US."

"C'est vrai, mon ami." His eyes sparkled with friendliness. "How long have you been in France?"

"Just a. . .a couple of weeks, less than two weeks."

"And what brings you to France?"

Philip laughed. He looked up at the stained glass window, searching for a reason, or for the wherewithal to explain himself. "That is a long story. I was in London, doing business. I met a man there who. . .well, I decided to come here in order to help some friends of his. That is, I'm taking some time off from business."

"Ah. . ." The curious man also looked up at the window, wherein was depicted the passion of Christ. "What is it that . . .what is your business?"

"I represent Brigham Tobacco Company of North Carolina."

A frown crossed the old man's face. He looked worried. It was the first sign of something other than lightheartedness in the stranger's demeanor. "I see. You should, you know, consider another line of work."

Philip was stunned. "Excuse me. Tobacco is one of the most potent growth industries of our time. People all over the world are gaining a taste for it every day. That is why I am here in Europe, developing new markets for our company."

Mel offered a muted, compassionate smile. He was looking at Philip again. "Certainement, mon ami, je comprends. I was, myself, a smoker, for a few years. And I have, in my life, been a businessman. But the expansion of this 'growth industry' will not always be so vigorous; nor is it beneficial. A day will come when the fortunes of tobacco will be reversed."

"Oh, pourquoi est-ce?"

"Tobacco is not good for you; it is not healthy." He looked up gravely at the Christ window again. "If you think about it, Philip, you know it is true."

But Philip didn't know what to think.

"Mais, mon ami, that is not what I came here to talk to you about." He smiled reassuringly.

"Oh?" Philip inspected the man's face. Wrinkles around his large, expressive brown eyes, seemed to indicate some unstated concern. "You, ah, you came here to talk to me?"

Mel chuckled. "Ha! In a matter of speaking. That is to say. I came here to talk to whomever would listen. I come here every day, or. . .almost every day."

"Oh. And why is that?" Now Philip was the inquisitor.

"Well, I, ah—for one thing—I like the window there, the Christ window, with the resurrection pictured in brilliant color." Mel raised his arms, formed his hands into a sort of frame through which he viewed the window, like an artist conceptualizing a scene that he is about to paint. "And I believe in it." He smiled broadly and looked at Philip.

"You believe in the window?"

"I believe in what is shown there—the crucifixion and resurrection of Christ." He looked up at it appreciatively. "It is a wonderful piece of work, n'est-ce pas?"

"Are you a Catholic?"

"No."

"But this is a Catholic Church."

Mel laughed loudly. For a moment, he said nothing, but only smiled, gazing at the window. The low, reverent murmur of pilgrim souls was ever-present. "I am a Christian; that is sufficient." The soft spark of vigilant faith could still be seen around them. "What about you? what are you?"

"I was raised a Christian. But from what I see in the world today—it doesn't make sense."

"What doesn't make sense?"

"Life itself. There doesn't seem to be any rhyme or reason to it."

Mel laughed again. "I hope you have not been infected with our French existentialism. It is an epidemic in Paris these days."

"Well, no. I wouldn't identify myself that way. But. . ." Philip had to think for a moment. He glanced around the chapel. "This place is—it makes a pretty convincing statement for the Christian way of seeing things, and, uh, doing things. I mean, look around. This place is gorgeous. I've never seen anything like it. Not even Westminster Abbey can compare. Well, Westminster is a lot bigger, but size is not everything. The room is light, bright. It is full of air." Philip laughed at himself. "I mean, every room is full of air, but . . . .this Sainte Chapelle is a very impressive memorial, a memorial to, ah, a life well-lived."

"The life of Saint Louis, King of France?"

"The life of Jesus."

Mel was looking steadily into the light as it flooded in through the high, multiple windows. The entire chapel was bright with sunshine, intensified in a prismy cascade of colors hung high in vertical space above them. The window tops, rounded at the top in delicate metal and stone tracery, curved overhead into a rayonnant ceiling of royal blue and gold. He nodded slightly in the direction of the Christ window. "You see that?"

"Yes."

"That is happening all the time. It is taking place every minute of every day, everywhere on this earth, all the time, wherever men live and breathe and find differences among themselves, and . . . make victims of each other."

"What do you mean?"

The old man said nothing for a minute. The soft rumble of some terrible history was crying out from the stones beneath their feet. Maybe it was calling out from the old man's heart, from a deep wound or wrong that had been done to him.

"What are you talking about? Crucifixion?"

The old man shrugged. "Not exactly, but, in some variation or another, someone, somewhere in this world. . ." He was speaking slowly. ". . . even now, perhaps people not far from us, are being falsely accused, unjustly convicted for crimes they did not commit, and, God forbid, executed by other people."

Across the room, a metal object dropped to the hard floor. The impact of it clanged sharply, echoing from smooth stone faces and glassy panels. Elaborately painted doorway lintels, mosaic-laden columns, hidden human eardrums, and the still, sanctified air itself vibrated in sympathy with the disturbance.

"God does not forbid it," said Philip.

Mel took his eyes off the window and looked steadily at Philip.

"God does not prevent the injustice," Philip continued, pondering aloud. He felt a kind of vehemence inside himself. "He does not remove the wrong that is done on the face of his earth. He tolerates the evil that men inflict on each other. He seems, too often, to overlook it."

Mel responded. "That removal is for men to do. That is what good men are called to do—identify the evil that takes place among them, judge it, and root it out, if it is possible."

"Good luck with that," Philip retorted. "Are you one of those good men? What are you going to do about it? Do you even know what can be done about it?"

At that moment, Lili appeared from behind where Philip was standing. She tapped him on the shoulder. Philip watched the old man's face metamorphose with curious joy. "Guten tag," she greeted them in her native German. She extended her hand to Mel. "Ich bin Lili. Comment allez vous?"

The old fellow was smiling broadly. "Ca va bien. Je m'appelle Mel Leblanc."

She returned the smile. "I can see you gentleman have been talking about something important. Am I interrupting?" she asked.

"Oh, no," answered Philip.

After a moment of watching her, Mel asked, "You are from Germany, Lili?"

"Oui, from Munich."

"And you are visiting us here in France? How do you like it so far?"

"I am not. . . visiting, just passing through." she said.

"Ah, and where are you going?"

She looked at Philip with a strange expression, something between amusement and alarm. "That is a good question." A little awkwardly, she turned back toward the Esther window, peered at it for a second or two, as if she were trying to remember something forgotten, then turned and caught Mel's eye again, repeating, "That is a good question."

Mel laughed easily. "Well, ok then, *ma chere*, where would you **like** to go?"

She grinned slightly. "Aren't you the bold inquisitor? Where would I like to go? California?" She glanced at Philip with a noncommital kind of ambiguity.

"C'est ca. Perhaps I can ask, then, when will you be going back to Germany?"

"Never. Ou, c'est-a-sat, I don't know. That decision is up to my father and mother."

Mel gazed at Lili with curiosity, leaning back slightly, as if to assess her. "You are Jewish, n'est-ce pas?" he asked her, rather bluntly.

"Yes."

"And you have discovered, I am guessing, that being Jewish in Germany is no longer an easy identity to bear?"

"Mais, oui, Monsieur Leblanc. How perceptive you are."

"Ah, you are not the only one, *ma chere*. There are others, you know. In fact, there are many others in your predicament. I have been noticing them for a year, or longer. I have spoken to a few of them. What is going on there, that so many of you are leaving?"

"Terrible things, Monsieur Leblanc. Terrible things are happening in the country. . . of my birth. But I am sick of . . . I am tired of thinking about it." She looked at Philip with exasperation. "There is so much, much more than I can . . ." Lili nervously shifted her weight from one foot to the other. "Hey Philip, I'm going to find the Ladies room. Please excuse me for a few minutes."

"Sure." He tried to smile empathetically.

The old gentleman merely nodded. Then Lili turned on her heel and headed for the door through which they had previously entered the chapel. "I'll be back," she said, departing.

Philip looked again at the old man's genteel expression. "What were you saying, Monsieur Leblanc?"

"I was saying, I think, that God does not prevent injustice, and this is for a reason. He wants to give Man—Man is, you see, the crown of His creation, and designed to reflect His own image—He wants to give Man an opportunity to oppose the evil."

Philip considered this thoughtfully. He looked up at the window, reflecting, with multiple colors, the last days of Christ's Passion. He could see miniscule dust particles floating in the light streams. "He wants to give Man the choice to do the right thing."

Mel smiled with satisfaction. He looked Philip squarely in the eye. "Exactly." He peered up at the window again. Then something new crossed his mind. With a curious anticipation, he turned to look behind them. Revolving to a prospect of the chapel's other end, he said, "If you've a few more minutes, I'll show you something."

Philip chuckled. "Something?"

"It is something I've noticed. And come to think of it, it relates, I believe to what is happening now. Would you like to see it?"

". . . to what is happening now?"

"Yes. What we see depicted here in stained glass tells a very long story. It is the biblical account of God's activity among His people through millennia of time. Although the events shown in these windows are unique and real, there is an eternal sense in which historical events of the same order are always taking place, happening again and again, in perpetuity until the second coming of Christ. Thus the good work of God is always going forth upon the earth, being actualized by the faithful efforts of His people. Conversely, His people are always being opposed by the evil. But just now, a new, mounting immensity of this ancient war lifts its deplorable violence to a more obvious level. I just now realized this—when your friend mentioned that something terrible is happening," He raised his eyebrows. "in the 'land of her birth.'"

"In Germany."

"Yes." He stepped in the direction of the far end of room. "I will show you what I'm talking about. I have thought about this a lot. Perhaps you can help me evaluate it."

Philip, puzzled as ever, followed the dapper old fellow as he initiated a trek to the far end of the sanctuary. Mel halted at a vantage point about twenty meters from the wall. Directly before them was a towering golden wall. Within its lower half were three high, equilateral arches, each one curving to a slightly pointed apex. These three constructs dominated the entire aspect. The middle arch, wider than the other two, housed a pair of huge doors, now closed. Set within the three arches, and a cubit or so back, an omnipresent background of gold shone heaven-like with earthly glowings. A myriad of painted saints and angels swirled in adoration around the central Christ figure. He was crowned in gold and clothed in ethereal blue.

The upper half of the end wall presented a very large circular, traceried rose window, almost as wide as the entire wall itself, backlit in sunshine through stained glass.

From the inner pocket of his suit-coat, Mel withdrew a small spyglass. It was very similar to, but smaller than, the one that his friend Nathan had handed to Philip in London a couple of weeks ago on Coronation Day. The old fellow was rolling the tubular instrument gently between his fingers as he looked upward at the rose-shaped window. "That, my friend, is the last book of the Christian bible, rendered in stained glass."

"Revelation," said Philip.

"Yes, the Revelation, or Apocalypse as the Catholics call it, of the apostle John. Do you see it?"

"As sure as you're born, Monsieur Leblanc, I see it." Philip laughed. He had not expected, when he woke up this morning at the Hotel d'Orleans, that anything like this would be presented to him today.

Then from behind them Lili stepped in, next to Philip, to his right. "I'm back," she said.

Philip was surprised when she placed her hand into his. Basking in the glow of the Sainte Chapelle, and the warmth of Lili's touch, he was gazing at the window in question, afraid to look at the lovely young woman beside him, content to just feel her hand in his, acting nonchalantly as if her sudden touch was just an expected development, neither here nor there.

20

9:11

This unusual man, Mel Leblanc, was gazing up at the rose window. He lifted the spyglass to his right eye and focused it. As he was doing so, he spoke to them. "If you can think of that large circle as a compass, it is divided into four quadrants, n'est-ce pas?"

"Okay," said Philip.

"Imagine a vector originating at the center, and pointed directly north, at zero degrees."

"Yes. I understand," Philip affirmed. He looked at Lili. She nodded.

"Now. From where that line would meet the window's edge— at the circumference, drop back down, about a third of the way down that radius toward the center. . ." He paused. "Look over to the right of that line—it would be east on a compass—look to the second tear-shaped panel. There is a man riding on a horse. Do you see it?"

"Yes," Philip said.

"Yes, I see it," said Lili.

Mel handed the spyglass to Philip. "Take a closer look," he said.

Philip took the instrument from the old man's hand. He started, instinctively, to focus it, but remembered that he had watched as Mel had focused it. Peering now at the telescoped detail of a crowned king riding upon the horse, he could see that the rider was carrying a golden scepter, sitting upon a white horse with a wide red collar around its neck.

"Describe the horse to me, Philip," he said.

"It is white, prancing with its left front leg lifted, like a show horse. It has a wide red collar around its neck, and a golden mane, and . . ."

"And what?" Mel's voice was quick with excitement.

"And . . . a face." Philip chuckled, perplexed.

"A face, what kind of face?" Mel prompted.

"It is—I don't know. See what you think, Lili. What does it look like to you?" He released her hand from his, and handed the spyglass to her.

Lili lifted the tube to her left eye and spiraled it around until she could position it on the appointed detail. "Oh, I see it." She laughed innocently. "The horse . . . the horse does have a face, and it is . . . a face like a man. A human face."

"What king is that?" Philip queried, peering at the illumined, teardrop-shaped panel near the window top.

"The king of the Abyss," Mel answered, as if the abyss were a common location.

"Abyss? What is that?" was Philip's retort.

"Some have translated it as the bottomless pit."

As Lili placed the spyglass in Philip's hand again, he was amused. "Strange. . . he doesn't look like any sort of king that would have come up out of a. . ." He looked carefully at Mel, who now seemed as ageless as a sage. Their eyes met. ". . . he doesn't look like anything as sinister as a person from a 'bottomless pit.' It seems to me, uh, with the fair hair and beard—even the horse is blonde—this king does represent anything as dark as an abyss, or a bottomless pit."

Mel chuckled. "Things are not always what they appear to be."

"The blonde hair," said Lili, "is a bad sign, if you ask me. The Nazis want to lift the blonde people—the 'Aryans' as they call them—to some kind of privileged status above everybody else. Maybe their 'king', the *feuhrer*, is from the abyss."

Philip asked, "Where is this abyss?"

"For that information, my friend, you will have to read the book of Revelation, in the Bible, if you can interpret it."

"I have read the Bible," said Philip, casually. "I was raised on it. Where is this king from the abyss in the Revelation?"

"9:11."

"Ah, and what can you tell me about this 'abyss,' of which that little, barely visible stained glass figure is said to be the king?"

The old man was amused at Philip's enquiry. "Smoke."

"Smoke?"

"Smoke comes out of it," said Mel. "Look it up some time. You will see."

"Smoke comes out of the abyss, yes. Revelation chapter 9, verse 1."

Philip was astounded. Why was this happening? He questioned, "What then?. . . out of all these windows in this spectacular chapel, and of all these detailed glass panels, would you choose to bring this particular one—this king, riding on a horse with a. . . a human face," Philip laughed. ". . . to our attention."

The old fellow was looking around the room with an amused kind of nervousness. "Ha! I. . .well, I, myself, have seen this. . . I have seen the effects of this abysmal king's authority."

Lili interjected, "Maybe it is King Louis, who commissioned this chapel to be built. He let the Catholics burn Talmuds in the streets of Paris. That must have sent up quite a plume of smoke."

Philip peered at Lili with a newfound curiosity. "What?!" Confused, he turned to Mel. "Yes. Who's to say that the king is not Louis, who had this place built, even as was persecuting the Jews?"

Mel was rocking on his heels. On his lips was the most miniscule hint of a smile. "I. . .I. . ."

"Or, let me put it to you this way, Monsieur Leblanc, **where** have you seen the 'effects' of this king from the bottomless pit?"

"Ah, in Jerusalem, eight years ago."

"What happened?"

The old man inspected Philip's face carefully. Then he turned aside, surveying the long north wall of the Sainte-Chapelle. Directing his attention slowly again on Philip, he said, "Let's have a seat on that bench over there."

"Sure," said Philip. He glanced at Lili; their eyes met and she nodded slightly, and began stepping toward the bench. Gently, she took his hand again. "C'est une bonne idee ," she agreed.

When they were seated, Mel looked up at the window again, disoriented, as if he were trying to decide where to begin. "I don't really understand what this abyss is, and surely I do not know who the king of the abyss is. All I can truly tell you is that somehow this biblical scenario makes sense to me, based on what I have seen in my long life. I am eighty-one years old."

"You are a blessed man," said Lili.

He looked at her with appreciation. The slight smile lit his face for a moment. "C'est vrai. God has given me many good years. I was able to share forty-eight of them with my wife, Agnes. She died three years ago." Mel's demeanor lightened a bit, and he gestured vaguely with his hand, as if waving one topic aside to be replaced with another.

"But she was there with me in Jerusalem, in 1929. We were in the Old City, in the Maghreb quarter, very near the Wall where Jews go to pray."

"I have an uncle who goes there at least once a year to pray at the Wall," Lili said.

He looked carefully at her. "C'est bien. I suppose then, that, if you have ever spoken to him about what it is like to go to the *Kotel*, then you can understand how important it is to these devout people to pray there."

"Oui," she affirmed, not wanting to interrupt.

"But what Agnes and I saw there in 1929 was a tragedy. It was in August. It was hot. We had been shopping for a special kind of candlesticks that she had seen somewhere. We were making our way back to a certain shop that was very near the Wailing Wall, and Agnes wanted to stop there to—I don't know what to call it—to pay respects, or something like that." Mel paused, as if remembering some detail. "We didn't actually pray there. It was more like. . .we went there to watch the people pray at the wall, like they do." He peered at Lili. "You know how they pray."

"Yes, with the rocking back and forth," she said.

"That's right. But where they go to pray, it is a small place, and crowded. It is hardly more than a little alley. The awkwardness of it is a source of constant disagreement and skirmishing between the Jews who pray there and the Arabs and north African Moslems who live nearby. The Arabs call the wall 'al-Buraq,' after the name of Mohammed's donkey, which he had tethered to the wall when he went up to the rock on the Temple Mount, the *Haram al-Sharif*, as they call it, in the year 622. From there, he is believed to have been taken up into heaven to visit with Allah."

Within the Sainte-Chapelle, a whispering reverence prevailed. Mel realized that his voice had escalated, so he resumed the recollection in a lower tone.

"So, you see, the wall has a special significance for the Moslems, and they are sensitive about the Jews' presence there, and more and more so, since the Zionists have lately prevailed upon the British authorities to allow more and more Jewish immigrants into Palestine. This is how it has been in the last fifteen years or so. There are probably as many Jews in and around Jerusalem now as there are native Arabs. The Arabs are—I think, nine out of every ten of them are—Mohammedans. Well . . . on that particular day in August, 1929, it was Friday, the Sabbath not only for Jews, but also for Moslems. We were there in the Old City, and had just left the alley where the Wall is. Suddenly, from behind us we heard loud shouting, and—it got louder and louder, until after a minute or so it was more like screaming and shrieking. Then we were surrounded by Jews who were running past us in a panic, almost a stampede of them. Some of them we recognized as the same ones who had been praying at the wall. We did not know what they were running from, but the noise and confusion from behind was growing louder and more desperate."

Mel paused for a deep breath. He surveyed the chapel, as if to remind himself where he was. All around, the few dozens of pilgrims of Sainte Chapelle were caught up in stained glass reverie and sacred circumspection. "I am. . .this is taking more time than I had thought . . ."

"Please continue," Lili urged, "Monsieur Leblanc. The time is of no consequence. What was it that had upset them?"

"We began to run with them, because the fear was. . . ah, contagious. I say 'run.' You can see I am . . .I was seventy-three years old at that time, and Agnes a few years younger. So we were having trouble attaining to the 'hind's feet in high places' pace that would have been required to keep up with that retreating throng. Agnes tripped and was almost overrun by the frenzy, but somehow we managed to get out with no injuries except a few scrapes and scratches, and a real hell of a scare. We changed direction at the first opportunity and headed directly for the house we were renting in the Montefiore district. We did manage, after a frantic retreat, to get back to the house safely. By that time, there were hundreds of people running through the streets—but not all of them were Jews. Many of them appeared to be the Arabs, pursuing the Jews. They were trying, or so it seemed, to run them out of Jerusalem, and probably all the way out of Palestine. . .The Moslems in the sacred area of the *Har-haBayit* had come down, a few minutes after their prayers had ended, from the high place—that is, the Al Aqsa and the Dome of the Rock—down to the Wall. It was, I thought later, as if they were descending into an abyss of vengeance and murder. The British called in their troops to put the riot down, but more than two hundred people died in Jerusalem that day before the chaos was reigned in."

It seemed to Philip that the old man had worn himself out with the retelling of this traumatic event. Mel was looking again up at the rose window, shaking his head. Lili was inspecting the floor, and Philip was speechless for a couple of minutes. The mild roar of whispering silence still prevailed in cavernous space. Finally, Philip broke the silence. "So what has this to do with the king of the abyss?"

Mel gestured wearily up at the rose window. "You saw that, in the window, as in the Revelation, the king of the abyss rides upon a horse with a human face."

"Yes," replied Philip, peering up again at the detail near the top of the window, this time without aid of a spyglass. He could barely see the horse's face, though he remembered, from his previous sighting with the instrument, that strangely human feature on an equine creature.

"Mohammed's donkey, al-Buraq—the Prophet had tied it to the Wall before going up on Haram al-Sharif—is pictured, from ancient times, with a human face."

Philip looked at Lili. He didn't know what to think about it. Her face registered nothing more than a similar puzzlement. Turning again to the old fellow, he inspected the wrinkles around his eyes, which were more pronounced now than before. Then he asked, "Do you think, then, that Mohammed is the king of the abyss?"

Mel blew out a heavy sigh. Wearily addressing his new companions, he opined, "Not necessarily. All this art. . ." He was gesturing broadly toward the panorama of Sainte-Chapelle, "this artwork—the imaginations, the toils, the sweating agonies of mere, fallen men like myself—they represent entities, or identities, of a spirit realm. The spirits have ways of manipulating us fleshly beings who dwell down here in the confusion of the world. I can't say that Mohammed is the king of the abyss. He is revered by millions of Moslems as the greatest prophet of all. So who am I to argue with them?" Mel shrugged, arching his eyebrows and his voice.

Lili thought he looked so Yiddish when he asked that.

"Maybe not Mohammed, but. . .the Mufti. . . the leader of Jerusalem's Mohammedans. After the Friday prayers that day, he provoked the faithful, with his fanatic jihad rhetoric, to descend from Al Aqsa after their prayers and rid their al-Buraq wall of Jews. And from what I saw, the Mufti must have also instructed his followers to kill those sons of Abraham. The whole desecration might have been a massacre sent forth from the bottomless pit of hell—the abyss."

After a moment, Lili said, "They're doing it again, you know."

"Doing what? Who is doing what?" asked Philip.

"Rioting—the Moslems in Jerusalem. They're still trying to drive Jews out of Palestine. That's what Hannah told me that night we were on the train from Perpignan. And if that's the way things are in Palestine, I don't want to go there." With a curiously unexpected vulnerability, Lili said to Philip, "Take me to New York, will you?"

After a moment of recovery, he answered, "You know I can't do that, Lili. You need to talk to your father. Besides, I don't live in New York. Where I come from, you would probably be bored to tears."

Lili laughed. "I'm not talking about marrying, Philip. I just need someone to take me to New York, or Los Angeles would be better, and right away."

Philip studied Lili's face. Maybe it was the German accent, or, he wasn't sure if he understood what she had just said. Her eyes were cast down, and she seemed to inspect her fingernails for a moment, as if to negate some affectionate slip of tongue with a practiced nonchalance. Then she looked up at him, with a flicker of smile, like a sudden sunbeam from a cloud that is there and then it is gone. She was too beautiful for him to dwell on, with the taut skin across her cheekbones having a kind of rosy translucence, and dark brown eyes flashing with a mystery unknown to him. She was not like an American girl, not like any woman he had ever known, but he had never known many women anyway, not intimately, since college a few years ago. . . He set his eyes awkwardly back on the stained glass, trying to locate again the king on the white horse. He knew for the first time that there is a deep hole in his heart. "Before I go back to America, I. . .I'm going to Belgium, to visit my father's grave," he stammered. He watched as she lifted her eyes again to the multi-hued prism of glass enlightening them from above.

This unsteady silence was punctuated by Mel. "Your father's grave?"

Philip, with relief, turned his face to the old man. "Yes. He was killed in the war, in October of 1918."

"Ah, I see." Mel rocked slowly on his heels, casting his eyes heavenward, in a tactful kind of imitation of what the two younger ones had just been doing. "Where in Belgium?" he asked.

"A place called Flanders Field."

Mel was considering his words carefully. "October. . . that was the very end of the war."

Philip began to shake his head, regretfully. "Yes, some have said . . ."

"Ecoutez!" Mel interrupted, raising his voice for emphasis. Then, placing his hand gently on Philip's shoulder, he spoke softly, "There is only one thing to be said. Your father died in defense of my home, La France. He did not die in vain. There are millions of Frenchman who are eternally grateful for his sacrifice. The Russians had pulled out, you see, after the Bolsheviks took their government. Then the Germans were able to send many troops from the eastern front to fight us here, and in Belgium. We would have been overwhelmed. But when the Americans landed on the Nord, they were absolutely the fresh reinforcements that our exhausted boys needed. I don't know that we could have turned Ludendorf and those well-disciplined Prussian troops back if your father and all those Yankees hadn't shown up when they did. There's no telling. . ."

Philip was surprised when Mel's face lit up, unexpectedly, and the old fellow volunteered, "I will take you there, if you like."

"To. . .to the battlefield?:"

"Yes. I have not been there since the war. My brother's son, Phillipe, died near there, at about the same time, in the last battle of Ypres."

"Is he buried there?"

"No, we brought him home, to Dijon, for burial. But I have, in recent days, thought that I'd like to go back to that place before my days come to an end. It was a terrible time, that war. But to see it now. . . with vast fields of green grass, and long rows of white crosses perfectly in line, and . . . to hear birds singing, instead of artillery shells whistling through the air, and, blue sky with clouds instead of the foul—the abysmal—smoke of warfare. You would, my young friend, do me a great service to allow me to accompany you there."

Philip had not expected to be considering, so soon, the Flanders visit, which would be for him the final leg of his Continental sojourn. A mild confusion must have registered on his face.

Mel was looking at him kindly, a fatherly smile on his face. "You think about it. What is it that you are doing in Paris?"

"I came here with Lili, and her family. They are en route to the United States, or, somewhere . . .they are trying to decide where to go from here."

"Anywhere but Germany," Lili added. "My parents are applying for visas. And you know what? Philip. . ." She looked at her wristwatch. "We need to go to the American embassy. It's one-thirty. We will be late if we do not leave here very soon. Mother and Hannah will be upset if I am not there at two o'clock for the appointment."

"That is true, Lili." agreed Mel. "You should be punctual. But it would take you at least half an hour to walk there. We can make it easy for you. I come here almost every day in a taxi, and I know all the drivers who work this area, the Ile. I'll get you a cab, and, if you will allow me, I will accompany you there. Mrs. Deegan, the receptionist, is a friend of mine."

21

Paper

At the moment Lili stepped through iron gates onto Boulevard de Palais, she was preparing, in her own mind, a path of departure.

Would she accept the thorny path of struggle toward a promised land? Would she take unto herself a shedding of bitter tears, the pouring forth of profuse toil and sweat, yes even the shedding of blood, for the ancient Zion quest of her people? In such a time as this, what is to be done from here, from this point of Parisian respite and repose? Whether 'tis nobler to oppose the slings and arrows of outrageous misfortune which were now being flung upon her race by that dark angel of the abyss whose mein kampf nine-eleven mayhem was even now conjuring a flood of murd'rous hate to be unsloshed upon the world?

Or go to New York.

At Mel Leblanc's hailing hand, a yellow taxi stopped at the curb in front of Palais de Justice. Philip ushered Lili into the cab first, then followed. Taking the front seat, Mel directed the driver to their desired destination. "American Embassy," he said to the driver.

Arriving at the northwest corner of Place de la Concorde, their cab passed beneath a stony landmark long cherished by French patriots—the Lady of Strasbourg, a statue symbolic of French independence from German domination. As the car slowed, Lili's alert eye glimpsed: a detail on the sculpture; it was a rolled-up scroll beneath the Lady's feet. With her mind still lingering on the significance of the scroll, Lili's attention was diverted as the taxi, having turned onto Avenue Gabriel, wheeled beneath high, pedestaled double eagles. They had arrived at the Embassy of the United States. Their taxi halted directly in front of the high front doorway, which, centered in a classic large-blocked marble exterior, was open. A uniformed doorman approached the cab. *I am ready for you, America,* she thought.

"Attendez vous, s'il vous plait," said Mel to the driver. The old Frenchman accompanied the youngsters through the entrance, into a spacious, gray marbled foyer. Immediately to their right, a lovely middle-aged woman with elegantly waved, brown hair was seated to receive visitors. The ceramic vase on her desk displayed a petite bouquet of magenta peonies to match the floral print of her dress. On the wall above and to her right a black marble bust of George Washington surveyed the scene.

The lady smiled at Mel. "Monsieur Leblanc! Whom have you brought to us this time?"

Mel, returning the smile, and bowing slightly, responded. "Mrs. Deegan, I have here Fräulein Lili Eschen, and Mr. Philip Morrow, a citizen of your country."

"Thank you, M. Leblanc," said Lili, then, "Hello, Mrs. Deegan. My family has an appointment with your personnel at two o'clock."

Glancing down at an open calendar book atop the blotter, she confirmed, "You are with the . . .Eschen family."

"Yes, Madame."

"They have arrived. You will join them in the Immigration room, n'est ce pas?"

"Yes, thank you."

"If you will please, then, walk back here, to your left. Enter that hallway and turn left again. Go through the last door on your right. Your family is waiting there for you, and you will all be interviewed. You will have to wait for a little while. This is a busy time for you Germans. There are several more of your countrymen in there now."

"This is my friend, Philip Morrow. He is accompanying us."

Mrs. Deegan smiled at Philip. "Mr. Morrow, where is your home in our United States?"

"North Carolina, ma'am, in the Blue Ridge mountains, the town called Trail."

"Ah, a mountain man!" Mrs. Deegan's voice took on an unexpectedly jocular tone. "Do you ever see ole Dan'l Boone 'round them parts?"

Philip laughed, taken aback. Then, slipping nonchalantly into character, he responded, "No ma'am. I haven't seen ole Daniel . . . but I hear tell he founded the place about a hundred years ago. In fact, my granpa tells me that Dan'l was our kin."

Mrs. Deegan was laughing. She looked up at Mel. "Dear me, Monsieur Leblanc, a lady never knows who is going to show up at the American Embassy!" Fixing her eyes again on Philip, she continued, "And what brings you to France, Mr. Morrow?"

"I am here to accompany Fräulein Lili, and to act, insofar as I can, as an advocate for her and her family, in their quest to become citizens of the great United States of America!"

The lady laughed again, enjoying the moment, luxuriating in this serendipitous association with someone from back home. "Citizens? Oh my! I hope your friends have their ducks in a row, their I's dotted and T's crossed. There seems to be a run on applications for U.S. citizenship these days, especially among the Germans. I don't know if we have a place for all of them."

"Well, Mrs. Deegan. . ." The salesman in Philip was taking command over all potentialities. "It's no secret that over there—across the Rhine—in the so-called Third Reich, Herr Hitler and his gang are doing all they can to run the Jews out of their German domains, and the SS goons are absconding hard-earned Abrahamic assets as they enforce their newfangled pogroms. So I am here to help the Eschens get the hell out of there before it is too late."

"My, my, Mr. Morrow, aren't we blunt in our assessments of this present situation?. . .before it's too late? too late. . .for what?"

Philip had stooped down slightly, intensifying the momentary exchange with the receptionists. He straightened himself, and sighed.

Mel Leblanc "Too late, Mrs. Deegan, for these people who have been deprived of their German heritage, and their livelihood has been removed from them, and even their son—the Eschens' son, Lili's brother. . ." He gestured in her direction. ". . .their son, Heinrich, has been taken away to Dachau prison, and they know not when, or even if, he will be returned to them."

A man was entering the room from outside. Mrs. Deegan's eyes caught sight of him, and the re-assuming of her receptionist duties became once again the foremost matter of her attention. "Can I help you, sir?"

"I am here to see Ambassador Bullit. My name is Josef Reznik, from Czechoslovakia."

"Do you have an appointment, sir?"

"I do not, but I have met with him before. Please let him know that Josef Reznik is here."

"I will do that. Please have a seat over there." She nodded in the direction of the opposite wall, which was furnished with comfortably upholstered chairs around a low table.

"Thank you."

Mrs. Deegan set her eyes again on Philip, and sighed. "What do you do, Mr. Morrow, besides advocating for refugees from the Third Reich?"

Philip chuckled. "I represent the Brigham Tobacco Company." He withdrew a wallet from his pocket. "Here is my card," he said, proffering it to her.

"I will pass this along. I can say that our people here are in full support of your company. Why, the ambassador, and his assistant, Mr. Ofie, light up Bullseye every chance they get."

"Here's a complimentary pack for you, Mrs. Deegan,," he said, offering.

"No, thank you. But you are welcome to accompany Miss Eschen back there if you like. I hope you can be of some help to them. Sometimes, I think our people stateside are doing all they can to keep these. . .Hebrews from getting in. You know how it is back home, not a lot of jobs to go around." She looked at Lili. "Where is it you are wanting to go in America?" she asked.

"My family wants to go to New York, but I would. . .I'd settle for California."

Mrs. Deegan laughed. "Well, good luck to you, Miss Eschen. Your people have got quite a little community going in New York. As for California . . .ha!" She squinted, looking intently at Lili, with a hint of smile. "You have to have stardust in your eyes to make it out there."

"I do," answered Lili, chuckling. "I have stardust, like Shirley Temple."

Mrs. Deegan was quite amused. Then another thought changed her expression. "Although. . .I hear the Okies are taking the place over."

"Okies?" asked Lili.

"Farmers, from Oklahoma. The huge dust storms have blown them out. I read in the papers that most of them are headed for California, and there isn't enough work there to keep 'em all busy. As a matter of fact, there probably isn't enough work in the whole U.S. of A to keep all the Americans busy. As for you refugees. . .I hate to be the bearer of bad news here, but the land of opportunity back home is not, just now, what it's always been cracked up to be." She lowered her voice. "Don't tell anybody I said so, but those fellas in the back room may have more hoops for you to jump through than you can manage. I think some of them have been trying to convince Germans to head for Palestine, or Uganda, or at least somewhere where there's no Depression going on." Mrs. Deegan looked up to see another gentleman, and a woman with him, approach her desk. The couple was quite dapperly attired.

"Bonjour, Madame. Je suis Otto Meszner, with the Berlin Philharmonic. I am here to submit my application, and the other required papers, for citizenship in the United States, and my wife here, Clara."

"Ah, Herr Meszner, I heard you would be here today. You are the oboist, n'est ce pas?"

"Yes, madame. I am pleased to make your acquaintance. He bowed slightly, and nodded courteously to the others present.

"Why, certainly, Herr Meszner, it is my pleasure to admit you to our Embassy. Perhaps these two young ones, Fräulein Eschen and Mr. Morrow, will lead you to the Applications department, as I have already given them directions."

"We are happy to do that," said Philip, looking the oboist in the eyes.

Then Mel stepped, rather abruptly, toward Philip. "I can see, Philip, that you and Lili are well on your way here, and I must be going." Proffering a card, he added. "Here is my address on Boulevard Saint-Michel. Please telephone me, if you like, when you decide to go north, as we discussed earlier. I would welcome the opportunity to travel with you to Flanders." He turned to Lili. "Mademoiselle, it has been a pleasure meeting you. My prayers go with you as you and your family find a way to your destiny, whatever that be." With that brief conclusion of their short afternoon together, he bowed slightly to her, glanced at Philip purposefully. "Adieu, mes amis," and he was out the door as quickly as he had first spoken to Philip in L'eglise Saint-Chapelle.

"Well then," said Philip, "shall we?" and he began walking to the adjacent hallway. "Merci, beaucoup, Mrs. Deegan. You have been very helpful." She smiled a farewell.

Venturing along the hallway with the German couple beside him on one side and Lili on the other, Philip followed her simple directions, arriving soon at a door with opaque glass on which "Applications" was printed. He opened it. The nondescript room was a large office, with three desks facing the door. Behind each desk sat a neatly attired clerk facing applicants. Behind the applicants who were being advised, an orderly array of chairs, probably two dozen of them, were nearly filled with the hopeful immigrants-in-waiting. In three chairs against the wall sat Hezekin, Helene and Hannah Eschen. Lili moved immediately to be seated next to her mother, who was obviously glad to see her. Philip greeted Hezekin and Hannah, and took a seat directly in front of them. He turned his chair so as to face them. Herr

Meszner and his wife took chairs beside him, facing the front and the men behind desks.

"So, Herr Eschen, how has your day been so far?" he asked. He smiled obligingly at Hannah. But the look on Hezekin's face was not good.

"Not so well," said Hezekin. "We received a telegram from the Distribution Committee in the U.S, but it is not what we expected. My cousin Leonard in New York has not yet made the full deposit on our behalf. I was able to send him only half of the necessary amount before the SS restrictions in Munich prevented me from sending any further transmittals. In Leonard's telegram of two days ago—the one we received in Strasbourg— his message was that he was trying to get dollars together to supply the other half, but so far he had not been able to do it. As of this morning, he has still not made the deposit. Our account with the U.S. State Department is still a thousand dollars short. At this point, there is nothing we can do about it, except wait. Now, that is not our only problem. There are two other items on their list of requirements that we have not yet provided. So I don't know how far this interview will proceed."

"What are the other two items?" Philip asked.

Hezekin's face turned from worry to something worse. "They are both documents from our household in Germany. We are expected to provide certified copies of our most recent tax returns, but I was unable to do this when we were leaving Munich. We were in a hurry, and to put it simply, I could not get my hands on them before we had to leave the house and lock it up before catching the train to Stuttgart. The other missing item is a statement of our accounts from our bank in Munich. The bank had refused to give them to me, the day before we left, and I think I know why. The SS is behind their refusal; it is because they are locking up our assets. . ."

"Stealing from you," Philip interrupted.

"Well, yes Philip. I don't what else to call it."

"Damn!" Philip's voice raised in sudden ire. "You are caught between the devil and the deep blue sea in this. It is ridiculous. The U.S. government is—I hope it is not so—aiding and abetting the Nazis in expropriating your money and your property. I just wonder if they know what the hell they're doing by putting forth this policy." He looked over at the three clerks behind desks, who were quietly doing their jobs, speaking in controlled tones to applicants from a controlled country. Philip noticed that Lili was watching him, from several seats away, with some alarm on her face.

"And our son!" Helene interjected. "They have taken Heinrich, and that is the worst of all." Mother's agony was in her eyes.

"But that is not all, Philip," Hezekin continued. "This list, which that fellow behind the desk handed me a half hour ago, also requires something called a 'Certificate of good conduct' from the police authorities in our country of origin. This requirement I had not heard about before today. I do not know how this happened. It must be a new requirement."

"Damn! Itmar had said this would happen. The British have been tightening their policy, and now the U.S. is doing the same thing. I can't believe this! Don't they know what the hell is going on in Germany? Certificate of good conduct!, issued by good Germans to certify good German Jews?"

The low hum of measured conversation droned on from across the room, even as the civilized world now was being torn asunder. Outside the U.S. Embassy, beyond the pedestaled double eagle entrance, beyond the statue of the Lady of Strasbourg, across La Place de la Concorde and past the Louvre where women come and go speaking softly of Michelangelo, and beyond the Saint-Chapelle, farther afield than Alsace and the Rhine and the frontiers of common sense and all decent human enterprise, the civilized world was ripping apart at the seams, while suited men in silken ties speak softly in controlled tones to people made desperate by the heartless vagaries of very specific, calculated larceny. Philip's father had died at Flanders Field almost twenty years ago, to put an end to this—to rid the world of Teutonic hegemony and such finely constructed highway robbery. Now the telegram had come from New York that the Lady of the harbor was trimming her wick, and the lamp beside the golden door would be smoldering under the power of darkness.

"Eschen. Hezekin Eschen," called the clerk from his desk, as he surveyed the room with spectacled eyes.

Hezekin took a deep breath, clutched his briefcase, stood up and approached the desk where a young U.S. State Dep't. clerk awaited his next case. The German couple sat squarely in front of the desk, with Hannah and Lili on either side. Philip dragged a chair forward so he could be positioned behind and between Lili and her mother, within earshot.

"What can I do for you, Mr. Eschen?" The young man was thin and pale. His brown gabardine suit sported a grease spot on the lapel. With a head balding prematurely, and thin, light brown hair greased back, his ears seemed too big. The voice from his lips was a bit too squeaky for a prospective immigrant to find comfort in.

Hezekin had opened his worn attaché case, retrieved a handful of documents, which he carefully laid on the man's desk, with the right-side-up orientation neatly arranged so the man could read them. Then Hezekin extended his hand, smiling sheepishly, and said, "I am Hezekin Eschen, from Munich. I have operated a delicatessen and meat business for thirty years. This is my wife, Helene, and our daughters, Hannah and Lili. We also have a son, Heinrich, who is still in Germany." He glanced back at Philip. "And our friend Philip is here to help us with translation if necessary, or any other matters. He is, like you, from the United States."

After shaking Hezekin's hand., the clerk said, "Very well then, Mr. Eschen. My name is Lou Breckenridge. I see you have what appears to be an impressive collection of papers here. Let's take a look at them. But first, let me ask you, have you been, before today, to this embassy, or any other embassy or consulate of the Department of State of the United States?"

"This is our first visit to this embassy. Before leaving Munich, we went to the U.S. consulate there, and received a list of what documents your Department would require for obtaining four visas, one for each of us. Here is that list." He handed a single printed paper across the desk. "And here, of course, are our documents, as specified on that list."

"You may retain this list, Mr. Eschen. You may need to refer to it from time to time. Do we have here all the documents specified?"

"I am not sure."

"Not sure?"

"There are. . .one or two of them that we could not obtain from the government of Germany."

Mr. Breckenridge had begun thumbing through the three stacks of papers, his hands busily sorting, re-categorizing, and thereby assembling two new stacks. His perfectly manicured thin hands, which Philip thought resembled two big pink spiders, romped nimbly to and fro on his desktop territory, carefully constructing a web of perfect, paperly documentation. "I see you have all five copies of each of your four visa applications. That's a good start, and copies of your birth certificates, and . . . your quota number? Did the consul in Munich assign you a quota number?" He looked through his glasses like a bureaucratic eagle.

"They did not assign me a number."

"Hmm. That is unfortunate. This is an important component of the procedure. You could have saved yourselves some wait time if you had gotten one."

"The official in Munich had said he would assign us a number, but he could not do it on the day we were there."

"Did you not go back later to get a number assigned to you?"

"Unfortunately, Mr. Breckenridge, I had to leave before I could go back to the American consulate in Munich. I am sorry. Can you assign us the number?"

"This is done after your documents have been reviewed by our staff here."

Hezekin's voice took an edge. "Yes, well, that is what the official in Munich told us.

"Perhaps you should have returned to the consulate to get the number before leaving Germany. It would have made your submittal package much more complete."

"Certainly, you are right. I am sorry I was unable to do that."

"Excuse me," Philip inserted. "What does that number assignment entail? Who actually selects the number?"

"It is an internal matter, sir, having to do with policies of the U.S. Department of State, as determined by quotas that have been established by the Congress and the Secretary of State."

"Mr. Cordell Hull?"

"Yes, Secretary of State Hull, although he of course does not assign the numbers themselves."

"Of course," said Philip. He found himself leaning forward, in anticipation of some development, but then, leaning back in the chair he felt a release of tension that expressed as a sigh. "How long will this take?"

"Not long." Mr. Breckenridge eyed Philip like a vigilant rooster with his thin neck. "And what was your name, sir?"

"My name was Philip Morrow, and uh, still is . . . from Trail, North Carolina, home of Daniel Boone. Have you heard of him?"

"Of course I have heard of Daniel Boone, Mr. Morrow."

An awkward silence followed as Mr. Breckenridge dutifully inspected all the papers, once again lifting them deftly, surveying their contents, checking signatures and stamps. After a while, looking down at his pulpy caseload, he said, "The Eschens are not the only applicants for visas to the United States, you know. There are many, many others. The list is quite long. You can hope that your application is not classified as LPC."

"LPC?" asked Hezekin. Philip wasn't touching that one with a ten-foot pole.

"Likely Public Charge," said Mr. Breckenridge, still inspecting. "We've got enough people on the dole in America as it now. We cannot take on new immigrant risks for dependency when we can't even keep all our American workers employed."

"I built my business in Munich from nothing," said Hezekin. "I started working as a butcher on a Bavarian estate, in 1907."

"You have done well, Herr Eschen," said the clerk, lightening his tone. "But I daresay," he said as he looked up, "that was before the Crash."

"The Crash?"

"The stock market crash on Wall Street, in 1929. Everything in the United States has changed drastically since then, and not for the better."

"What has a stock market crash to do with cutting meat for people to eat? Everybody needs food." Hezekin retorted, straightening himself in confidence, with eyebrows raising.

Philip was laughing. These two men were obviously from different continents, different eras, and the difference was not making Hezekin's plight any easier. But Mr. Breckenridge was in the driver's seat, and he knew it. It was a role he was accustomed to.

"Well, I can see, Herr Eschen, that you are not cut from the same cloth as many of these other Jews who are looking for an entrance into the new world. If they are looking for a new world, they should at least try to look like modern people, instead of walking around with their big hats and their curly hair. Those are the LPCs. I cannot imagine many of them making a good way in America."

Hezekin shrugged. "Eeh, to each his own. Isn't that what they say in America? Everybody doing what's best for them. Those are my people you're talking about. I've sliced many a salami for them. They can work hard and spend their money like anybody else."

"Be that as it may, we have some more work to do here." Mr. Breckenridge resumed his careful inspection of the Eschen credentials. "I see you have affadavits, and deposits from a relative in the United States, Leonard Herschel. He's in New York City. Is that where you want to go?"

"Yes," Hezekin affirmed.

"Or California," Lili piped in.

The man looked curiously at Lili. "Well now, that's not a bad idea. I wouldn't mind being in California myself just now."

"It couldn't possibly be better than Paris, Monsieur Breckenridge," Hannah ventured.

His inspection shifted to Hannah. "You may have a point there, mademoiselle. Perhaps you Eschens could do well in the United States after all, although there are plenty of LPCs in California too. Times are tough all over, and there are not enough jobs for everybody in the United States.

That's what I'm trying to tell you. Honestly, you may do better somewhere else."

"As God wills, we will go somewhere, Mr. Breckenridge, but it will not be back to Germany." Helene said with finality.

"The Nazis were giving you a hard time there? I take it."

"To say the least, sir. They have used their new Nazi laws to steal our business from us," Helene continued. "And then they arrested our son and took him away, although he is guilty of no crime. He is guilty of . . .nothing! Heinrich has never done any bad thing."

"What was the charge?"

"They don't need a charge. They don't need a court order. They do what they want, whatever they want, to rob us, Jewish people, of all that we have worked hard for, for generations."

"What was the charge, Herr Eschen?" He looked at Hezekin, seeking, in this case, actual information.

"The charge was kosher killing. This!—this I have been doing all my life, and I taught him the trade, and now these brutish goyim take over and decide it is illegal."

"And where is Heinrich now?"

"He is in Dachau prison," said his mother, beginning to display her grief.

For the first time, young Mr. Breckenridge leaned back in his padded chair with a relaxed demeanor. He swiveled slightly in his swivel chair. He glanced at the wall behind them, looked up at the ceiling, tossed his pencil on the papers. He looked directly at Philip, then at Hezekin. Slowly, he said, "So I suppose this is why you have no dossier from the German police? If there is a dossier on you, it probably will be of no benefit to your cause."

"What difference does it make? Hezekin asked, sincerely. "The police in Munich are now criminals. They are controlled by the SS!"

"Surely, Mr. Breckenridge," said Philip gently, "this is not the first case of this type that you have seen."

"No. We can see from here what it is happening in Germany. But we do have rules."

"Ah!" exclaimed Philip. "But I bet your rules were written before the National Socialists stole the government of Germany from the German people. So, perhaps, Mr. Breckenridge—what was your first name?"

"Lou."

"So perhaps, Lou, it is time that the U.S. State Department change its rules pertaining to political refugees, to reflect what is actually happening here and now in Europe."

"Easily said, Mr. Morrow, easily said. But that would require an Act of Congress."

"I think not. If you look into this, you will probably find that these restrictions are administrative rules that have been promulgated by people in your own State Department."

Lou looked sideways toward the man behind the next desk. "Hey, Earl," he called.

The man redirected his attention away from his own dutiful inspections. "Yeah, what?"

"This requirement for the good conduct form—how long has that been on the visa list? And is it from Congress, or administrative?"

"Ya got me, Lou. Ask Larry."

But Larry, in the third desk, was listening. "I don't know Lou, but it is still a rule. You know that."

"I suggest you look into it, Lou," said Philip, calmly.

Lou peered at Philip again. Then he glanced sideways at his peers again and said. "It looks like we got us a mountain man here, trying to blaze a new trail for the Jews through the State Department."

Philip looked kindly at Mr. Breckenridge. He could feel an amused smile on himself as he said softly. "I'm not the only one. There are **more** of us coming."

It almost seemed for a second that Mr. Breckenridge was amused.

Behind him, against the back wall of the room, two expansive banks of wooden file cabinets held down the fort of Departmental record-keeping. Between these was an oaken door, which suddenly opened. An attractive gray-haired woman stepped through the door, then remained there with her hand on the doorknob. After a few seconds in which she could determine that she would not be interrupting, she called, "Mr. Breckenridge."

"Yes," said the clerk, still inspecting his charge.

"May I see you for a moment?"

"Certainly, Emma." He looked up at Hezekin. "Excuse me," he said, then promptly rose and left the room behind her.

"I think your daughters have special talents," Philip commented to Hezekin. "As soon as they started talking, he lightened up quite a bit."

Hezekin smiled. "I'll have to remember that," he said.

A minute later, Mr. Breckenridge returned. "I must conclude this interview for now. Please telephone in two days for your quota number."

22

Zion

"Now the deep currents of history have come to the surface," said Edmond Rougond. He was speaking to the Eschens as they, having wandered from the American Embassy into the nearby Tuileries Gardens, were sitting on a park bench. In the center of a large, stone-enclosed pool before them, a fountain designed to irrigate their vision, displayed silvery plumets of water that danced with the afternoon sun. Dancing droplets glittered before the party of seven souls, only one of whom was a resident of Paris. Very near to them, by the edge of the pool, a pair of black swans, with their necks swaying, floated effortlessly.

Two gentlemen, friends of Itmar, were there to provide yet another perspective on where the rising currents of history may propel, from this juncture, the now-homeless family Eschen family. Afternoon sunlight cast a warm glow on their little interlude, illuminating the riot of spring flowers blooming around them. "The current erupted to the surface in Russia about fifty years ago," Monsieur Rougond continued. "Before that, the flow of it had been, as it were, subterranean, mostly in the east of Europe, ever since the Diaspora that Titus provoked when he ran our people out of Eretz Israel, eighteen hundred years ago."

Philip was watching with curiosity as M. Rougond spoke. A balding, middle-aged professor with, Philip thought, a striking resemblance to Lenin, he stood in front of the park bench as if delivering a private lecture to the Eschens. The man was quite comfortable addressing this hapless German family in such a manner, as he was a lecturer at the Sorbonne, albeit it in physics. He had already explained to his audience that the scholarly awakening of his youth had propelled him into a scientific channel early on.

He had followed that inclination to an accomplished position in the world of academics. But events in the real world of human governments had imposed upon him an obsession with issues more fundamental to the human spirit, and specifically the Jewish expression of it.

"In 1881, Czar Alexander II was assassinated. This was a terrible loss. He was a man who had departed, courageously, from the ancient Russian policy of oppressing us Jews. He had set the serfs free. Our people were able, for the first time, to openly attend schools and universities. But when he was killed, a new repression began with the 'May Laws' of 1882. Among our people, there were two different strategies of resistance against Czarist repression that materialized in the following years. We had some relatively influential men—*shtadlonim* we called them—who took it upon themselves to represent our interests to the authorities. But these leaders, enjoying the benefits of some wealth, were too timid in their advocacy of our generally desperate circumstances. They did not want to, as the Americans say, 'rock the boat.' This type of leadership was benevolent, but not very effective in resolving our disparities." He sighed, expecting a question or two. But none came. The Eschens were listening carefully. "My friend here, Gurion, probably knows more about this than I do." Edmond smiled and nodded to his friend. Gurion had propped one leg on the end of the bench and was leaning upon it, nursing his cup of coffee cup from the nearby open-air café.

"Please, continue, my friend," Gurion Salomon encouraged him.

Edmond gathered his thoughts. "But from deep within the folk a more resolute impulse came forth. This was a necessary and inevitable development, like. . . like the coming of spring." He gestured, smiling, at the flowers growing in orderly beds beside them. "This impulse was provoked by the very privation that we experienced, yes, but it was inspired by a much older, and more constructive, collective memory that our people had carried within themselves for many, many generations. It is memory—ancient, but quite potent, and very active—linked to a yearning for redemption." He chuckled. "I suppose that here in Paris, among these existentialists, it is thought of as purpose, or a reason for being. *What is my purpose for being here?* you see." He locked eyes with Philip, and for a moment, Philip saw the zeal of Joshua behind the gleam. "But for most of us Jews, not all of us, by any means. . ." He laughed, cocking his head to the side. ". . . it is a devotion, first to G_d, *Elohim* who created us, and who spoke to Moses through a burning bush." He smiled down at Hezekin. "You know this."

Reaching in his coat pocket, Hezekin retrieved a yarmulke and placed it on his head. There was joy all around in this simple, public act of identity, for in Germany the wearing of the yarmulke had long since covered Hebrew heads with officially sanctioned humiliation.

Continuing, "But this is more than devotion. It is emotional, visceral. It demands some kind of restoration of. . .something missing, something that has been lost along the way. . . and it becomes, for many, an ideological impetus, that is linked to a vision for collective life, rooted not only in Jewish tradition, but in a very worldly, tangible and practical way: it is rooted in the land itself."

"And what land is that?" asked Gurion gently, rhetorically, as if he did not know.

Edmond smiled. He peered at Lili. "And what land is that, young lady?"

"Palestine," she replied, looking up at him, in wonder at his zeal.

He looked into her eyes deeply. "Israel."

"I—Israel," she repeated.

"Oh, daughter of Zion, did you not know this?" Smiling again, he spread his arms, as if it were a given.

Lili, a little stunned, but recovering, "I do now."

Everybody was a little bit amused.

"And do you think, Lili, that Shirley Temple in California, USA, can compare with Eretz Israel?"

Turning red with embarrassment, Lili turned aside to her mother, who was, no doubt, the source of this breach of confidentiality, this divulging of the daughter's escapist California dreaming. She was embarrassed, yes, but nevertheless mildly pleased with the attention. "Mother!"

But her mother was laughing, with hand to her mouth. "I'm so sorry," she said, with little conviction.

Then, as the outburst of mirth subsided, Gurion Salomon began to speak. He was a short man, also balding but not as much. He had wild hair that stuck out from his head as if charged with electricity, and a large nose, between expressive brown eyes. "It is good that we can laugh in the face of such danger," he said, rather startlingly.

After an awkward moment, "You mean the danger that we have been through in getting away from the Nazis?" asked Hannah. This was the older daughter speaking.

"Yes, certainly," Gurion affirmed, softly. "But of course your brother has not gotten away, has he?" And the jocular mood was suddenly interrupted.

"No," said Hannah. "He hasn't."

"And you understand, Oh daughter of Zion, that this is not the end of our tribulations. Even as your brother Heinrich is suffering untold troubles now, agonies that he cannot communicate to us, we ourselves are destined to endure with him the terrible toll of this injustice."

"How's that?" asked Hannah.

"We are all in this together," Gurion answered.

"This? Life—you mean we're all in this life together."

"Certainly, but there is more to it than life itself. There is the replacement of that which is missing. It is a restoration, which makes life better, makes life more complete. This is something that, tragically, Heinrich is no longer in any position to do. But you—we, all of us here—are. We, as Boaz of old, can redeem the land. We can be agents of redemption here on earth, if we are willing to accept the call, because what has happened to Heinrich—it is not the end of this. It is neither the beginning nor the end. As Edmond told us a few minutes ago about the oppressive laws that were enacted in Russia fifty years ago, after Alexander II was assassinated—those restrictions were not the first laws ever promulgated to restrict our people from the privileges and opportunities commonly available to other citizens. This is a new pogrom in Germany, but it is really nothing new. Since the times, long ago, of Hyman, Antiochus, Titus—and there have been many others, Torqamada—we can know, through the counsel of those who have gone before—that these persecutions of our people are nothing new. This Hitler beast who has imprisoned your brother is but the latest manifestation of it. So it becomes obvious to us that now is the time to, once and for all, carve our way of deliverance out of the wilderness."

"Of course," Edmond added, "there is no better wilderness in which to carve than the one we started with four thousand years ago, Eretz Israel. In taking this course, we will circumvent the anti-Semites of the world by forging our own solution to their 'Jewish problem.' We would rather implement our own plan than wait for any ruthless, self-appointed regime of the goyim to undertake it. The British have helped us tremendously since the Parliament adopted the Balfour Declaration after the war, although. . ." The professor raised his eyebrows and looked knowingly at his partner-in-arms.

"It seems that, lately they are starting to get in the way a bit," Gurion said.

It was time for the American to speak up. Philip asked, "Aren't they reversing their immigration policy now, because of the Arab riots last year?"

"We hope not. We are waiting for the Peel Commission to make a decision about what policy adjustments would be in everybody's best interests, now that certain elements of the Arab community have decided to take issue with our settlements."

"Where do you live, Mr. Salomon?" Philip asked.

"I live in Tel Aviv. I moved there three years ago. Before that, I had lived in a settlement called Petah Tiqvah, which is Hebrew for 'Gate of Hope.' It was founded by Zionists in 1878. Before that, I grew up in Poland, but I left there for Ottoman Palestine in 1907, when I was twenty-two years old."

"And, I take it, you are hoping to recruit the Eschens here, to settle in Israel?"

"We have a place for them if they are willing to go. But Israel is not for everyone; it is not even appropriate for every Jew to immigrate there. There is much work to do there, and it is hard work, too. Based on what Itmar has told me about Hezekin, he could make a great contribution to our project. There are not many men whose work experience reflects expertise in business, such as he has developed in the cattle business, that originated in his own two hands—the hands of a working man who knows his trade from the ground up."

"And you, Monsieur Rougond, do you live in Israel?"

"Thank you, Philip, for calling our homeland Israel. That is what our forefathers have called it for several thousand years now. I have lived there. I made Aliyah two years ago to take a physics post at the new Weizmann Institute in Rehovat, which is just south of Tel Aviv. But I have taken a temporary assignment here at the Sorbonne, working on a special project. Dr. Weizmann thought, considering the work in physics with which I am presently engaged, this would be a good opportunity for me, as well as for our physics department at the Institute."

"What project is that?" Philip asked?

"It is called quantum mechanics, which is the study of physics at the microscopic level. Have you heard of it?

"I have. That has something to do with the structure of atoms—protons and electrons, and that sort of thing, right?"

"Yes, but on the smallest possible level that you can imagine. Within the realm of those protons and electrons, there are even smaller particles, if they can be called that, which sometimes display characteristics of energy, rather than matter."

"So that is related to Einstein's equation, E equals MC squared, correct?"

"Precisely." Dr. Rougond chuckled.

"Studying such small interactions as that is quite a different activity from dabbling in national politics, and recruiting people from one nation to another, n'est-ce pas?"

"That is true," answered the professor, amused. "But in this endeavor with my friend here, Gurion, I am just providing some assistance. It is a rather pleasant change from working in the laboratory with electron microscopes and such. But I will say, there is more in common between these two worlds—the atomic and the political—than you may think."

"Oh," exclaimed Philip, cocking his head slightly. "How so?"

Dr. Rougond laughed. "You are a very inquisitive fellow, my friend. Perhaps you should. . ." He was watching Philip with interest.. ". . . come to Israel as well."

Philip was taken by surprise. He felt himself turning red with embarrassment.

"As for the smallness of quantum physics, as compared to the relative largeness of political movements, I should say that I simply have large faith in the power of small things, small . . .beginnings."

"That is. . ." Philip was thinking out loud. "That is a fascinating way to put it, large faith in the power of small things. It is what Jesus called 'faith like a mustard seed.'"

"Ha! C'est sa. I have heard that he said that."

"If my layman's understanding of Einstein's equation is correct, it proves that there can be, in fact, very large amounts of power that can be released when those very small atom parts react in a certain way. Is that right?"

"Yes, exactly. Theoretically. If the bond that holds protons together in an atom's nucleus is broken, theoretically, energy in a very large amount will be released."

"Sounds dangerous," mused Philip.

"Oh, yes. But of course, it has not happened yet. Or, I should say, it has not happened in a way that men can discern or experience on this earth. But out in space, in the wide, wide solar system, the galaxy, the universe. . .anything can happen, and probably is happening, even now. This is, I suppose, how our universe was formed."

"What about God? Didn't Moses write that God created the universe?"

"Sure. It had to start with God. As the Frenchman, Rene Descartes reasoned, there had to be a Prime Mover." The professor checked the time on his watch. "Speaking of the Mover, I've got to be moving along, sorry to say. Itmar had asked us to meet you here, and I am happy that we were able to arrange this little rendezvous. But I do have a few errands to do before shul.

My wife and I will be at the synagogue, and Itmar, if he is not off somewhere being busy." Edmond looked at Hezekin. "Will you be joining us for shul this evening?"

"Yes. The Berrots have invited us, and they will be fetching us at our hotel soon. We do need to be getting back to the hotel. Thank you for taking some time with us here. Your presentation is, ah, very convincing." Hezekin glanced at Helene, who was smiling. Beside her, Lili was standing, looking a little disoriented.

"So what do you think about our 'presentation'? Did we convince you to join us in Aliyah Israel?"

"We will be considering it. Surely, it is, as Mr. Salomon mentioned, 'not for everybody.' It does sound like there is so much work to be done, and I am getting old."

"We are all getting old," agreed Edmond Rougond. He turned to Philip with outstretched hand. "Philip, it has been a pleasure meeting you. Perhaps we will see you at the synagogue."

"The pleasure is mine, Monsieur. Thank you for the invitation. We shall see what happens. We shall see how the Prime Mover moves in these coming days."

Out on the rippling pool, two black swans stretched their necks and their gleaming black wings, preparing to move. The red sun was pasted in the sky behind a host of descending birds. Along the edges of white-graveled Tuileries pathways, willow trees bowed in adoration of our Creator, and the City of Light prepared for another evening and another day, the seventh day. It was good.

23

Absinthe

"You go," Philip said to Lili as they were leaving Tuileries gardens, following some paces behind the rest of the Eschens. "Go and worship, and be with your family. It sounds like you have some decisions to make. I will be fine here. I'm going to take a walk. I have a few decisions of my own to make."

She looked at him with compassion. "You are so alone, thousands of miles from your home. You can come with us. You don't have to be Jewish to come with us to synagogue."

"Yeah, well . . .I'll be okay. I'm not the only one far from home, you know; you are far from your home too. At least I can go back to where I came from, whenever I choose to. That's not something you can do, unless you're willing to take a chance on. . ."

"On getting arrested for no good reason, like my brother."

"Yes." He grinned weakly at her, feigning nonchalance. But he felt, for some odd reason. that he could no longer look at her just now, and he needed to be away from her, away from her family. There was an intimacy among them that he could not enter into. It was so different from his family, so unlike his upbringing, in which his grandparents had raised him while they ran a general store in a little mountain town back in that other world. Indeed, America in Philip's memory was another world, the land of the free, where no strange political repression was happening, where no menacing presence of some ancient prejudice overshadowed, where no irrational grudge stretched back into the shadows of the Old World. Something was stirring deep within him that he could not contain. It was time to let this whole thing go. The Eschens could find their own way; they didn't need him. His expected advocacy for them at the embassy had turned into a non-event. There was now no longer any reason for him to follow them around this god-forsaken city. And seeing her in this late afternoon light was a kind of exquisite agony. He could endure seeing her while they were alone, but her family's presence cast everything into a different light. For the first time, he was wondering how Itmar had ever talked him into making this ridiculous jaunt through France.

Of course, it had not started this way. The assistance he had offered Itmar when they were at the docks back in London had seemed such a simple gesture at the time. But now, everything was difficult, and the journey was far too complicated. He had not signed up for this. She was too beautiful. The rosy hue of her cheeks was irresistible. He wanted to touch her face tenderly, but not while her family was present. He knew the cultural difference, the religious difference, between them was too vast to ever be bridged, unless he could get to a place of being alone with her for some long time, and he could not foresee that happening in any way, nor could he even fathom any true purpose for it than his own slow-boiling love for her.

Philip found himself wandering in Paris. Their late afternoon parting had unexpectedly provoked a strange, itinerant sorrow unlike anything he had ever felt before, and he set slowly across La Place de la Concorde, ambling aimlessly westward, through car traffic while Frenchmen and women heading home at the end of another Friday scurried on around him. Crossing the wide plaza, he followed the great, grand boulevard, Champs Elysee, and proceeded along the sidewalk on its north side. Philip slowly passed by the shops and small stores, open-air cafes and large department stores, patisseries, brasseries, groceries, vendors avec their carted flowers, books, les pommes, and les oranges; he trod beneath and among over-arching trees that bequeathed, with tender nature, their leafy green grace upon all that humans make and do as we pass below, amongst all our goings to and fro, displaying most of what we grow and know, while overhead streetlights cast their spotty, yellow glow o'er impressionistic Paris with all its starry, streety, post-impressionist smearings of Van Gogh.

L'Arc de Triomphe loomed over him but a block or two ahead when Philip glanced up a sidestreet on his right, peering into the darkening city's enticements. Blue and red neon caught his eye: the sign for *Cabaret Latrec* quietly beckoned in the darkening dusk. This low-glow beacon summoned, from deep within him, prospects of some exotic diversion, now being rarified as faint music, half-heard strains of an accordion and a woman's voice. Approaching an antiquish wooden door from which the melody emanated, he opened it and entered, unthinkingly. Through smoky ambiance and a small crowd of elegantly-appointed listeners, a crooning dame's sweet-sad song celebrated love, while romanticizing its loss. Soft, jazzy piano notes and the wispy accordion wove melodic embellishments in and out of her phrases. A standup bass thumped gently underneath, while a brushy little snare drum stroked the ensemble's moody rendition with soft rhythm from behind.

Philip was drawn in, feeling immediately an anesthetic comfort to sooth the piercing of Lili's unforeseen presence, or absence of it, into his awkward life. He moved closer to listen. A pale, dark-haired songstress, clothed in shimmering black glamour, poured forth the classic mood-altering lament:

Plaisir d'amour ne dure qu'un moment;
chagrin d'amour dure toute la vie.

He was standing beside a small table in the back of the room. "Monsieur," he heard a white-shirted waiter say beside him, as the man bowed slightly and withdrew a chair from beneath the table. A lit candle and a vase with two red rosebuds graced the tabletop, he noticed as he took the seat.

"Un verre de votre vin rouge préféré, s'il vous plait," he said, looking the waiter in the eyes.

"Oui, monsieur."

Philip listened to the singer, watching her with pleasure. She was a beautiful woman, though much older than he, probably about forty. In the smoky spotlight her eyes shone with a seasoned passion, while she offered the classic love song in a high, controlled vibrato. As a ritual libation, its dimly familiar melody flowed like aged burgundy from her blood-red lips.

J'ai tout quitta pour l'ingrate Sylvie.
Elle me quitte, et prend un autre amant.

Philip was sipping his burgundy, losing himself in the moment, and so the fresh poignancy of Lili's impact on his day was already fading. This was his intention. The two scarlet roses on the table became objects of intense study, interrupted only by glimpses at the glistening lady in black who commemorated the event in her bright spotlight. He knew his love for Lili would never bloom; it would remain in his memory as the perpetual rosebud on this table. The differences between them were too vast. He knew he'd be better off to move forward from here. Lili was not the sort who would seek another lover, as the song says; rather, she would find some other man better suited for herself, better prepared for her station in life, her family and her Jewish faith. It would be better to prick his finger on the thorn of this Parisian interlude with her, tossing the flower and then receiving the pain as a life lesson, than to linger longingly at the rose, and then be obliged by her family and their imminent untimely displacement to watch the petals fall one by one.

Meanwhile, the glittering singer's skilled performance, presenting a theatrical excellence rather than, say, the wounded innocence a younger singer would project, evoked "Sylvie's" perspective on the song's low glow of old love lost. She was the one who had forsaken some past lover, who had composed the song as a plaintive legacy of love's careless cruelty.

He ordered a second glass of the wine. Then the wise woman in black, who was so tunefully administering salve to his soul, transformed in his mind . . . he was imagining her now as a ballerina, not just any lovely pirouette from the Nutcracker or whatever, but rather the young woman he had seen in a Degas painting this morning. He had studied a print of the artwork in a shop window, near the café where he and Lili had lingered before visiting Sainte-Chapelle. Something about the way light was shining on this singer, in her illuminated garb, reminded him of that artful dancer, whom Degas had portrayed in his famous work as being in a pool of light.

Within his memory, there was a fondness for this picture. Back in '29, his second year at Carolina, Philip had fallen for a girl. She was a girl like no other. Charlotte was from a prosperous family of Charleston; she was studying art history. They would spend hours together in the campus coffee shop, smoking cigarettes and talking. Now and then she would let him kiss her. She had been to France. He had seen within her an intense preoccupation with the impressionist painters. Even as young as they were at that time, she had already been to Paris, had spent hours wandering in the Louvre and the Musee D'Orsay. Although Renoir and Monet were great in her mind, Toulouse-Latrec and Degas were her obsession.

For some unfathomable reason, this particular Degas image was etched forever in his memory. Charlotte had shown him a picture of it in a large book of impressionist prints. In the painting, a lovely dark-haired, white-skirted ballerina is dancing, *on pointe*, in a special kind of staged light, the depiction of which the artist had perfected as a favored characteristic of his signatory style. With her arms extended in a wide, celebratory movement, the dancer's blissful face is turned upwards to heaven, or toward the artist, who is positioned on a balcony or some such position above. Around her waist, an energy-charged red, orange and yellow flower bouquet burst color upon the white field of her billowing skirt. Other ballerinas in the background seem to step lightly, their toes pointing outward in classical ballet style. The overall feeling of the painting was of brightness and celebration.

Perhaps this wizened songstress, draped in sequined black and crooning of lost love, had been, in her youth, rather like the illumined ballerina, whose jubilant movement must surely outshine, when all is said and done and all stories told, the melancholy evocation of old love ballads.

"Are you an American?" asked a gravelly male voice from the next table, breaking Philip's reverie as some other French tune glided to an airy accordion cadence.

Philip turned to his left, and considered more closely the couple sitting there. The man, in mature middle age with a crown of white hair atop his head, sat looking at Philip, his face turned slightly upward in a kind of jovial welcome, expecting a response. The woman, tan and red-haired, appeared much younger; she was sipping from a glass of wine. Philip smiled at them, instantly recognizing the man's friendly accent. "Yes. How did you know?" he asked, across the empty table.

"You look like one!" The man smiled good naturedly, paused a second, relaxed his face a bit. "I oughta know an American when I see one; I am one myself! Truth be told though, ah . . . the waiter told us. Come over here and join us. What are you drinkin' over there by yourself?"

Philip raised his glass, looking at it awkwardly, as if it were an object of some curiosity. "Why, uh, one of the local reds, I guess." He chuckled; it seemed like the thing to do. Standing up, he walked gingerly over to the other table and sat with them.

"I'm Robert Jabbok, from the state of Washington, pleased to meet you. This lady here is Simone." His hand was extended with friendly ease, and Philip took it easily, finding himself strangely comforted to be in the company of a fellow countryman. A firm handshake it was.

Philip sat, placed his glass on the table. "I'm Philip Morrow, from North Carolina, pleased to meet you."

"Ah! well then, Philip, what brings a young fella like you all the way from the land of the free and home of the brave, to this Continental powderkeg?"

Philip, slightly amused at Robert's colorful language, responded dutifully, "I represent the Brigham Tobacco Company, of North Carolina."

"Ah! You sell cigarettes?"

"Well, yes, mainly. We have a whole line of tobacco products." But now Philip noticed within himself, a sudden, unprecedented embarrassment at the disclosure of that fact. The thought of Mel Leblanc, and the admonition that the Frenchman had spoken to him that morning about cigarettes, crossed his mind, inexplicably.

"Can I have one?" asked Robert, uninhibited as the day is long.

"Sure." Philip was chuckling. "In fact, take that pack. I've got plenty of them."

"You're kidding!" said Robert, accepting the pack from Philip's hand.

"Wow, how long has it been since I heard that?" Philip mused. "Only Americans say that—'you're kidding'. You won't hear that phrase from a Brit, and certainly not from a Frenchman."

"Ha!" He looked playfully at the woman beside them. "She's French. How about it, Simone? Have you ever heard someone say 'you're kidding'?"

"Non." She smiled easily too.

"What about you, Mr. Jabbok? What are you doing in France?" Something about Robert indicated that this fortissimo man was no tourist.

"I have just been released," Robert stated, rather matter-of-factly.

Philip's face registered a curious grin. "Released. . .?"

"Yes. I have been released," the bravado repeated. He looked knowingly at Simone. She was leaning back in the chair, smoking nonchalantly, and allowed him the minimalist hint of a smile.

Philip felt as if he were in a game of some sort. "You are the first American I have met since I came to this country two weeks ago, and. . .and you're telling me you have just been released?" He felt as if he had just taken on the Yiddish inflictions that he heard from Gurion only a couple of hours ago. "Released from what?"

"You have discovered, my friend, . . ." Robert's eyes wandered around the room. The accordion player had returned to the spotlight, this time with a violinist at his side. The two musicians caught the wily old fellow's attention for a moment. Then they began playing softly, the final theme from Dvorak's New World, a melody which some have named *Going Home*. Robert smiled approvingly. "You have, no doubt, discovered that this life is a game, n'est-ce pas?"

"A game?"

"Yes."

"And what, Robert, is **your** game?"

"Ah! The game is. . . whether you are to live, or . . ." He shrugged. "to die."

Philip wanted to accommodate this man in whatever point he was trying to make. "That is a simple enough game to play, I suppose. We—all of us here. . ." He looked at Simone. "We are masters of this game, yes? as we are all three are sitting here. . .alive, as it were."

Robert was silent for a moment. Then he laughed with satisfaction. He looked into Philip's eyes. "You play the game well, my friend." The man reached into the side pocket of a jacket that was hung upon the back of his chair. He reached into the pocket as easily as if he were wearing the jacket, and withdrew a leather-covered flask, which he twisted open at its top. On the table in front of him was a glass half-full of water. Setting the mouth of the flask carefully over the glass, he poured a small amount of greenish liquid into it, which turned the water in the glass a milky yellow.

Philip was curious, but said nothing.

Robert took a little sip. He smacked his lips with delight.

"Okay. You got me. What drink is that?"

"A medicine. Do you want to taste it?"

"What is it for?"

"It is for everything," he said, as if this requires no further explanation.

Philip was of course amused at this behavior. He did not want to pursue the matter of tasting. The air of mystery surrounding Mr. Jabbok was interesting, but not an attribute that he himself would want to take on.

Robert took another little swig. "This is, for instance, better than the evening papers."

Philip chuckled. "It's not difficult to be better than the newspapers, these days. There is so much bad news. Does your medicine medicate against the bad news?"

"It does." Robert lifted his head in a quick movement of affirmation. What's more. . . it is better than all the old evenings in Paris cafes, or even . . .Madrid cafes. . ."

The Madrid reference did not escape Philip's notice, but he did not mention it. Robert's quirky role-playing began to assume a spectre of comprehension in Philip's mind. He gazed at the accordion man with a moment of appreciation, then turned again to Robert. "You don't hear music like that in America," he commented.

"Oh yes you do," said Robert, quickly.

"Oh, where?"

"In *South* America." Robert was entertaining himself with this banter.

"Ah," Philip said, as if the syllable carried some arcane profundity. "You know, Mr. Jabbok, I did not come from London, to France, on the boat from Calais."

"Oh?" Robert was happy now. He had enjoined Philip to his pastime after only one mention of the game. "How *did* you come to France, mon ami?"

"I came on a boat into St. Jean de Luz."

Robert lifted his eyebrows. "I see. And why was it, mi amigo, that you entered Napolean's country way down there, instead of taking the short route from London?"

"Some business to attend to," said Philip, matter-of-factly.

"Your tobacco business? Don't tell me—cigarettes."

"Precisely. I was delivering cigarettes. I can have some delivered to you if you like."

Robert Jabbok laughed. "These cigarettes, the *Bullseyes*, you delivered a shipment of these." He nodded down toward the pack that Philip had given him. "You are doing quite well, mi amigo. I can see that. American cigarettes are precious cargo on this side of the Atlantic, as you well know, especially the Bullseyes; they are probably more valued than any other, especially . . . in Spain, n'est-ce pas?"

"Yes, especially in Spain."

Robert lit up another one, as if to fortify his point about Philip's leading brand. "And to whom did you deliver these cigarettes, in Spain?"

"A Spaniard."

Robert's gaze was steadily bullseyed on Philip. It was as if the absinthe had reinforced his bizarrely resolute behavior. "A Spaniard. . . of which side, Republican or Fascist?"

"I do not know. Does it matter?" asked Philip, honing, at last, to the point at which they had laconically determined to arrive.

"Oh, si, es importante." he exclaimed, nodding excitedly. "You should not be doing business with the Fascists." Robert's veiled ambiguity had turned suddenly to certainty. "I myself have shed blood for the Republic of Spain, mi amigo. And what is *muy importante* is I have just come from there, less than a week ago. I barely got out of there with my life."

"You were fighting for the Madrid government?"

"Si. But the government has moved to Valencia."

"Oh, yes. I read that. That is not a good sign for the Republic."

"It is not a good sign for anyone," Robert mumbled, almost groaning. His eyes wandered. He noticed the waiter. "Nicolas!" Another drink for my friend here," He looked at Philip. "What will you have? This is on me. Would like to try the absinthe?"

"Un peu du cognac sera bien," said Philip.

Simone added, just as Nicolas arrived at the table, "Je voudrais avoir une quiche, s'il vous plait."

"Qui quiche?" asked the waiter.

"Ratatoille quiche."

"C'est bien."

"Bring a whole one," Robert said. "We will eat quiche so the medicine does not get the best of us."

When Nicolas had taken the order and gone to fill it, Robert's attention was directed once again to the war in Spain when Philip said, "So you were fighting for the Republic. Where?"

"In Castile and Leon, but out in the countryside, in the Sierras near Avila."

"And you left the war to come to France?"

"I had to leave."

"Were you, ah, discharged?"

" Se podria decir. . .I discharged myself, " he answered. "I had signed up, in the International Brigades, for one year. My year had ended, almost."

"Almost?"

"I had a good opportunity to leave Spain, with only two months left in my enlistment. I had a good friend who had just been killed, and I myself had been laid up with a gunshot wound in a hospital in Barcelona for a week." He looked into Philip's eyes earnestly, for the first time expressing something besides confidence and machismo. *Was it fear?* Then he lifted his shirt to reveal a large bandage on his low right abdomen, still in place. He dropped the shirt. "When the Fascists were pressing hard on Madrid, and the government decided to withdraw to Valencia. . . as we said, esto no era una buena señal. You remember that we also said, a few minutes ago, what the game of life is all about, really. . .and I thought of Simone here." He looked at her and smiled. There was a moment of tender gratefulness between them.

"Whether one is to live, or die," said Philip.

"Si, mi amigo. So I was released from death, but my dear friend, Ernest— he was from Idaho—he did not escape that sentence. We had traveled to Spain together to join the Brigades, but he did not get out alive, although he did manage to complete the mission that had been assigned to him."

"What mission was that?"

"General Golz had sent us into the mountains to blow up a bridge—Ernest was an engineer—so Franco's army would not get through to Madrid."

"Your friend blew up the bridge?"

"He did. But it cost him his life."

"Did the explosion kill him?"

"No. The explosion was beautiful; it was perfect. It happened exactly as he had planned it. But afterward, very soon afterward, he was shot dead by a Falangist lieutenant."

"Oh. I am. . ." Somehow, sympathy did not seem appropriate to comfort this old fighter. Philip peered carefully into the man's eyes, seeing no expectation of comfort there, but only a stoic resolve. "Were you there?"

"I was not there, although I was nearby, and had already taken the bullet. Some peasant fighters took me to Avila on a horse cart. From there I was taken to Madrid, then to Barcelona. Barcelona is, you know, so very close to France. . .my year was almost up." He shrugged his shoulders. "I fear the worst for the Republic. The partisans are very disorganized. Lately, though, they are getting very good, disciplined support from the Russians, but the prescribed Moscow remedies are . . ." Robert glanced down at his absinthe glass, now nearly empty. His voiced trailed off, sleepily, or drunkenly, Philip could not tell which. "Their remedies are bitter, like the medicine here."

"You like the medicine, n'est-ce pas?"

"I like it, but. . .I do not like the Russians, although they are exactly what is needed if the Republic is to survive."

"The Republicans are damned if they do, and damned if they don't . . .submit to the Russians' organized warfare."

"Usted ha dicho exactamente," said Robert Jabbok.

Nicolas brought Ratatouille quiche, setting it on the table for them. Philip was so very glad to see the food. He felt as if he could eat an entire quiche by himself. "S'il vous plait apporter un autre," he said to Nicolas.

As the waiter was leaving, Philip interrupted his departure. "Oh, Nicolas, s'il vous plait, quiche Lorraine, ce temps, sur mon cheque."

Receiving food was a dénouement, of sorts. Robert and Simone ate hungrily, as did Philip, for a few minutes while the music continued, a spirited rendition of the Farandole from Bizet's L'Arlesienne, offered by the violinist, with the accordion accompanying. Its energetic conclusion was applauded by the thirty or so patrons of Cabaret Latrec. Robert seemed to be revived by the taking of food and lively music. The pianist came out again, opening his solo set with Debussy's *Clair de Lune*, which appropriately established a somber mood for what was to come.

Philip was mildly surprised when Robert, having refreshed himself and ordered espresso, appeared ready to resume his melancholic retrospective. "But I must tell you, mon ami, the deeper truth that, almost from the very start, predetermined my eventual departure from Spain. It was because of what I saw at an event that took place when I had been in Castile for one month."

"Do tell," Philip obliged.

"In the town of Abiesa, during the beginning of the movement—August of last year it was—much blood had been spilt on Spanish ground after Franco had sent his army of traitors into Castile and Leon to make a way for the Fascists to Madrid. Our fighting against the guardias was brutal and bloody, and all of it was ugly, even the glorious part that ended in our occupation of the town itself." Robert slurped his little espresso. His eyes reflected a weary urgency to report to Philip's willing ears an account of certain events that disturbed his soul.

"The nearby peasants, under the leadership of the *Partido Agrario*, had taken control of the town. They set up a revolutionary council in the *Ayuntamiento*, or city hall as we call it in the U.S., to administer justice to the fascists who had formerly controlled the town. There were about twenty of them, held prisoner and being tried—if you could call what happened there a trial—for their oppressions against the people of Abiesa and also against the peasants of that region. All of these men were known to the peasants and workers. Everybody knew everybody. There was a man named Pablo, a native of the village, who was in command. He ruled over the arbitrary proceedings inside the Ayuntamiento with a pistol at his side the whole time." Robert, having finished his espresso, summoned Nicolas and ordered a glass of the wine.

"Pablo sent word to the church that the priest should be brought over to hear the Fascists' confessions. And so, within a few minutes, the priest, trembling with fear, was brought into the big room to hear them confess their many sins and to make peace with God before they were to be sent out to their fate at the hands of the townspeople. The priest began praying with them—as I was told, for I was outside, with others of our Brigade, in the perimeter, and in the shade. I could see the front portico of the Ayuntamiento, as some people would, from time to time, be allowed to go in or come out. The plaza was filled with people. After awhile they arranged themselves into two groups, one group on each half of the square, with a clear path between them, about two meters wide, which went from the steps of the big hall all the way out to the cliff which was on the edge of the plaza, with the river far below it. I was told that the fate of the condemned men would be that they should be brought out after their confessions and then made to walk between the two lines of the townspeople, all the way out to the cliff, where they would have no choice but to jump, or be thrown off.

"This was a cruel arrangement, and crude enough as it was hastily organized by the Partido partisans. But the people waited for an hour or two before the first Fascist was turned out to suffer his fate. And while they lingered there, they were—it seemed to me, every one of them, except for the children—drinking continuously from their bottles, and disposing of any decency or semblance of legal legitimacy—and as the day passed they became more and more drunken, so that by the time the first prisoner was sent out, the mocking and jeering that they cast upon him—this was a man with whom they had lived and done business for all their lives—was disgusting. I was thoroughly disgusted, and went aside to vomit in the grass. I was not even drinking that day.

"There were to be twenty prisoners thrust out into the unmerciful hands of that mob. As the doomed men came out, one by one, with an agonizing half-hour or so, between each one, the drunken townspeople, incited with mounting rage by the most depraved, worthless ones among them, each prisoner was taunted differently according to his personal history among them. As the condemned souls were prodded and pushed forward like cattle toward their demise at the long falling into the river, they were also beaten with rods that are normally used to flail cattle into submission. The flails had been stolen, along with a bunch of pitchforks and other implements being used for their punishments, from a store owned by a man called Don Guillermo. But as fate would have it for poor Don Guillermo, he was one of the men ruled to be a Fascist among them, and so he too was sent out to be humiliated and executed by the drunkards of Abiesa. A few townspeople among them cried out for mercy to be shown to Don Guillermo, but there was no room for mercy in that mob. They were like a pack of wolves, and so he too was thrown to his death after being beaten wih tools from his own store. After that, many of the people retreated from the spectacle of injustice. Yes, justice had been turned on its head that day, in a carnival of reprobate malevolence. When I saw two men falling down drunken, and passing a bottle between them as they shouted 'Viva la Anarquia!' the depravity of it all overwhelmed me and I had to get out of there. I was a witness as the town of

Abiesa, a village of decent, hard-working people, descended into an abyss of hate, shame and senseless atrocity."

The music had stopped. Robert's voice had dropped, almost to a raspy whisper, and tears were welling in his eyes. He drained the last of his concoction.

Outside Cabaret Latrec, just down the street or next door, a churchbell could be faintly heard tolling through the sudden silence.

"What happened after that?" asked Philip, slowly, hesitantly.

"Don't ask," said Robert Jabbok. He was looking a little unsteady, with eyelids slowly occluding, then popping open in a sort of alarmed wakefulness.

"He's getting sleepy," Simone said to Philip. "It's time for us to get a cab back to the apartment."

"Where is that?" asked Philip.

"Montparnasse, near the Luxembourg."

"That's near Rue Bonaparte, n'est-ce pas?"

"Oui."

"May I ride with you? I will help with the fare."

"Certainement," she said. "You can be of some help to us. I may need you to steady him on the other side." Raising her head to her left, Simone called, "Nicolas, le cheque, s'il vous plait."

Twenty minutes later, they were crossing the Seine at Pont de La Concorde, turning onto Boulevard Saint-Germain. Robert was dozing in the back seat with his head on Simone's shoulder.

Simone gave the driver instructions. "Mettez Saint-Germain et aller a l'Hotel d'Orleans, Rue Bonaparte. Ensuite, nous irons a 38 rue Vavin."

She was instructing the driver to deliver Philip to his hotel. "Are you sure you can manage with him at your place?" he asked her.

"Certainement. We do this all the time, probably once a week anyway. Once we get to the apartment, he will realize we are almost home, and rouse himself for the climb to the second floor."

"Do you always go to Cabaret Latrec?"

"Mostly, yes, not always. Sometimes we go to Montmarte. But if we go there, there is a chance we will see people who Robert would prefer not to see. So the Latrec is our favorite. We like the music there. Robert says it is better suited for an old fellow like himself, not too raucous."

"The music was perfect. I enjoyed every minute of it," said Philip. "Thank you for inviting me to your table." They were stopping at the Hotel d'Orleans. He paid the driver.

"Merci," she said. "Do come and visit sometime, at 38 Rue Vavin, number 23, very near Boulevard Raspail at Montparnasse. Or, often you will find us during the daytime at Café La Rotonde, on that corner."

Shutting the cab door and climbing the stairs to his room at l'Hotel d'Orleans, Philip was burdened with thought about all he had heard that night from the once-soldier who had given up his cause because of the cruelty he had seen at Abiesa.

24

La Mostarde

Philip awoke with a headache. Someone was knocking at the door, but it sounded to Philip's fogged brain as if that person was attempting to break down the door.

"Heinrich is in Switzerland!" Lili blurted excitedly, as soon as he had opened it. Her bright eyes, her cheeks, rosy with rest and joy, were beyond beauty. He felt himself in a stupor just looking at her, as if he were still sitting at the Cabaret hearing a tender song about the pleasures of loving a woman, or as if he were still dreaming and had been arraigned to some French court of love for sentencing. Perhaps he would be doomed, to ever remember her in this rose-cheeked way, like the ballerina in Degas' painting suspended in perpetual youth and beauty, but never to partake of her charms, for just the night before he had decided, down in some rational part of himself, to spare himself the disappointment of further entangling their divergent lives. But . . . but then he had been dreaming, and in the dream his sister, Sylvie, was weeping, and trying to tell him something. He could not hear her. Maybe she was telling him to scoop Lili up from the detritus of this. . .this crumbling, humpty-dumpty old empire, with its green mold on angelic statues and its warlike divisions with dictators and pogroms and radical politics and refugees and Dachau, and maybe he should just take her up in his arms and bring her to America, no matter what anybody said, her father, mother, Moses or Maimonides.

Not going to happen. Although. . .she had said, while they were on the Pont Neuf yesterday morning, had she not said?, that he should take her to

New York right away. What was that all about? But she had sounded more like a comedienne in a Hollywood movie when she flippantly said that to him, as if she were just leading him on, just playing some Marlene Dietrich trick on him. Actually, she was cruel, putting him through this and not knowing the power of her own beauty on him. She was young, for crying out loud. She didn't know. . . no; it was him, he didn't know. . .

"How? . . . how did this, er, . . . that happen?"

"We got the telegram an hour ago. He is in Interlaken, something about a train and a mountain trail. Father is going there to get Heinrich and he has said I must go with him."

"Uh, when?"

"We leave from Gare de l'Est after two o'clock."

"What time is it now?"

"Ten twenty."

Philip was not comfortable, and he needed to go to the bathroom. Totally at a loss, he said, "Well, go on then." He stepped back, in a manner to indicate, dishonestly, that he was about to close the door.

Lili obliged him by setting her foot between the door and the jamb. "What do you mean, 'go on then'?"

"I mean, go to Switzerland and get your brother. Nothing could be more important than that. To be honest with you, Lili, based on what we've been hearing about the Third Reich, I'm surprised he has been released. Hey, I need to go to the bathroom."

She stepped toward him, halfway in the door. "I don't think he was released, Philip. I'm going to sit here in this chair and wait while you go in the bathroom."

Philip was caught in some kind of purgatory, between bladder discomfort, annoyance at Lili leaving Paris suddenly, compassion for Heinrich and yet inexplicable joy that she seemed to be pursuing him into a corner, as if to capture him. This was a problem, because she had already captured his heart, but he could see no way for this relationship to blossom into anything beyond a few romantic days by the Seine in this City of dreamers and lovers.

"What are you telling me? He escaped from a Nazi prison?"

"I don't know. He can tell you himself when he gets back here, when we return. Mother and Hannah are staying here."

"Why don't you stay here, and Hannah go with your father to Switzerland?"

"I do not know. Father made it very plain to me he wants me to go with him. Philip, go in the bathroom. I'll be here when you're done. We can talk."

"Talk about what? What's there to talk about? You are going to Switzerland, and I'm here and I'm running out of money. I need to get back to London, and work, or hell, just go back home. I could never live here in Europe. Everything is so. . . unmanageable."

She looked at him seriously. It was an expression somewhere between pathos and wonder."Ok, Philip, I can see you have some feelings in there somewhere. I was beginning to wonder about you, being an American. . . I'm going out in the hall; I will wait for you. When you're done refreshing yourself, and you are feeling better, I'll be out there. We'll get out and get some breakfast."

"It doesn't make sense to split your family, two of you going backwards, back in the direction of Germany, and the other two. . ."

"You are right. It doesn't make sense. Nothing makes sense any more." She grabbed the door handle, cast a look of feigned annoyance over her shoulder at him, like a mother at her child, stepped back into the hall, and closed the door silently behind her.

She would make a good mother. The thought leaped into his head from somewhere. *What?!* He had dreamed about his sister, who is a good mother. That was it. *It doesn't make sense?* He wanted to impregnate her. He was glad she didn't insist on waiting in the room; it was a mess. He rushed into the bathroom, took a shower, put on clothes, got ready for another day of whatever might happen. Why would she be lingering here at his room—he was thrilled at the thought that she would wait for him—as if something good could happen between them, as if the gulf between their separate lives was not too vast to be bridged. *Maybe if they can get to New York, instead of going the other way, something good could happen, something happy and free, like the way things are done in America, where people can do what they please, not being bound by antiquities.* Twenty minutes later when he opened the door and stepped out, there she was waiting for him at the end of the hall, looking out the window, just as she had done yesterday. Twenty-four hours had passed since they had started yesterday from that same window. *Why couldn't we just have another day like yesterday, a day of wandering along the river, Lili perching, stretching on tiptoes on the bridge bastion , him watching with exquisite desire, the curve of her thighs beneath a skirt, the two of them watching the ducks and then being amused by a 700-year-old masterpiece of architecture?* Instead, she would be stepping into a rail car to go back east a long, long way, to cross a border, a border that presents

unknown shifting political perils. *What if the Nazis have taken over Switzerland?*
What if this is a trick? What if the Germans had released Heinrich to lure his father and the
lovely daughter back into their grasp, their Germanic grip?

No. Switzerland is a neutral country, has been since forever. Be rational.
This is about her brother, who may be emerging, by the grace of God, from a
fate worse than death.

"What are you doing here?" he said to her roughly, as he approached the
window."

"What do you mean what am I doing here?" A fierce beauty flashed from
her eyes as she challenged him.

"You should just get on the train and go to Switzerland with your father,
and find out from Heinrich, what the hell is going on Germany."

"I will be," she stammered, "getting on the train, but I wanted to see you
first."

"What for?"

"Why are you being so mean, all of a sudden?" She glared at him, tears
welling. Maybe it was not a glare; maybe it was something gentler,
something more vulnerable.

He wanted to take her in his arms. "Look Lili." He stepped over to the
window and looked out. A gentle rain was falling; it was a gray day. "Your
family was almost torn apart by this. . .this Nazi thing, whatever the hell it is
they're trying to do over there. And now. . .now it looks like, since Heinrich
has gotten out, your family will be together again, and your parents will
decide what direction they want to take, and then they will move on that
decision, and you will go somewhere where you will settle, and life will
eventually become normal again for you, for all of you, and all of this, this
Paris diversion, ths Parisian dream, will become a memory, a fading memory
and you will tell your grandchildren someday about those few days back in
Paris, back in '37, when no one knew what would become of Heinrich, and
you were confused trying to decide whether to go Palestine or to America,
and it all seemed so precarious. But then, wonder of wonders, suddenly
Heinrich is in Switzerland instead of Dachau and everything will be back to
what it was."

She looked admiringly at him. "But we have lost everything, Philip."

"Nah."

She was looking at him incredibly. This was terrible. She was becoming
even more beautiful to him, with every second.

"Nah. You still have each other. *That* is precious. Listen. . . I know. I grew up without my father. There's a lot to be said about a family that can stay together, especially in treacherous times like these. Heinrich getting out of prison, and out of Germany, I mean—that is huge. And not only that, not only will you all be together again, but you have your faith. I know that is important for your father and mother."

"It is precious, yes, but . . . I don't want to live with my father forever."

Philip laughed incredulously. "Lili, a day from now, when you see your brother again, when you leap into his arms, and he is delivered once again into the warmth of your family, it will all be—everything will be different then. There is no telling what you will want to do then. You just need to go to Interlaken and get him, and then you can collect yourselves, assess your feelings about the options, and you will. . .you will forget about me. Come on, we'll go get some coffee." He turned to walk down the hall, expecting her to follow.

She grabbed his hand and pulled him toward her. "No!"

"You don't want to do this," he said. She was looking up at him, eyes glistening, and they were so very close. He instinctively put his arms around her. She responded willingly and before anyone knew what could happen or not happen, their lips were locked together, and it seemed the world stopped spinning on its axis. But, giving himself only a moment to appreciate it, he forced himself to end the kiss, pulling his head back slightly so he could peer into her eyes again. "Lili, I'm in total confusion."

"What do you mean? Does it matter?"

"I need to go back home. This company thing I'm doing now—it's going to end. I mean, I'm going to end it. I can't go on selling cigarettes any more. It's not right for me, not right for my company. I don't know what the hell to do. I let Itmar talk me into coming over here. For what reason, I don't even know, except. . . ."

"To meet me."

He stepped back from her, not wanting to be caught in this position if sister Hannah should wander in their direction. They were still holding hands between them, as if praying together, huddled together in an intimate . . . conference. "That's the real beautiful thing about it. But it didn't start out because I wanted to get on a boat, come to France, and meet a girl like you sitting in a restaurant down on the south coast. It started because I was just so tired of working, and coming to the realization that there's something else I should be doing, though not knowing exactly what it is. But what that old fellow told me yesterday, before you came over to us—it has really stuck with me."

"What did he tell you?" She was happy to be included in his life deliberations.

"He said a day would come when the markets for cigarettes would get smaller and smaller, because most people would quit smoking."

"For health reasons," she surmised.

"Yes, mainly that. I suppose the old fellow has been around long enough to know what he's talking about. And I had already been feeling a discomfort, and, to be honest, feeling a little guilty that I'm over here on the company's expense while coming to the conclusion that something has to change. But the thing is—I don't know what that change will be."

She stepped back from him, but now there was a satisfaction between them, like some rare truth had been quietly affirmed at the momentary mingling of their lips, and intensified, as the stars would have it, by the coming of spring. A bond of some indeterminable support had been created, an earth-old partnership between one lonely man and one unique woman that could in the end, or even for a moment, enrich and fortify life for all their time on this troubled earth. In the long run, who knew?, such sacred coupling could bear tender fruit never before put forth by the labor of a woman, nor seen by the eye of man.

She looked up at him with a newly formed, intimate discernment. "You want to go back home to America then?"

"It kind of seems that way." Relief was entering into him from some indeterminable fountain of goodness.

"Well then," she crooned, turning her smile up at him again. "Take me to New York, will you?"

He laughed. "You don't understand. I don't know what the hell I'll do when I get there!"

"Does it matter? You'll think of something."

"It's not as simple as that. Times are hard back home."

"So, really, America is not quite the land of milk and honey that you were suggesting it is, a minute ago when you compared it to this place?"

"You mean, compared to where we are now, France?"

"Ah, Europe, you know, France, Germany, the Continent."

"It's a great place, I mean, the United States, but there are an awful lot of folks desperate for work, and. . . if I went back there after quitting my job, then I'd just be another one of those unemployed guys looking for work. There's a million of 'em."

"You could go back to your home town then, to help your family with the store. Your grandfather has died, and your family could probably use the help, especially since you're a bona fide business man now, with experience in international markets and all. . ."

"Oh, you can't go home again," he said, as if it were common knowledge.

"Why not?"

"It's a small town. It's . . . I don't know. I mean, what goes on in a little Podunk town like Trail, where I come from, well, it's nothing like calling on clients in the city of London, which is what I've been doing for the last eleven months." He released her hands, stepped over to the window and looked out. "But hey, you know what? I'm hungry. Here you've dragged me out of bed at this early hour, and we're standing in the hall trying to solve the problems of the world, and I haven't even had coffee yet." Philip grabbed her hand and began walking down the hall toward the stairway; Lili followed. "Let's find some breakfast."

"Where are you going?"

"I don't know. What does it matter?" he asked, appropriating her phrase. "That place down the street, where we were yesterday, across from the Art School. It will do just fine."

They emerged in the lobby. Philip, holding her hand tightly, was intent to spirit her through the foyer and outside so they could get to the place down the street without being noticed by Hannah or anyone else. If this was to be her last hour with Lili for who knows how long, he wanted it to be of a certain private quality.

"My mother will be looking for me," she protested, lamely.

"It's all right. You've got some time. Let's get some breakfast. Then I'll bring you back here before noon. I promise."

The couple did not, however, slip through that hotel lobby before being noticed, and interrupted, by someone. "Philip Morrow!" he heard, from an authoritative voice somewhere behind him. Philip turned toward the caller. There, sitting in a wing chair, in a gray suit and yellow silk tie, with umbrella in one hand and newspaper in the other, was the old man of Sainte-Chapelle, Mel Leblanc. "I would very much like to talk to you, Philip. I have a business proposition for you, " he proclaimed, so as to ensure the termination of Philip's hasty departure.

Philip, doing an about face, returned a few steps into the lobby, peered at the old man in mute surprise. He stopped again at the man's chair. "What is it?" he asked.

"What is what?" said Mel Leblanc, good naturedly.

"What is the business proposition?"

"I'll explain it to you—definitely worth your consideration. For a young man like yourself—the world is your oyster, you know—it will take some time. Where are you going?"

"We were. . .ah, just about to go down the street for coffee, and maybe a little breakfast."

"Breakfast, mon ami. Allow me! This restaurant here, right here in the hotel, is a good one. Allow me to order breakfast for all three of us, and I will explain to you what I have in mind."

"I've been waiting for a man like you to come along," Mel Leblanc said when they had been seated, as Philip at last gratefully received a cup of coffee.

"What kind of man do you think I am?" Philip asked. "You've only known me for a day."

"Smart."

Philip chuckled. "There are plenty of smart people around. You probably meet at least one smart person every day, with the way you get around this city."

"In your case, Philip, I can see not only that you fulfill the first qualification, but also another one that is just as important."

"And what is that?"

"You are well-positioned."

"To do what?"

"To represent my company in America."

"And what company is that?"

"*La Mostard*," he said.

Philip looked puzzled. Lili was chuckling. Then she chimed in, "It's mustard, Philip. He wants you to go to America and sell his mustard there. And his mustard is, by the way, the best in France."

"C'est vrai, mademoiselle, exactement," said Mel LeBlanc, pleased with the speed with which they had already arrived at his proposal. "My family has been growing mustard in Bourgogne for four hundred years. My nephew, who administers the company now, has often mentioned to me that we should be exporting our mustard to the United States. What do you think of the idea?"

"I'm sure it is good idea," Philip obliged. "Americans like hamburgers and hot dogs, and most people put mustard on them, along with catsup and onions, and pickles. Most places where you would see folks eating hot dogs, for instance, at baseball games, amusement parks, casual restaurants, you will see mustard in a yellow container, next to the catsup. So there's a huge market that has already been developed. There is, ah, one particular brand that seems to have established itself in public places like that; it is the *French's* brand. Is that one of your products?"

Mel smiled. "Our competitor. Both companies originated in Dijon, where I come from, which is the mustard capital of the world. The French's company has seen great success with its yellow mustard. They make it bright yellow by adding a spice, turmeric, and this colorful condiment has a kind of visual magic when it is applied to the hot dog, or a bratwurst. So it makes a kind of festive food for eating at a sports event."

"A fun food," said Lili.

"Haha. I like that, a fun food." said Mel. "But that yellow mustard you see at the ball game, at the amusement park and so forth, it represents only a small part of the mustard world, and so it represents only a small part of what the market for mustard could be, and certainly will be, when our other varieties of mustard are presented for people to enjoy."

"So what kind of mustard does your company make?"

"La Mostard is a brown mustard; it is spicier, a little hotter, and it looks more like the real thing."

"The real thing?" Philip mused. "Hmm. That has a ring to it. There may be some advertising possibilities there."

"Ah ha! Philip, you are already confirming my intuitions about your potential for this business venture. You'll have to use your imagination if you want to compete with French's in the United States."

"Well, Monsieur, do you suppose you can convince large numbers of Americans to spice up their hamburgers and hot dogs with brown mustard instead of the yellow stuff?"

"Hmm, probably not." Mel had a mischievous smile on his face. But that would not be our intent anyway, although it would. . .it would be nice if such a thing could happen. But brown mustard, our La Mostarde, is especially suited for other foods that generally satisfy a, shall we say, more refined palate."

"Such as?"

"Well, here is our special idea for this very special mustard. You have in the United States a very popular way of preparing meats that is called *bar be que, n'est ce pas?*

"Oh, yes," said Philip. "People do it in their back yards."

"Well, I am here to tell you, mon ami, that this *bar be que* that you Americans have come to enjoy so much—it is a very special food, n'est-ce pas?"

"Sure."

"Your very special *bar be que* deserves a very special, spicy preparation— *La Mostarde, le condiment a faire ressortir le meilleur dans votre bar be que!*"

"Hmm, sounds tasty, it does. You may be on to something there," Philip agreed.

"Even so," Mel continued, "although such strategy has, probably, the greatest potential for expanding new mustard applications, there is another type of food market in which the brown mustard is already a standard of excellence, and so if La Mostarde can be presented in a convincing, appetizing way, we have possibilities for large sales to the delicatessens. You see, the delicacy meats—salami, pastrami, bruschetta, and other spiced sausages and prepared meats of that type—these specialties have refined flavor that demands a zestier mustard."

"C'est vrai, Monsieur," said Lili. "My father uses your La Mostarde at his delicatessen in Munich, and he sets it in the serving areas for diners to use on their sandwiches—or that is to say—he did, before the store was taken from us." Lili's face became occupied with a sudden startlement. She looked down at her coffee, as if the cup contained some mystery that puzzled her. With furrowed eyebrows, her face turned up again, and toward the door that opened into the hotel lobby. The waiter was arriving with food, but she took no notice of him. With no explanation, she rose, with an apparent expectation of leaving. Philip grabbed her hand, but gently, as gently as he could. "Wait!" he commanded softly. "Where are you going?"

"I must go, Philip. We are to leave for Switzerland and find Heinrich."

"That is two hours from now? Don't you want something to eat before you go?"

"I. . .I am, I was not expecting this so soon. My father is. I just need to—"

"Is this your goodbye?"

"No, no!" Her eyes returned from their distracted thought, whatever that had been; then she directed them to Philip's eyes. He could see a pleading in there, a confusion, almost a panic—so suddenly it had come upon her.

"I'll go upstairs with you. You're going up to the room, where your father and mother are." He stood quickly, still holding her hand, now tightly, attempting, for the first time it seemed, to actually compel her into, or away from, some directional change she was about to take. She was still hesitant, indecisive, although the suddenness of her intent to depart indicated otherwise; now she was hung upon a thread of some imminent grief, or dread, and her eyes clearly registered the panic. Philip kept his hand tightly on hers, stepped around her chair to be in a position to accompany her out of the restaurant.

Looking back at Mel LeBlanc, Philip said, "Excusez-moi, Monsieur. Nous partirons maintenant. Je vais, si Dieu le veut, revenir plus tard."

25

Passage

To make another person happy is a good thing. To do so through your whole life, for one woman whom God has chosen for you, is the greatest good, and also the greatest joy. This has been my experience.

If you would like to talk some more, Philip, please call on me at 44 Boulevard St. Michel, No. 7.   Mel Leblanc

This was the entirety of the enveloped note Philip received at the hotel desk, when he returned to the restaurant an hour later to find that Mel was gone and the table had been reset for other diners.

Hezekin's rather formal greeting to Philip outside the hotel had been a little stiff, although cordial enough. Now Lili and her father were in a taxi to Gare de l'Est, and from thence on a train bound for Interlaken, Switzerland. Philip's parting with Lili had been thoroughly unsatisfactory, and awkward, though he did manage to communicate to her that this would not be the end of whatever it was they had come to.

Once again, Philip was wandering in Paris, but this time with the uncomfortable awareness that his funds had been steadily diminishing all this time, and the Brigham Company was no doubt expecting him back in London, probably yesterday or the day before that. The time was fast approaching when he would have to leave France and return to work, or even return to the U.S.

Philip had already decided that it had been a stupid maneuver to be diverted by Mel into the hotel restaurant, instead of walking down the street to the café, just he and Lili alone for an hour before she would be leaving with her father. But that was water under the Seine now, and he found himself caught between a resentment of Mel's untimely intrusion, and a strange expectation of dependency on this very friendly, very helpful old Frenchman. Philip had returned to the Pont Neuf, the overlooking bastion where he and Lili had stood yesterday, watching the river flow beneath them, amused with the ducks and their silly little waddling motions of webbed feet beneath the water. Ducks have not a care in the world. The Lord and little old French ladies feed them.

Somehow, it seemed that on this spot yesterday a new thing, very precious, had begun, something as-yet unformed and incomplete, but suspended now on a bridge that could not adequately span the time or space between them. Philip felt as if his heart had flown from his body and it must be trundling on a locomotive through French countryside, only to encounter on the other end some desperately tragic prison tale that would rudely confirm the truth of every terrible damned thing that was happening in this world, and carelessly dispose of all goodness and all joy. What's the world coming to?

He had decided, the dearth of funds notwithstanding, that he would take her to New York, if she was serious about such a request, if she was. . .even capable of emancipating herself in such a way as to accomplish such a thing. She is not yet twenty years old. Philip pulled out his pack of cigarettes, started to light one, as he had done a thousand times before. *Oh what the hell!* He tossed them into the river with a flip of the wrist, and watched as they struck the current and, borned up by it, floated beneath the bridge. What kind of purgatory will this be? To endure the withdrawal, with all that is happening now, or not happening now. Bring on the pain, the drain, or whatever it was they had said happens to a person when they quit smoking. Bring it on. Let it sap me of all false feelings of security. I am ready now to address this life thing without feelings. Just toss these feelings to the wind. Just cast these cares into the current of all that this world gives and takes away and rushes with swiftly splashing removals and departures. Let me be robbed of nicotinal comforts; let me be separated from smoke. Let the smoke fall and rise upon me, within me, no more.

He began to walk southward off the bridge, turning left at the quai to go along the river. After a short distance, he turned again, to the right this time. Philip was wandering now on the Boulevard St. Michel. After an hour and a half of trudging numbly through the most romantic city in the world, he arrived upon an elegantly appointed apartment building with the number 44 in gold on a sculpted capital above the doorway. Beneath the address was a name gilded in smaller letters: Le Bourgogne. A uniformed doorman greeted him and inquired about whom he was visiting.

"Monsieur Mel LeBlanc," he answered looking past the man into a courtyard beyond. The place was constructed around a very green courtyard, bursting with spring verdure and, daubed intermittently with blossoms of many colors. Peonies of lavender. Oleander and azaleas of fuschia and magenta. He could see perfectly tended, delicate fern-like borders encompassing raised beds that punctuated the patterned courtyard, which was paved in between the planters with old worn brick.

The doorman smiled curtly at him, extended his hand toward the entrance to the center. "S'il vous plait, go into this courtyard. Go to the left. Enter the door in the center of that wall and walk along the hallway until you arrive at No. 7. It will be the last one on your right. Monsieur LeBlanc lives there."

Philip followed the doorman's suggestion and arrived at Mel's front door, barely having a chance to knock before the old Frenchman opened it and invited him into an apartment of rare perfection. The whole place gleamed. It was old fashioned, furnished with French Provincial style, but Philip could appreciate, for the first time, it seemed, the appeal of this dated adornment. The long couch was upholstered in maroon velvet, which contrasted its mahogany-trimmed edges. A thick Persian rug lay in the middle of the room. An ovular marbletop table displayed exquisite matching ceramic vases brimmed with fresh white roses. A gold-faced grandfather clock, its pendulum gently swaying, occupied the center of the left wall. The large, multi-paned window occupying the right wall admitted afternoon light from what appeared to be a different, though very similar to the one he had come through, courtyard. Philip felt very strange to have been received into this very regal comfort, though he felt as disjointed as a cast-off wandering fool on a Paris sidewalk. Not knowing what would be an appropriate thing to say after their suddenly rude departure from the hotel restaurant, he blurted, to the point of his striven thoughts:

"I am ready now, to go to Flanders Field." Philip could not explain why he had deemed himself ready for such an undertaking, except that it was a visit he had resolved, early upon arriving on the Continent, to make, and he was running out of money and time and he knew that there could be only one thing awaiting him there. Death itself, not his own of course but his distant father's death on the battlefield in defense of Belgium or France and the freedom of the whole world. Mel, peering at him curiously, appeared suddenly to have switched patriarchal roles with his grandfather Roby, who had raised him and taught him business back in the mountains of North Carolina. And oh, that was another death to commemorate in some strangely, probably inappropriate way, for grampa Roby had also died just a couple weeks ago and Sylvie had called to tell him, but they didn't talk long before the trans-Atlantic connection was cut off, but he had dreamed of Sylvie just last night--or was it the night before?—but anyway grampa Roby was dead. And so, Philip would consider their lives, the lives of his grandfather, so familiar, and his own father, a shadowy unfamiliar, when he got to Flanders Field. Meanwhile this old Frenchman had somehow by the grace of God managed to facilitate a host of good things, even in the midst of all this European trouble and displacement and an unjustly imprisoned brother, and the young, wave-haired fair ashkenazi woman who was now on a train bound for nowhere. . .Philip thought mel did look, in a funny way, like grampa Roby, although he was quite a bit taller, and apparently, a lot richer.

Mel could see, with his seasoned discernment, that young Philip was not prepared to talk about mustard. Perhaps he was not the best candidate after all, being a little disoriented, maybe unstable. "Would you like a glass of wine?" he asked. It is our best old Burgandy, grown in my back yard, so to speak, bottled in '29."

Philip had never believed in angels before now. "Sure," he said. That would be great. "I quit smoking today."

"That's a good start," Mel affirmed.

"A good start on what?"

"A good start on a healthier, more productive life."

"I'm sure you are right about that, Mel. But it goes against everything I was raised in. Back in the Appalachian hills where I come from, tobacco was just as commonplace as supper and church on Sunday."

"That church on Sunday part would be worth holding onto," said Mel, with a curiously pastoral tone in his voice. He handed the glass half-full to Philip. He poured the wine from a bottle on the sideboard and handed the glass to Philip. it from a bottle on the sideboard. "When would you like to go to Flanders?"

"When would you be free to go?" Philip asked, accepting the proffered glass half-full.

"At eighty-four years old, I am always free to go." He smiled largely.

Early the next morning, Philip joined Mel in the cab he had arranged to take them to Gare du Nord. From there, the plan was to board a northbound train for Lille, and Belgium. After a mile or two riding in the cab down

Boulevard St. Michel, they had crossed the Seine onto Ile de la Cité, past Palais de Justice with the Saint-Chapelle steeple looming behind it, where they had met yesterday, which now seemed so long ago, for much water had passed beneath the bridges of time since then. Crossing the River again over Pont au Change they were going along on Boulevard de Sebastopol when Mel, looking out the car window, noticed on the sidewalk an old soldier hobbling along with a cane. The man's uniform was an outdated, 19th-century infantry style, with red squared-off cap at the top, red pantaloons, and the diagonal crossing of gold-braid straps across his blue shirt. Philip saw a faraway look cross Mel's eyes; then the old Frenchman began to speak about what had happened soon after the war had started in 1914, when the Kaiser's army had damn near blasted their way all the way to Paris.

"It was a deathly desperate situation. But the cab drivers of Paris, along with many other Parisians, answered the call to duty. Many French citizens say those cabbies made the difference between victory and defeat. General Joffre and General Gallieni, the military governor of Paris, had sounded the 'all hands' call. The taxi men got organized, and they hauled 6000 reserves out to the battle, to reinforce the French army regulars. Together they stopped the long German advance, which had begun all the way back at Mons, in Belgium. The German army was turned around at Meaux, on the River Marne, about forty kilometers miles east of here. 'T'was then and there that the beginning of Germany's defeat was sealed."

Philip was listening intently. These events had set in motion a bloody four-year military stalemate that finally culminated in the autumn of 1918, when, at last, with the intervention of British, Canadian, Australian, New Zealander and American forces, the French were able to eject the German army from France and Belgium. Philip's father, Clint Morrow, had been one American soldier of that campaign, one who had contributed to their unified effort, and one who had ultimately sacrificed his last full measure of devotion in the Allied cause of freedom. Philip had never heard, in such an intimate, first-person voice, an accounting of the military events that preceded his father's death. He had never heard words so personal, so intimately spoken by a person whose life was directly related to the consequences of that war. Philip had nothing to say. He was hanging on Mel LeBlanc's every word.

Mel continued, "But it would take four more years of trenched hell between the Hindenberg line, where the German army stopped to refortify, and Gent, in the heart of Belgium, before we could muster the force to chase their kraut arses back to Berlin. Your father, and all those other Americans who come in with General Pershing in the spring of 1918—they were as green as soldiers on a field of battle could be—but they sure stood in the gap, and did what needed to be done to enable the army of France to take our nation back."

At that, the old Frenchman's countenance changed from reminiscent gravitas to a fateful solemnity. He gazed right into the younger man's eyes, and Philip could see an aged weariness, as if Mel, and the French nation itself, were presently worn out with the disdain that would envelope any renewed provocation of that very old, stalemated German/French coexistence. "Sad to say, now the Germans are back to their old bellicose habits, but with a new twist—that bizarre symbol, the swastika—as their battle standard. How they came up with that crooked emblem as a means of drumming up the devotion of their people, I will never know—and in the middle of Christian Europe! Whatever their scheming leaders are up to, I fear they are, yet again, dragging that dark angel of death up from the abyss to torment us."

~

Half a morning later they were boarding the northbound train. By that time, whatever it was that had brought together this aged Frenchman and his young, attentive American charge had been uncorked to its full expression. The old fellow was intermittently pouring out his life's vintage in a slow trickle of memory; its balmy flow had begun to endow their embarkation with a kind of therapeutic anointing, the beneficiary of which was neither the young man nor the old, but that Man of the ages whose fermented wisdom percolated through deepened souls of both men.

Now they were walking beside the train, small luggage in hand. Pausing in mid-stride, Mel managed to recap, in the midst of crowd and bustle, a simple advisement that he had begun last night and had already landed upon this morning. "Half the battle in this life, I think, is deciding what to keep and what to let go. You have got to know when to hold them."

They arrived at the railcar to which they had been billeted. Philip appropriated Mel's briefcase, collecting it with his own, both in his left hand. Placing his right gently hand on Mel's lower back for support, he waited patiently as the old fellow carefully climbed onto the steps to ascend into their coach. As Mel's bony, spotted hand grasped a vertical brass handrail inside the little stair, it seemed to Philip that the ghosts of ten thousand French souls were lingering there. The rail's brass patina had been worn to a dullish sheen as ten thousand reaching hands had, in the beginnings of their ten thousand journeys on this train, taken hold of it. Thus the passenger citoyens of the Republic, the old and the new, the young and the old, some yet alive and some now dead, over years and years of time and millions of miles sliding along the steel rails of La France, had climbed all aboard, heaving themselves up and swinging themselves in a ninety-degree arc at the top of the metal steps, and after steadying themselves and catching balance again, proceeded through the breezy passage space between cars and through the metal door, into the little railway world of a train's cozy interior, where they were and would be locomoted to Strasbourg, to Nimes or Toulouse, to Bordeaux, La Rochelle or Le Havre, to Orleans or, as in this case, to Lille.

So now they were on a train for Lille; they seated themselves.

Mel had been saying you gotta know when to hold 'em, so he hit the ground—or, in this case, the seat—running, which is to say he continued to talk just as soon as they had sat. "My ancestors decided to keep their land in Burgundy. This was a very difficult choice—a terrible decision to have to make—in 1685. Louis XIV revoked the Edict that had permitted Huguenots to worship and live according to their own conscience. So, with much prayer, but in an agony of decision, they relented, and converted to the Catholic side, but in so doing, they were able to keep their land, their heritage, their home and work."

"Did they do the right thing?—you are wondering," he continued. "They have long since stood before God, who is the author of all this, and given their account of what happened and what had to happen, and why they chose—if God asks such questions—to succumb to the Catholic enforcements. I hope they did the right thing, and are safely with the Lord in heaven now. But the result of it on this earth was that my people were able to prosper, while still professing their faith in Christ, even to this very day, and I was able, two hundred years later, to take hold of the resources they cultivated. And that, of course, is why I can present to you an opportunity to export a spicy little taste of France to enhance the culinary horizons of people in faraway America."

Philip had to laugh at the context in which this ancient gentleman had unexpectedly renewed his business proposition.

"More about that later. I hope you are considering it. What I am telling you now is: Religious unity imposed by the Church, the State, or by the King, is, as my friend Grant says, a burden too large to be dropped without entailing some great effort and sacrifice. Nevertheless, it was lifted from the French people, at least statutorily, when the Revolution came. So it turns out, since the Revolution, that the State, instead of the Church, has assigned itself to wield the heavy hand of imposed uniformity on us, in so-called

Enlightened ways that aspire, by political ideology, to transcend mere religion. But we are just as human, and therefore depraved, as we ever were, whether by religious, or secular convolution. We still have a long way to go to ever achieve any kind of universal *egalite* or *fraternite*, if such a thing is even possible. Personally, I don't think it is possible for the State or even the King to do what only God can do—enable men to live together in any semblance of true peace. It ultimately falls to one group or another to have the role of scapegoat imposed on them, so that the favored groups who wield the power can proclaim excuses to the people of why things never happen as they should. Thus they can justify why justice is never fully implemented but is perpetually subverted by greed and corruption, and why we always have the poor among us and why they always get poorer while the rich get richer. And some groups, even some individuals, are sentenced by the powers that be among men to be crucified on the cross of all our depravity. The Dreyfus affair, forty years ago, demonstrated that. And the persecutions—all of what is happening to the Jews in Germany now—such as were imposed on my ancestors, the Huguenots, in the French Catholic way hundreds of years ago, instead of the German Nazi way that now rears its ugly head. That's why I say you've got to know when to leave something behind, as my people did long ago, when they sacrificed their religious affiliation in order to hold on to what they had worked so hard to get."

"You gotta know when to fold 'em," Philip affirmed.

"That's right. My people had to leave something behind. In their case, it was their Calvinist doctrines. If my people had allowed Catholic religious manipulations and Reformed doctrinal hair-splitting to control their fate, they would have lost everything this earth has to offer; they would have had to leave and start again in another country. The Catholic Church, under the authority of the King of France—or **over** his authority, however the case may be—had the power, rightly or wrongly, to promulgate such persecutions."

"It seems very much like what the Eschens are having to suffer now," Philip observed, thinking out loud.

Mel let out a long sigh. He looked out the window. The train was taking them beyond Paris city now, into the suburbs. "It is similar, but not the same. Your friends the Eschens are Jews, and that is a different matter altogether. They have taken the road of emigration that my ancestors chose not to take. The Eschens have chosen to leave, rather than to stay in Germany. In their circumstance, I cannot blame them. The war between Nazis and Jews is not being fought over mere doctrinal disputations, but rather upon something much more fundamental—that is to say, the question of who is Messiah—and so they had to leave Munich, because the Nazis who have taken over the government of Germany have selected an identifiable group of well-endowed victims, the Jews, to rob them and to fleece them as sheep. The Nazis expropriate the sizable wealth of the Jews in the name of the Third Reich, and thus identify for the common people a scapegoat upon whom the sins and economic failings of all can be laid, therefore banishing that sacrificial animal to wander in the wilderness, and to be sacrificed on the altar of human law and reason, which is fickle and fallible. It has always been so for the Jews, for thousands of years. They are the smartest people on earth, and, for the most part, nobody else can understand them, so it is best to leave them alone. Let them go the way of their choosing. In so doing, they travel and settle through the whole earth, thereby enriching life for the rest of us. You can hear the excruciating passion that this life extracts from all of us human souls, when Mendelsson or Haifitz take up the violin; in those notes, you can hear and empathize with the deepest human suffering, which is intimately and necessarily joined to the deepest human joy. But that is a hard road to travel, my friend, the one that the children of Israel have chosen. I would not wish such a troublesome diaspora upon myself. As for me and my house, we follow Christ in his path of salvation for the world. Along the way, we have found a little mustard seed. And so we cultivate it, so that the wanderers of this world—such as you, Philip—can find a place of some comfort and safety, if you are willing to accept it."

Mel's soliloquy had landed upon a promontory of repose. His eyes, which had been gathering inspiration from the Parisian environs blurring outside the window, now fastened themselves squarely upon the younger man, as if to throw down a gauntlet, as if to challenge Philip in a way that he had never anticipated since first he had landed upon this Old World.

Then old weariness took up new residence in the old man's face. His gaze lingered momentarily in the passing countryside before he inserted a small pillow beneath the back of his head and relaxed his lanky body. His wrinkled eyelids closed, and Philip was left to his own thoughts. The fields and forests of Picardy were passing silently, except for the low rumble of locomotive wheels, while Mel descended to slumber and the morning sun ascended to gray and silvery clouds. Philip found himself considering, yet again, the plight of Lili and her family, and wondering what would be the impact of Heinrich's entrance into their refugee odyssey.

About an hour outside of Lille, the old man stirred, sat up straight, and looked around to gather himself. "Let's find the dining car and get coffee."

Philip had learned, from listening and hearing other passengers, that the dining car was two cars behind them. So they roused themselves, ventured carefully into the aisle. Philip followed closely behind Mel, hands ready to steady him if any sudden movement should necessitate it, as the old man swayed with the train's trundling and once almost stumbled, and detoured for one toilet stop, then entered the dining car, whereupon they happily descended into the first two seats and received coffee.

Then Philip posed a question that he had pondered while Mel was sleeping. "What did you mean, Mel, when you said the Nazi policies against Jews resemble persecutions that the King and the Church had inflicted on your ancestors?"

Mel took a big slurp. "Ah, just what an old man needs before rolling into Lille," he said, with a satisfied grin. A few years ago I met a fellow who researched this. He was an American, like you, and he lives in New York. His name is Archon Grant. What he presented in his little book of Huguenot history was consistent with what has been passed to me through my family and others I have talked to over these many years. It seems that King Louis the Fourteenth, as he was getting quite old, wanted to mend some fences with the Church in Rome. So he set out with a renewed zeal to affirm his authoritarian proficiency for identifying heretics and dealing harshly with them, in order to purify the Church in France from Calvinist and Reformed influences.

"So, Louis promulgated, with the dutiful assistance of his loyal scribes and fawning bureaucrats, a series of documents—over a hundred of them—that carefully and systematically curtailed the liberties of the Huguenots and inflicted, over several years, penalties upon them that became more and more restrictive. The result was an array of punitive restrictions that amounted, in an almost scientific way, to a very systematic persecution.

"You need to understand, Philip, that these people were not criminals; they were not wine-swigging urchins of the streets. Nor were they Jacobin anarchists like those that have plagued France for the last hundred and fifty years. These Reformers were Calvinists, hard-working people who, for the most part, wanted to keep to themselves, raise and teach their children in the Biblical faith that they had accepted as truth directly from Holy Scripture. In faith, in education, industry and thrift, these good people generally surpassed most of the subjects of the French King. This systematic persecution culminated in the revocation of the Edict of Nantes that King Henry IV had promulgated about ninety years before.

"Here are the cumulative effects of those anti-Reform laws: Huguenots were excluded from public employments, barred from practicing law and medicine, and forbidden to print or publish books. The internal legal counsels and courts that these Protestants had instituted were rendered illegal and illegitimate in French courts.

"Mixed marriages were outlawed. The children of Reform families could legally be compelled by Catholic clergy and schools to forsake, at the age of seven, the faith of their parents. All souls who were persuaded by any means to accede to papist conversion were awarded with benefits in which their Calvinist peers could not partake, such as being relieved for three years from the payment of their debts.

"Huguenot temples were destroyed, and their worship was suppressed with brutal cruelty, while their properties were routinely destroyed or stolen by priests and their accompanying dragoons.

"This sentence of unyielding harassment and brutality is what my forefathers escaped when they capitulated, for a generational season, to the bullying of the State Church. There were many Huguenots who did buckle under the strain. My ancestors were among them. Nevertheless, by the grace of God, and with help from the Republican government of France, I am a Christian who is, today, free to practice my faith as I determine, according to my own conscience. The cruel oppression by which the Crown and the Church sought to enforce religious uniformity ultimately served only to disgrace Christendom.

"Louis the Fourteenth blatantly disobeyed God's second Commandment when he commanded that dissident Christians be tortured and executed in the very name of Christ and his so-called 'holy' Church. A century later, the godless Jacobins and Gerondists incited the Revolution, and wrested power from his grandson Louis the Sixteenth, then sent him to the guillotine, which added the merciless judgment of man to the righteous judgment of God upon that arrogant king and his royal house—the house of Bourbon. It was a monarchy that had, by its crimes, forsaken any legitimacy or presumptuous 'divine right of kings' and replaced it with debauchery and injustice. Therefore God enabled the vain philosophers and vindictive orators of a new doctrine—not a doctrine of God who is almighty, but a doctrine of Man, who is vain and violent and arbitrarily cruel—to rise up, in 1789, and replace the Crown's bloody persecutions with a Reign of Terror administered by the vengeful, anarchic spirit of the age. The Revolution and its long, violent aftermath demonstrated to all who have eyes to see that the righteousness of man is like filthy rags—bloody rags.

"This could only happen because the philosophers of that age, the nineteenth-century, were so readily able to compile a long list of indictments against the Crown and its Church, oppressions and crimes against not only the Reformists of faith, but also against the people of France, by their heartless exploitation of the poor.

"And so the religious anarchy that the Regents of France had so feared would destroy their Kingdom was ultimately given free reign by a mob of peasants and anarchist firebrands in 1789. Unrestrained violence and blood-seeking vengeance were the order of the day. A new kind of judgment was instituted, at the passionate urging of the so-called philosophers of Reason. Religion was dead; it had been crushed by the fears and abuses of unrighteous kings.

"Certainly, Philip," the old man said, raising his coffee cup in a toastful gesture, "it had to die. Religion had to die. How else could it be resurrected from the sinful condition to which it had fallen?"

"France had fallen from a Reign of Religion into the Reign of Terror. Now a century and a half later, the good people of France have managed by the grace of God to stabilize this unwieldy ship of State. But it has taken a toll on us. We French are weary of the fickle instabilities and inconsistencies of human government. We are not agreed, as a nation, in what we believe; we are not united in any formidable resolve to defend France.

"Now, at such a time as this, while we languish in disarray and faithless vulnerability, we look across the Rhine at Germany, a country boiling in the fierce heat of their new experiments in godless government. And we see a dreadful thing. We see, we hear reports, that the smart Germans are preparing for themselves, probably for us, and perhaps even for the world, a new Reign of Terror. It is a reign—it is a Reich—devised with heartless, calculating Germanic precision. And what is it that they are doing there? What do they do there? First they come for the Jews. Everybody hates the Jews, they think. Or, everybody can be made to hate the Jews. But I ask you this, Philip?"

In spite of the coffee, the weariness had again overtaken Mel's face. His small brown eyes, close together, narrowing now with resignation, were attempting to express profundity, but were instead presenting a question that was rooted in fear. "Who will be next on their list? "Who will they come for after the Jews?" Philip could see the fear behind Mel's eyes, fear that was hollowing out his faith. But there was a battle being fought behind those ancient eyes; it was battle between faith and fear, and Philip could see it plainly now. It was a very old war. Philip just happened to get a view of it in here in this person, but he knew—he could plainly see—that the war between these two was as old as the man himself, as old as Man himself. "They will soon come for us, the people of France, especially those of us who are unwilling to stitch their crooked cross onto our sleeves and our French hearts."

26

Roses

"Jacob isn't here," she said.   The woman stood timidly, half-hidden by her front door, which she had opened only wide enough to negotiate a brief encounter with Philip, an encounter which it seemed, would conclude as soon as possible.

"Are you expecting his return home?"

"I am . . .expecting him, but I do not know when." She was looking at the unfamiliar visitor now. Her eyes met Philip's; he detected something very sad. . . not sad. Desperate. She seemed confused. He could see now, as she hazarded a little more gap in the open door, a frumpy housecoat hung over her thin body. She was an attractive woman, about forty, but not content, not comfortable with the unexpected intrusion of an American knocking on her door. Her eyes were red around the edges.

"Itmar Greeneglass sent me," he announced to her.

She was surprised. Her eyes flashed with a new interest in this visitor, or was it a flash of . . . hope? Had the mention of Itmar's name struck a resonant chord within her? "Where is Itmar?" she asked, hesitating.

"I was with him in Paris just three days ago. He sent me here with a delivery."

"Where is it?"

Philip was somehow surprised by this question, although it had been his intention to deliver the small package. "I've got it here, in my pocket. It is . . . small." He lifted the very small black jewelry box from his pocket so that she could see it. He smiled at her, watching her eyes.

The woman's face softened. "Who are you?"

"My name is Philip Morrow."

"You are American."

"As I'll ever be," he retorted, smiling again, with more confidence than is appropriate for a man to have, still holding the little black box where it would not escape her interest, which it did not.

"Is Itmar here?" she asked, still insensitive to the awkwardness of carrying on a conversation around a half-closed door.

"No. He is in Paris, I suppose. That's where he was, ah, three nights ago when we talked, and he gave me this, which is for . . . Jacob. Are you Jacob's wife?"

"Why isn't Itmar delivering it himself? Is he still alive?"

"He was still alive, as of Thursday night when we were together."

"Why were you together?"

"We had just eaten dinner. We were having cognac in the lounge of the Hotel d'Orleans."

"What did he say?"

"He told me to give this to you." He was holding the little box up again.

With still no apparent interest in the little box, "What else did he say?"

"He had just arrived on a train. He was telling us about his trip."

"His trip from where?"

"From Calais."

"Was it a good trip from Calais?"

"Well, no. . . it was not, a good trip."

"No. It was not a good trip. He was supposed to have met my husband at Calais, but that never happened."

"Why did it not happen?"

"You tell me," she said, her lower lip protruding like a child's. She appeared on the verge of tears.

"Listen. I am sorry I have disturbed you." He looked down at a little flower bed beside the front stoop. Bright red poppies were growing there. It was a quaint, stucco cottage on the edge of Lille. Philip had almost decided to leave. "I'm going to leave this little item for you, as Itmar asked me to do. I'm going to leave it right here on the top step, next to this flower. Who planted the, ah, lovely poppies?"

"I did."

"Ils sont tres beaux," he said. Setting the little box down, he was preparing to leave.

"Wait!" she commanded. "You may come in now," she announced, opening the door to a passable width for entry.

Philip retrieved the little item from that spot where he had just laid it, inserted it into his shirt pocket, straightened himself, then entered the cottage. He found himself in a very cozy home, humble in scale, but richly furnished. She ambled into a sitting room on the left side of the hallway, and motioned for him to sit on a small, golden velvet sofa. "Thank you," he said, accepting the seat.

"Excuse me a minute." She left the room. Philip felt as if he were sitting in a time capsule. Against the wall on his right stood a fine, shining black upright piano, with the name *Pleyel* embossed in gold leaf above its keyboard. On its top, a gold menorah had been placed in the center. Two small rolled parchments, tied with black ribbon, had been laid beside the candlestick to its left.. On its right side two crystal wine glasses had been set, with a simple, pearly-white ceramic vase between them, displaying a single, fresh white rose. A sculpted rosebud, identical to the fresh flower in its whiteness, but forever unbloomed, adorned the slender body of the vase.

The walls of this room reflected family history, with intricately placed old photographs, some in golden frames, some in white. On the opposite wall, a window allowed the mellowed sunlight of a partly cloudy day to enter, brightening the room with an otherworldly luminescence. On each side of the yellow-draped window hung a white picture frame with a bright impressionist painting, a Monet table bouquet displaying splotches of yellow and blue.

The woman re-entered her living room, set a glass half-full of white wine on the low wooden table in front of Philip's knees. Then she sat in the high-backed white armchair next to the sofa. She had changed into a smart, rather formal longish blue dress with a gold brooch above her breast, which was modestly concealed in the dress.

"I have not seen my husband since the day that he was to have met Itmar at the Calais train station," she explained, forthrightly. Now she looked at him directly, as if expecting an explanation.

This was not good news. "You have not . . . heard from him at all?" Philip stammered.

"No."

He was waiting for further comment, more information. But it seemed that she was the one expecting to be informed. "I must explain, I . . . have not known Itmar for a long time, only a couple of weeks actually. So I am not the one, unfortunately . . . I mean, I am not the one who knows anything about, ah, where your husband is."

She was studying his face. "Il se passé bien. Je comprends. These are dangerous times." She had not brought out a wine for herself, but she asked, do you approve of the wine?"

Philip had not yet tasted the wine, but now he did. "Merci. Il est tres bon vin." Her mention of dangerous times did not comfort him; it did not explain anything. He was beginning to understand the fragility of this Continent's patched-up peace.

She resumed. "If you have known Itmar for only two weeks, why did you, or, why did he, recruit you to deliver this?" She seemed to have no interest in the box's content.

That's a good question. He was considering this when she interrupted his thought.

"I have no interest in what is in the box. I only want to see my husband again. In fact, you may have it, whatever it is."

Philip was stunned. Seeking an explanation for himself as well as for her, he offered, "Itmar said—it was Thursday night when he told me—that he had found this little box in the attic of his flat in London, when . . .I think, shortly after he had moved into it. He found it in a trunk with photographs."

"Ah!" she blurted. For the first time, he gleaned what might have been the hint of a smile on her face. "Now those, I would like to have. They belong to my mother-in-law, may she rest in peace."

"Yes," said Philip, with some excitement. "Itmar said that he was quite sure the trunk belongs to Jacob's mother, who would be . . ."

"My mother-in-law, yes. Magda. The trunk disappeared from her apartment in Paris during the war."

"I think Itmar thought it was important that this be delivered back to the family—that is, to Jacob."

"Mais, certainement, but what about the photographs? Itmar has it backwards. That little pearl, or whatever it is, has no significance compared to the other contents of that trunk."

"Well, but you know where the trunk is now. It is in London, safe at Itmar's place, and can be readily obtained at any time, n'est-ce pas?"

"C'est vrai. But I don't know if anything is safe in the keeping of Itmar Greeneglass," she blurted. "I mean, that is not what I meant to say. What I meant to say is, I don't care about the safety of anything except my Jacob. This is not the first time that someone associated with Itmar and his clandestine activities has gone missing. Excuse me." She left the room abruptly.

When she returned to the room a couple minutes later, this time with a small wine glass for herself, she sat again in the armchair. Her eyes were red around the edges and Philip knew she had shed tears during the absence. He had risen to inspect a photograph on the wall by the piano, It was an old, yellowed sepia of a proud woman with a muted smile, bright eyes and a full head of wavy hair tied back and arranged atop her head. She was wearing an old-fashioned smocked, high necked dress and apparently, a brooch that was similar, or perhaps the same one, that this woman now was sporting.

"I'm sorry," Philip said tactfully, after seating himself again, "what did you say your name is?"

"I did not say. Mimi. My name is Miriam. They call me Mimi." She sipped the wine and looked at him squarely again.

"Mimi Bruchis," he said.

"Yes. I still do not understand why Itmar would trust you, having known you for such a short time, to deliver this pearl to me. Are you part of his network?"

"His network. . . I, ah, don't know anything about that, although he did mention he was involved in some projects over here on the Continent."

"Projects. Such as. . .?"

"Well, he was involved in some collective efforts to supply provisions to some Republicans in Spain. That's how we met."

"So you are a part of that network?"

"No." Philip chuckled. "Okay, let's back up a bit. You remember that a new King of England, George VI, was crowned in London, just a few weeks ago?"

"Oh yes. May 12th."

"Right. Well, on that day, I was out on the streets of London, like a million English people were. I was with a friend of mine, and we were trying to work our way through the crowds to Trafalgar Square to get a view of the royal procession after the coronation. We were having a hard time of it. We stopped in front of a tobacconist's shop on Haymarket. I was looking in the window, when the next thing I know my friend Nathan was talking to an old fellow, and Nathan had his arm around the man, trying to help him because, as it happened, he was faltering. Nathan tried to keep him from falling on the pavement. The old guy was mumbling about the gold standard, or somesuch, when he just up and dies. Right there in Nathan's arms, he passes into eternity, and . . . well, anyway, a few minutes later, after a bobby had come along and called for an emergency team, I met Itmar. That's when I met him. And. . . I suppose you could say the circumstances were so unusual, so, uh, grave, there was a profundity about it, like something sacred—a man passing from this life into, whatever, heaven, and I think we were all a little shaken. And so, a little while later we went up the street to Itmar's flat where he explained to us that that man—Paul Wallris was his name—had been working with Itmar and some other people to transport food and supplies through Bilbao into Spain, and now I am wondering, Madame Bruchis, was your husband Jacob one of those people that Itmar is working with?"

She peered at Philip for a moment, as if still deciding about the reliability of what he had just said. "Not exactly." Her eyes were fixed steadily on him as she continued, "Jacob is working with Itmar, but not in Spain. There are other places here in Europe where the need is even greater than it is in Spain."

"The need? for what?"

"For protection, ah, . . . for emigration."

"Emigration from where?"

She looked at him with incredulous wonder. She did not know how to answer. He had, after all, appeared on her doorstep only an hour ago.

"Wait, wait!" he exclaimed. "I mean, I know what you are talking about. I am myself involved with an expedition to bring some Jewish refugees out of Germany."

Her face morphed, for the first time, from stony objectivity to something resembling interest. "So Itmar did recruit you to assist in getting Jews out of Germany?"

A light bulb went off in Philip's head. "Yes! He did. He recruited me. I had not realized . . ." For Philip, it had seemed more like just doing a favor for a friend, although Itmar wasn't really a friend, because Philip had not known him long enough for such terminology to be attached to their relationship. However, as he considered this, he understood that Itmar **is** a friend. What else would you call him? Philip liked him from the start and that is why he trusted Itmar, and Itmar trusted him, and if that was not friendship, then what is?

While Philip was ruminating on this, she said, "I only wish I knew where my husband is. He was supposed to have been back here three days ago. If you cannot tell me where my Jacob is, you can at least tell me what you do know. You can tell me what happened three days ago at Calais, and how it was that Itmar turned up in Paris instead of coming here to this house with Jacob."

This was not good. Philip was thinking back to Thursday evening, when he stood outside *Les Deux Magots* with Lili and Hannah, and the other girl, Helene. At the curb, he had spoken with the Eschens while they were in the backseat. Monsieur Berrot was driving. They went to retrieve Itmar from the nearby Babylone-Sevres metro station. When the parents arrived at the restaurant later, Itmar arrived bruised and injured. He had been beaten somewhere outside the Calais train station, where he was supposed to have met Jacob Bruchis. He had been tossed onto a cattle car and somehow got into Paris, and it was amazing if not an outright miracle that they had dinner together. Philip regretted that he had not questioned Itmar more thoroughly about the sinister circumstances that had diverted him, not by any means of Itmar's choosing, to roll into metro Paris on a cattle car instead of meeting Jacob Bruchis in Calais and then coming, it seemed, it must have been intended, to this very house. Philip was regretting that he had not asked Itmar more questions, but then Monsieur Berrot had walked into the bar of the Hotel d'Orleans and they talked about French industry and chemicals and the destructive politics of France and, in truth, whatever the hell did happen to the man that Itmar was expected to meet at the Calais train station that day? And so . . .

"What has Itmar told you about that?"

"Nothing. I know nothing, my friend. Anything I can know about my Jacob, you must tell me."

Philip wanted to speak carefully to this woman. In fact, he knew nothing about what had happened to Jacob that day. He only knew one thing, and he decided that it was only right that he should tell Jacob's wife, "I do not know where Jacob is. I do not know why he didn't return to your home that night with Itmar at his side. I can only say that . . . when Itmar did manage to get to Paris that night, it was because he had been apprehended at the train station, and beaten, and then thrown onto a cattle car that brought him—whether Providentially or by chance I do not know—to Paris. That is all I know."

It was then that Miriam Bruchis began to cry. Philip rose from the sofa and awkwardly placed his hands on her shoulders, hoping to comfort the woman as sobs began to thrust her shoulders into convulsive heaving. For the first time in many a year, Philip began to pray. He didn't know what else to do.

With Philip's gentle touch, her sobs now slowed to a whimper. Miriam's doleful cries cast a heavy cloak of interment over the room. The meticulous parlor, which had been a decorous tribute to her life of cumulative love with Jacob, was now bereaved of all capacity to afford comfort, or to manifest any sense of orderly wellness. Instead, draperies of despair now shrouded those furnishings with which she had, over many years, lovingly woven every fabric of their nest. Philip's gaze was fixed on the back of her head, brown hair tightly curled; he could not see the face of her unbridled grief, but could feel it palpably. Miriam's head was hung in sorrow, and as he was feeling powerless to extend any solace to her, he himself was taken into another time and place.

Philip's mother, Rose, hung her head in the sudden grief. Sobs began to thrust her shoulders into convulsive heaving. As her composure withered, Rose collapsed. She would have fallen to the floor, had not the soldierly messenger extended his strong arms in time to prevent it.

Philip, eight years old, was peering up at his mother's face writhing in agony, until the olive green and brassy regalia of the messenger's military uniform obscured her face from his sight. The news had come that infantry man Clint Morrow, son of Roby and Daisy, husband of Rose, father of Robert, Philip and Sylvie, would never return from the fields of Flanders. His last full measure of devotion to the cause of freedom had been poured out. It had bled into the mud trenches of the last twelve days of the War, when a bullet, fired by a retreating German soldier, struck Clint while the 37th Division of the American Expeditionary Force advanced to a Belgian village called Oudenaarde.

A place called Oudenaarde, in Flanders Field, forty-seven kilometres from where Philip now stood sheepishly praying for this woman as she wept. The eight-year-old boy Philip never saw his father again, but tomorrow he would see, for what it was worth, the plot of ground where his father had been laid. And why had Clint Morrow left his young and beautiful wife, his three children, and crossed the Atlantic with a bunch of starry-eyed smelly doughboys from Ohio and West Virginia? Why had he harkened to the call of Uncle Sam in Washington, and the command of General Pershing, after they had trundled off the boats at Calais? Philip did not know why, but he wanted to understand. That quest for an explanation, or at least a visual confirmation, that it had all actually happened here as he had been told, and that was the reason he had never seen his father again. His father? What is a father anyway? Just another carrier of the human condition, that haplessly fickle condition which had nevertheless been, in a moment of passion, inserted through his father's intimacy into the fertile womb of the good woman, Rose, twenty-nine years ago, just like the white rose atop Miriam's piano—and he was focusing on it while she wept—had been lovingly placed into a slender, perpetually budding vase that stood between two empty glasses.

Now all those questions had been raised again. These testings of human purpose and reason had been brought to the embattled forefront of the world again, by an upstart Austrian corporal with a chip on his shoulder and a diabolical thirst for vengeance. Now the dispute, whatever the hell it was between these Frankish and Germanic peoples, had been dragged up from the mud of Flanders again and it had, among other disruptions, prevented the planned rendezvous of two men who had scheduled themselves to meet a few days ago at the Calais train station, a few miles down the road, a few kilometers from here, down on the Channel coast. But the meeting had never happened, and so for whatever reason, if there were in this world a thing called reason or some entity called purpose, now a clueless young American stood in this perfect parlor having no wherewithal to bring comfort to a lovely, grieving woman as he felt her body vibrate with cries of anguish, for now he held her tightly, kneeling awkwardly on one knee, as if he were somehow a surrogate for Jacob her husband, as if her were an angel sent to her. But now there was a knock at the door.

Miriam dutifully roused herself from the sudden bout of bereavement. She removed herself carefully from his embrace, looked up at him. "Thank you." Now she was rising from the chair. Wiping the tears from her eyes, she said, "Please, do sit. I will see who is at the door." She stepped noiselessly into the foyer, opened the door. A moment later her rabbi entered the room with a grave look on his face. He was a dignified patriarch with a ring of white hair beneath the yarmulke that capped a balding head. Philip wanted to stand, to shake the man's hand, American style, but felt such a greeting would be inappropriate at just this moment, and so he sat there on the couch, leaning slightly forward while the two embraced, even as he and Miriam had embraced only a moment before, although her greeting to the older man appeared sacramental, rather than awkwardly tearful.

Then the rabbi stood just inside the room, having no awkwardness in his countenance. With hands grasped together at his waist in a relaxed demeanor, he waited patiently, allowing Miriam to manage their unexpected encounter. She said to Philip, "This is Rabbi Ben Moise." Philip nodded. Moise moved forward to greet him, and so now Philip rose to shake hands with him. "Shalom," the older man said, with bright eyes that cloaked, with ceremonial grief, a respectfully subdued joy.

"Hello. I am Philip Morrow. I am here at the request of Itmar Greeneglass."

Miriam looked from Philip to Rabbi Moise. "Itmar is Jacob's associate, from London," she explained.

"I see," said the older man, with a curt nod. The rabbi seemed expectant, perhaps on an errand of some confidence, but he was hesitant to offer explanation. His perusal of Philip's face was friendly, but brief. Then he turned again to Miriam.

And she turned to Philip. "I want to thank you, Mr. Morrow. for your timely visit, and for your empathy, ah . . . here." There was still no mention of her husband's whereabouts, or his condition. Jacob's circumstance would remain a mystery as far as Philip was concerned, although the unspoken truth was that his present absence was related somehow to that scheduled, unfulfilled meeting with Itmar Greeneglass at the train station in Calais.

Philip readily interpreted from Miriam's tone that now was the time for his departure. He nodded courteously at the rabbi and moved in the direction of the front door. She followed, opened the door for him, and he stepped across the threshold. Now a step below, he looked up at her. Retrieving from his pocket the small jewelry box, he lifted it, and was prepared to open it for her final consideration.

She raised her hand, palm outward. "No. I do not want that. I appreciate your bringing it. I know what is in the box, but I must tell you that . . . it is reserved for you, Philip. It is, ah, as they say, . . . a pearl of great price."

He smiled dumbly at her, not having expected this, nor comprehending its significance. "Very well then." He stepped back, stumbling slightly. "I will be on my way. You can, ah, contact me if it is ever necessary, through Itmar."

"Yes. C'est ca. Your presence here has been well-timed, a helpful comfort to me. I had not realized . . . until you told me about what happened to Itmar that day . . ." Her goodbye was breaking in a quiver. "Go in peace. Shalom."

"Shalom to you," he said, and turned away, in a slow walk to the street. He saw that a car was waiting at the curb, with Mel and a driver inside. Thus ended Philip's fleeting moment of intimate grief with Miriam Bruchis, one very brief encounter in this troubled universe of severe events and sometimes merciful interludes.

27

Poppies

"What did she say when you gave her the pearl?" asked Mel, after Philip had climbed into the back seat with him.

"She never said anything about it, except that she had no need of it. She only wanted to know where her husband was. She had no interest in recovering it for herself, or for anybody else." He looked Mel squarely in the eye. "She said I should keep it, and that it was, ah . . .reserved for me."

"That is a curious thing. May I see it again?"

Philip handed him the little black box. Mel opened it and, after removing his glasses, held the precious object, round and luminescent against the black velvet, close to his eyes. "Oh my, it is such a large pearl. Hmm. . .I never have known much about these things." He lifted his head, sparing his eyes from the strain of close inspection. "I did buy a string of them once, for Agnes. She gave them to Marieke, a young friend of ours, a Flemish girl, just before she died." Then, remembering something special, Mel peered at the driver and spoke to him, "Jacques, you used to sing that song—the song you wrote—for Marieke. What was that song? I always loved to hear you sing that melody. Sing some of it for us, would you?"

"The song for Marieke? It's in Flemish, and Dutch, and also French, together in the same song," said the driver, turning his head slightly to the side, looking in the rearview mirror at Mel.

"Yes, yes, that lovely Flemish song. It is a masterpiece. Chantez pour nous, s'il vous plait."

And so baritone Jacques began to sing, and the car was at once filled with hauntingly beautiful melody:

> *Ay, Marieke, Marieke le ciel flamand*
> *Couleur des tours de Bruges et Gand.*
> *Ay Marieke, Marieke le ciel flamand*
> *Pleure avec moi de Bruges Gand.*
> *Zonder liefde warme liefde.*
> *Waait de wind c'est fini*
> *Zonder liefde warme liefde*
> *Weent de zee dj fini!*
> *Zonder liefde warme liefde;*
> *Lijdt het licht tout est fini.*
> *En schuurt het zand over mijn land,*
> *Mijn platte land mijn Vlaanderland.*

After a long silence, Philip asked the driver, "How can this be? I have never heard such a beautiful song. It is a pearl of a song, Monsieur Brel. You wrote it?"

"I did. I wrote it for Marieke."

"And you sang it for her?"

"Oh, yes, many times I have sung it for her."

"And did you, ah . . .did you love her?"

"I did."

"Yes, well, and then what happened? Did she return your love?"

"She did, for a while. Then she went back to where she came from."

"Oh, and where is that?"

"In Bruges, near the north coast, in Belgium."

Now they were approaching the border. Jacques stopped at the low gate, opened the window and displayed his passport to the guard. Mel and Philip rolled their windows down and likewise produced their passports for Belgian inspection. Then their pilgrimage to Oordenaarde continued.

Philip left his window down, breathing in deeply the cool, thick lowland air. Flat, greening Vlaanderland rolled by beneath late afternoon clouds. The country was bursting with spring freshness and new life, *Mijn platte land, mijn Vlaanderland,* Jacques continued singing in low baritone.

By and by, "That could be a pearl of great price, you know, Philip," Mel said. "You should have a jeweler look at it."

"Oh, I will. I will do that, when I get to New York," Philip answered, wispily. He was lost in thought. The value of this new acquisition was far from his mind. Something about the spring air, the mists at the edges of the fields, the lush, lowland foliage, the shadowy light, *lijdt het licht het donk're licht*, something was moving deeply inside of him. "Mel?"

"Yes?"

"How could this place have been a battlefield for a world war?"

The old Frenchman cast his eyes on the passing landscape, and seemed to join Philip in this musing. He answered slowly, "War is a terrible thing, an ugly thing. I did not fight in the war; I had already served my military duty, long before the Archduke was assassinated in Sarajevo and the whole damn world flew apart, like shrapnel. But I had many friends who fought here, and back there, where we just came from in my France, back there at the Somme, the Marne, Amiens. Our soldiers drove the Germans back across their fortified lines, the Hindenberg line they called it. By summer of 1918 the Germans were in full retreat, although it took them a hell of a long time, and rivers of spilt blood, to admit it. And so it all ended here. Those trenches, over there in France, that had been held and occupied for two hellish years by both armies, those muddy hellholes were finally left behind, vacated, and afterward . . . filled up again with the soil of France and Flanders and Belgium, and green grass was planted where warfare had formerly blasted its way out of the dark human soul and the dark humus of lowland dirt and now we see that grass, trimmed, manicured and growing so tidily around those rows of white crosses out there, most of them with some soldier's name carved on them, many just unknown, anonymous, and how could this have happened? You might as well ask how could. . . a grain of sand get stuck in an oyster? And how could that oyster, in retaliation against that rough, alien irritant, then generate a pearl—such a beautiful thing, lustrous and white—coming forth in response to a small, alien presence that had taken up unwelcomed residence inside the creature's own domain? The answer, my friend, is floating in the sea, blowing in the wind, growing green and strong from soil that once ran red with men's blood."

Now they were arriving at the battlefield. Jacques parked the car, leaned against the front fender, lit a cigarette. Mel and Philip walked through a stone arch, along a narrow, paved road lined with flowering linden trees, spring green with their large spadish leaves, sprinkled with small white blossoms. The sun was getting low behind them. Shadows of these trees had overtaken the narrow lane, turning it cooler than the surrounding fields, acres and acres neatly arranged with white crosses and gravestones, and continuous green, perfect grass between all. Having reached the end of the linden lane, the stepped slowly, reverently, along straight pathways, passing hundreds of silent graves on either side. The setting sun was still warm here, after their cool approach from beneath the trees.

At length, they came to the row that Philip had been looking for, the one he had read about in the army guidebook, where his father's grave was nested precisely and perpetually in its own place in eternity:

Clinton Aaron Morrow

born July 13, 1895 in North Carolina, USA   died Oct 30, 1918
in defense of Oordenaarde, and the free world
". . .and upon finding one pearl of great value, he went and sold all that he had and bought it."

After a while of silent consideration of this, the sun, like a red wafer in the sky, descended below Flanders Field. The crossed battlefield became filled with lengthening shadows.

Then Mel asked his young friend the question, "Philip, those words about your father are carved upon a cross. Do you believe that the one whose crucifixion is represented by that cross was raised from the dead?"

"I do, Mel. I do believe it. And my father will be raised with him, if he hasn't already been."

"Who told you that?"

"My mother, my grandfather . . . a few others whom I have trusted, and God, who has brought me to a place of. . . knowing this. It is a small thing, just a kernel—this faith of resurrection."

Mel smiled with a curious satisfaction. "Like a mustard seed," he said.

"Yes."

Peering at Philip, then at the darkening horizon where the sun had just disappeared, Mel concluded, "Very well, then. Let's go back to France."

And so they did go back to France. When they arrived at the hotel in Lille, a telegram with Philip's name on it was waiting for him at the desk:
PHILIP: HEINRICH SAYS WE SHOULD GO TO NEW YORK STOP NOW MY FATHER AND MOTHER AGREE WITH HIM STOP I HOPE TO SEE YOU THERE   LILI